ABOUT THE AUTHOR

BARBARA MANDELL has had a varied career writing mainly for radio and television. Her occasional broadcasts for BBC radio included writing and presenting a weekly series of travel programmes; she was the first woman newscaster in Britain for Independent Television News where she also worked as a reporter and script-writer. She wrote a Yachtsman's Guide to the Fal while living on a boat in Falmouth but has spent the last few years in Europe. She lists her present occupation as 'travel for pleasure' and is currently based in Luxembourg.

CADOGAN GUIDES

CADOGAN GUIDES

THE
SOUTH
OF FRANCE

BARBARA MANDELL

Illustrations by Pauline Pears

CADOGAN BOOKS

LONDON

ACKNOWLEDGEMENTS

I would like to thank the many people who gave me their time and help in writing this book. Special thanks are due to the French Government Tourist Office and to the Monaco Information Centre in London for their kind assistance; to Tourist Offices throughout the South of France for their patience and endless stream of information; and to friends too numerous to mention, both those living in the South of France and those who are frequent visitors, for their invaluable advice and support.

Phototypeset in Ehrhardt on a Linotron 202,
printed and bound in Great Britain by
Redwood Burn Limited, Trowbridge, Wiltshire

CONTENTS

Chapter IV

Cannes to Toulon

Chapter V

Toulon to Marseilles

Chapter VI

Marseilles to Arles

LIST OF MAPS

INTRODUCTION

The very words 'the South of France' have an exotic quality about them, always appearing complete with capital letters like the South Seas or the Far East, and in just the same way they are a composite title for an area of infinite variety.

The Mediterranean follows the French coast like a shallow inverted 'S' from the Alps to the Pyrenees, covering some 560 kilometres (350 miles). All along the way the scenery changes dramatically, from the impressive mountains that cascade down to the shore near the Italian border, past the red crags of the Esterel Massif, one of the oldest land masses in Europe, to the salty half-deserted plains of the Camargue. After that the sea turns southwards along mile after mile of sandy beaches and shimmering lagoons until it reaches the Vermilion Coast where rocky cliffs and sheltered bays provide the last contrast before the Spanish frontier.

Once you turn inland it is a little more difficult to decide exactly where the South of France ends and the rest of the country begins unless, of course, you divide it up into the official coastal departments, namely the Alpes-Maritimes, Var, Bouches-du-Rhône, Gard, Hérault, Aude and Pyrénées-Orientales. This is all very logical if you happen to be an administrator or a local resident, but most visitors have their own entirely personal and sometimes quite restricted ideas of where the boundary lies. Winter sports enthusiasts will include the ski resorts of the Alpes-de-Haute-Provence, while the archaeologically-minded tend to concentrate on the areas along the Rhône and the rich rewards to be found in ancient cities like Aix, Arles, Avignon and Orange. Followers of contemporary art head straight for the Riviera with its wealth of museums and art galleries, many of them dedicated to such masters as Picasso, Matisse, Cocteau and Chagall. For sophisticated holidaymakers the South of France is personified by the bright lights and luxurious hotels of Cannes, Nice and Monte-Carlo; ornithologists prefer the wilds of the Camargue; Juan-les-Pins is the haunt of the young, St-Tropez of the curious.

Until quite recently few tourists gave a thought to the coastline beyond Marseilles, probably because there were only a handful of fishing villages and a great many mosquitoes there. Ancient towns like Montpellier and

Perpignan were generally regarded as overnight stops on the road to Spain; Carcassonne was famous but Aigues-Mortes and Pézenas had still to be discovered. Skiing in the Pyrenees came a poor second to a winter sports holiday in the Alps. Now the whole scene is changing. The mosquitoes have gone and holiday resorts are springing up at frequent intervals overlooking the magnificent sandy beaches and offering a tremendous variety of sports and entertainments that need space to develop their full potential. Ruined castles stand guard over forest-filled valleys where rivers have eaten away deep gorges and the hills are honeycombed with exceptionally beautiful caves and grottoes. There are ancient manasteries like the Abbey of Font-froide, medieval villages such as Castelnou and prehistoric remains that are said to pre-date the original inhabitants of the Côte d'Azur by more than 300 000 years.

The vineyards blanketing the area between the Mediterranean and the foothills of the Pyrenees and the Cévennes, where Robert Louis Stevenson travelled with his donkey, produce an abundance of wine much of which finds its way into the co-operatives. However, a considerable amount is still personalised by the numerous châteaux where visitors are welcome to call in and sample it for themselves.

Generally speaking, the South of France from Marseilles to the Spanish border is a good deal less sophisticated and less densely populated than the eastern section, but it is catching up fast with modern hotels, furnished villas and apartments, efficient marinas and attractive sites for tents and caravans, although some can be rather short on trees. Like all the other regions along the Mediterranean seaboard it has its relics of history, its national costumes, local customs, traditional music, dancing and celebrations as well as local specialities and individual dishes.

Probably because the Riviera has been part of the British holiday scene for 100 years or more, one thinks of the Italian border as being much closer than the Spanish one, but in fact the distance from Calais is exactly the same, give or take three or four miles.

Like so many other people I have had to define my own boundary for the South of France and originally it was intended to be a line running parallel with the coast and about 40 kilometres (25 miles) inland all the way. In fact this line has veered to the north or south occasionally, because there is always something to tempt you round the next corner, across a valley or up a mountainside. It would be unthinkable to drive along the Route Napoléon without inspecting the Canyon du Verdon, said to be the most outstanding of its kind in Europe, or visit Arles and ignore the brooding hill village of Les

Baux or the ancient border towns of Beaucaire and Tarascon, followed by a quick nod in the direction of Avignon, Orange and the Pont du Gard. Few people on a day's outing from Nîmes or Montpellier can resist a visit to the famous grottoes of the Cévennes or drive inland from Narbonne without being tempted by a signpost to Carcassonne. But one has to draw the line somewhere and so it marks, very roughly, places which can be visited on a day trip from one or more popular holiday resorts in the same area and yet still leaves a lot to be discovered along this narrow strip edging the South of France.

Every effort has been made to ensure the accuracy of the information in this book at the time of going to press. However, practical details such as opening hours, travel information, standards in hotels and restaurants and, in particular, prices are liable to change.

We intend to keep this book as up-to-date as possible in the coming years. Please write to us if there is anything you feel should be included in future editions.

Chapter I

GENERAL INFORMATION

Montmajour Abbey

Getting to the South of France

Having once made up your mind to holiday in the South of France, the next thing to do is to decide how to get there. The choice of ways to travel is fairly wide.

BY AIR
The following airlines fly direct to cities in the South of France: Air France (158 New Bond Street, London W1Y 0AY. Tel. 01–499 9511): Heathrow to Marseilles, Montpellier (in the season) and Nice; Manchester to Nice.
British Airways (PO Box 10, Hounslow, Middlesex. Tel. 01–759 4000): Heathrow to Marseilles, Nice; Manchester to Nice.
Dan-Air (Newman House, 71 Victoria Road, Horley, Surrey. Tel. 897 4000 02934 5622 (reservations): Gatwick to Montpellier, Perpignan (in the season).

The cost of a return flight from London to Nice at the time of going to press can vary from £344 to £188 (Superpex—high season).

5

Pan Am fly non-stop from New York to Nice four times a week (cheapest return tickets: low season—$548; high season—$837). Other major airlines only fly to Paris from the USA and Canada. Air France flies to Paris from New York (888 7th Avenue, New York, NY 10106, tel. 212–247 0100); Chicago (John Hancock Center, 875 North Michigan Avenue, Chicago, tel. 312–440 7922); Houston (1 Allen Center, Suite 3220, 500 Dallas Street, Houston 77002, tel. 713–651 0415); Los Angeles (8501 Wilshire Boulevard, Beverly Hills, Los Angeles, tel. 213–274 8381); and from Toronto (151 Bloor St West, Suite 600, Toronto, tel. 416–364 0101) and **Montreal** (2000 Rue Mansfield, Suite 1510, Montreal, tel. 514–284 2825). For information on other airlines which fly to Paris, contact your local travel **agent**.

The national domestic airline, Air Inter, operates flights from Paris to Marseilles, Montpellier, Nice, Nîmes and Perpignan. For details, contact Air France (addresses above). Details of other independent internal airlines can be obtained from your travel agent.

BY RAIL

French Railways operate an overnight service from Calais to the Riviera throughout the year, and from Calais to Languedoc-Roussillon in summer.

Motorail from Boulogne, Calais, Dieppe (and Paris) provides a car-sleeper service to main holiday areas to save you the trouble of driving down.

The TGVs (Trains à Grande Vitesse) are the new high speed trains which run from Paris to Avignon, Marseilles and Montpellier. You can now get from Paris to the South in approximately five hours.

For the under 26s, Transalpino (71/75 Buckingham Palace Road, London SW1, tel. 01–834 9656) give up to 50% discount on travel to various destinations in the South of France including Cannes, Toulon, Saint Raphaël, Atibes, Nice and Marseilles. Tickets are valid for two months and you can stop off along the route. Under 26s also qualify for up to 50% reduction on rail travel with a 'Carré Jeune' or 'Carte Jeune' railcard, available from French Railways London.

If you want to start from somewhere other than the Channel coast, or stop off along the way, you can plan your arrivals and departures exactly as you would at home. Information and bookings can be obtained from French Railways Continental Shipping and Travel, 179 Piccadilly, London W1V 0AL, tel. 01–409 3518 (Motorail) and 01–409 1224 (for other passenger services); also from main British Rail Travel Centres, stations, and all ABTA travel agents.

BY SEA

There are quite a few different ways of crossing the Channel, either with or without a car:

Brittany Ferries (Norman House, Millbay Docks, Plymouth P11 3EF. Tel. Plymouth 0752 21321, Portsmouth 0705 27701) run from Plymouth to Roscoff; from Portsmouth to St-Malo and to Caen (starting 5 June 1986); from Poole to Cherbourg, starting 13 June, 1986 to 7 September 1986 which may be extended; and once a week from Cork to Roscoff (seasonal).

Hoverspeed (International Hoverport, Ramsgate, Kent CT12 5HS, tel. 0843 595555 or 01–554 7061, Birmingham 021–236 2190 or Manchester 061–228 1321) takes you from Dover to Boulogne or Calais.

Sally Line (81 Piccadilly, London W1V 9HF, tel. 01–409 0536) runs from Ramsgate to Dunkirk.

Sealink (PO Box 29, Victoria Station, London SW1W 0AG, tel. 01–834 8122) operates from Dover to Calais and Dunkirk, from Folkestone to Boulogne, from Newhaven to Dieppe and from Portsmouth to Cherbourg and Weymouth (seasonal) to Cherbourg.

Townsend Thoresen (Enterprise House, Channel View Road, Dover CT17 9TJ, tel. 01–734 4431 and 01–437 7800, Dover (reservations) 0304 203388) runs from Dover to Boulogne and Calais and from Portsmouth to Le Havre and to Cherbourg (seasonal).

BY ROAD

There are very few long-distance bus services in France so if you opt for a coach you should plan to start from London.

Euroways (52 Grosvenor Gardens, Victoria, London SW1W 0AU, tel. 01–730 3433) operates regular services to Aix-en-Provence, Antibes, Cannes, Juan-les-Pins, Marseilles, Montpellier, Nice and Perpignan.

Riviera Express (8 Park Lane, Croydon CR0 1JA, tel. 01–680 8787) will take you to Aix-en-Provence, Cannes, Nice and Ste-Maxime.

Supabus (172 Buckingham Palace Road, London SW1 W9TN, tel. 01–730 3453) run to Aix-en-Provence, Cannes, Frejus, Marseilles, Montpellier, Nice, Perpignan and Ste-Maxime.

If you want to hire a car, airlines and tour-operators have fly-drive schemes and French Railways offer similar train–car arrangements. Alternatively, contact one of the international car firms like Avis Rent-a-Car (Trident House, Station Road, Hayes, Middx, tel. 01–848 8733); Godfrey Davis Europcar (Bushey House, High Street, Watford, Herts, tel. (central reservations) 01–950 5050; Hertz Rent-a-Car (Radnor House, 1272 London Road, Norbury, London SW16, tel. 01–679 1799).

Whichever way you decide to go it, it is a good idea to get advice if it is your first visit to the Continent. A good travel agent will help you with hotels, provide general information and handle your bookings as well. The motoring organisations will not only book you and your car across but also tell you what documents you require and advise you on all the things you need to know when you arrive. If you want to arrange the whole trip yourself, it would be wise to call at the French National Tourist Office (178 Piccadilly, London W1V 0AL, tel. 01–491 7622) which will supply you with all the information you want. They even have a Yachting Department where, should you want to take your own boat, you can find out if your craft is the right size and has sufficient power for the route you hope to follow.

French Tourist offices in the USA are in New York (610 Fifth Avenue, New York, NY 10020, tel. 212–757.11.25); Chicago (645 North Michigan Avenue, Suite 430, Chicago, Illinois–60611, tel. 312–337.63.01); Dallas (World Trade Center No 103, 2050 Stemmons Freeway, PO Box 58 610, Dallas–Texas–75258, tel. 214–742.70.11; Los Angeles (9401 Wilshire Boulevard, Beverly Hills–California–90212, tel. 213–272.26.61.) and in Canada in Montreal (1981 Ave McGill College, Suite 490, Montreal – Que H3 A2 W9, tel. 514–1.288.42.64; Toronto (1 Dundas St. W, Suite 2405, Box 8, Toronto – Ont M5 G1 Z3, tel. 416–593.47.17).

DRIVING DOWN

Driving through France is no problem as long as you remember to keep on the right side of the road, have all the necessary documents and observe the rules. For example, you must not have a child under ten on the front seat, a 'stop' sign means coming to a halt and not just slowing down to a crawl, and your headlights must be properly adjusted (yellow tinted headlights are advisable). There are random breath tests for drinking and driving. On-the-spot fines are payable in cash and can be heavy.

It is quite a long haul from the Channel coast to the Mediterranean— 1066 kilometres (662 miles) from Calais to Marseilles and 1221 kilometres (759 miles) from Calais to Nice—so, unless you are a dedicated driver or start out at crack of dawn, it is as well to stop for a night on the way. Out of season there should be little difficulty in finding a hotel but do not leave it until the last moment, especially if you are on a main route. Most places fill up in plenty of time for dinner which is usually served at about 7pm and may well be over if you arrive much later than that. In the summer try to ring ahead and book, and even then try to be in good time or you may find they have given you up for lost and let the room to someone else.

The quickest way to the South of France is obviously on the motorway *autoroute à péage*, which will cost you in the region of £40 for the privilege. You collect a ticket, often from an automatic machine at the barrier, and pay in cash for the distance covered wherever you decide to branch off. The main roads are a bit slower but there are no charges. On the whole the minor roads are good but can be costly in both time and distance.

Petrol is available almost everywhere and the majority of garages, like most hotels, will accept credit cards. However, it is as well to have some ready cash because you could land up somewhere that refuses all the usually acceptable ones like Carte Bleue (Visa), American Express, Eurocard (Access) and Diners Club.

GETTING AROUND

Once you arrive in the South of France you will naturally want to look round and there are several ways of doing it. If you have your own car, the problem is solved. Most villages, apart from the deserted ones, have a petrol pump attached to a small garage that can cope with ordinary repairs. Garages specialising in most of the better-known makes of car can be found in the large towns and they will deal with more serious matters, speeding the work up as far as possible for tourists in distress. Parking can sometimes be difficult but a great many hotels make provision for their guests.

BY AIR

There are a number of airports along the coast from which internal flights can be made: Cannes, Carcassonne, Marseilles, Montpellier, Nice, Perpignan and St-Tropez. A helicopter service operates between Monaco and Nice.

BY RAIL

You will find excellent train services all along the coast and details of times, fares and so on are available at the local stations.

BY ROAD

Buses are a good way of getting about whether in town, between the different centres or to outlying villages. The timetables and prices are obtainable from local tourist offices and from the bus stations which are often quite close to the main square. Coach operators lay on excursions and conducted tours at quite reasonable prices. They take you to the better-known and therefore more crowded places of interest which ensures that you do not miss anything important but leaves no time for exploring on your own. Lunch is seldom if ever included in the price and nor, for that matter, are entrance fees to museums and so on.

HIRE
One or more of the international car firms can be found in the major towns and the price you pay depends on the type of car and the length of time you keep it. Bicycles can be hired at any number of railway stations and most coastal resorts have their own arrangements as well. Prices vary between 25–45 F per day but you must expect to leave a deposit (about 150 F) against any damage but not reasonable wear and tear.

Horses are available in a surprisingly large number of places for lessons, short rides and pony trekking. The usual method is to join a party and the prices, in general, start at about 35 F.

Boats, whether you want to sail, water-ski, fish or simply mess about, can be found at the majority of seaside resorts, the cost depending on what you want. The best place to go for information is the local yacht club or the port authority, and you will quite likely have to prove your ability and get a temporary certificate in return. However, no certificates are necessary if you want to cruise the Canal du Midi, the Canal du Rhône à Sète or the Canal de la Robine between Easter and the end of October. Over and above all this there are boat trips along the coast, to offshore islands and between some of the resorts.

Where to stay

HOTELS
The hotels in France fall roughly into six categories, ranging from the outlandishly expensive to the extremely modest. The star system of classification is used. Hotel prices are fixed and displayed for all the world to see but they vary according to the season. In the majority of cases the figure applies to a double room, which costs more than half the usual price if you take it on your own but not a great deal extra if three of you pile in together.

★★★★★★

Anyone who is going to the **Paris** in Monte-Carlo or the **Château du Domaine St-Martin** at Vence, to mention only two, needs no help from me. Just warm up the executive jet and leave the job of booking to your secretary. These hotels will cost you well over 1000 F a night at the very least and breakfast in bed will probably be extra.

★★★★★

One step down, for which you need a healthy bank balance or a reliable expense account, will run out at somewhere between 600 and 1000 F, but you can rely on being very comfortable.

★★★★

In a lot of places this is the most expensive hotel available and offers a high standard of comfort in an unexpectedly wide range of prices. Some charge as little as 350 F while others with something exceptional to offer can ask as much as 900 F.

★★★

These hotels are described as good, average establishments and can range from the delightful to the merely acceptable. Their rooms work out at between 250 and 350 F and it is worth going in to look at them. You can always say that it is not what you want and no one minds in the least.

★★

Once again, there is no harm in looking at these small hotels because they are usually clean and comfortable but without a lot in the way of optional extras which is why you can book in for around 120 to 250 F.

★

At the bottom of the list you come to places which are frankly basic. They can be full of atmosphere or extremely forgettable but then you cannot expect the full treatment for about 100 F.

On the general subject of hotels, one or two small points to make your stay more comfortable are worth bearing in mind, especially if you are not paying the earth for a room.

Pillows, for example. You will always find a bolster at the head of the bed and it may be deliciously soft or more like a sausage full of gristle and very little else. Look in the cupboard to see if there are any pillows and if you draw a blank ask the management for some. If you are ultra-particular or are staying at the very cheapest hotels, it might be as well to take your own.

Towels, for some reason, are seldom large and fluffy, so to avoid patting yourself dry with something a fraction of the size you are used to, why not

11

pack a towelling dressing gown? Soap also comes in tiny packages and therefore a cake or two would not come amiss.

Railway lines and main roads are something else to watch. If your room
looks out on either of them, it is likely to have double-glazing, which cuts
down the noise, but in this case make sure it is air-conditioned as well. If
not, you will be faced with buying ear plugs or suffocating in the heat.

When it comes to paying the bill, you will usually be able to do so with a
credit card, but make sure beforehand: it could be awkward if the banks are
closed. Remember most banks usually shut early on the day before a public
holiday, on the holiday itself and at weekends.

If you are touring during the high season and have not booked for the
following night, ask the hotel to do it before you leave or you may find
yourself sleeping under the stars.

LOGIS AND AUBERGES
These are scattered all over France, mainly in country areas but very seldom
near large towns. They provide comfortable rooms, some have added
attractions like tennis courts and swimming pools and, as the majority are
family concerns, you can often sample some very tasty local dishes. A guide
is brought out every year and it is well worth buying a copy.

APARTMENTS
Nearly everywhere you go along the coast it is possible to rent an apartment
or a villa and this is ideal for people who prefer a self-catering holiday. In
most cases there are shops and supermarkets nearby and the whole thing
works out much more cheaply than a hotel.

GÎTES
These come in all shapes and sizes, being anything from part of a manor
house, an eight-roomed villa or a flat down to a rural cottage or a room on a
farm. Some are self-catering while others provide bed and breakfast and
occasionally an evening meal. They are priced according to size and lists
are available for each area.

CAMPS
Spending a holiday in a mobile home, a caravan or a tent is very much part of
the French way of life and every resort has at least one site and often
considerably more. They range from the four-star luxury variety with a
restaurant, supermarket, bars, take-away meals, and facilities for all the usual
sports, to very modest set-ups where the amenities are minimal. Some of

them have tents, caravans, mobile homes and chalets to let and all the details are set out in comprehensive lists published for the various areas. No matter how large the site you choose, book ahead if you are going in the summer or you may find there is not a single corner where they can fit you in.

BOATS

Charter companies operate in most places where there is a port or a reasonable marina and it is not too difficult to find the sort of boat you want. Naturally the prices vary as much as they do in Britain, pride of place going to the ones that come complete with a skipper and crew. The local yacht clubs will point you in the right direction, tell you what is available in the way of services and facilities and see that you understand the rules. Every marina has its quota of cafes along the quay and the *ports de plaisance* along the Languedoc–Roussillon coast offer an amazing selection of other attractions as well.

Eating out

As with hotels, so with restaurants. They range from very expensive indeed to extremely cheap and cheerful and it is seldom that you will have a bad meal, although it may not always be good value for money. They are all required to put up a list of prices outside so there is no excuse for finding that you cannot pay at the end. The custom is to provide up to three set menus of different lengths and prices as well as an *à la carte* where you can order anything you like and pay accordingly. The more up-market restaurants usually have a list of specialities that may have been invented by the chef, conform to well-tried recipes or are traditional cooking at its best. Some less expensive restaurants make a feature of local dishes and in small family concerns the cooking is usually simple and frequently delicious.

Now and again you may come across a restaurant which leaves a lot to be desired and there are a couple of pointers that do not always apply but could put you on your guard: for example, the cheapest menu hidden away where it is liable to be overlooked, a refusal to serve wine by the glass in an area where the vines are practically climbing in through the window, and a complete absence of local people when everywhere else around is crowded.

Unless you go to a cafe or a restaurant which offers a snack lunch, it is false economy to order a sandwich or an omelette which usually turns out to be quite expensive by comparison with the set menus.

Although there are obviously places in the more swinging resorts and larger towns that stay open late in the evening, it is a mistake to assume that eating after 9pm is a national occupation. To be safe you should aim for about 7 to 7.30pm unless you have discovered otherwise. Lunch usually starts about noon and stops abruptly at 2pm, but during the season quite a few cafes will feed you at any reasonable hour.

Wines

Good wine, like good food, is very much part of everyday life in the South of France, although the coastal regions do not produce many of the really outstanding examples that are so highly prized by experts all over the world. On the other hand, the region produces quite a few excellent wines, some interesting varieties that you might need to know better before you grow to like them and endless local products which are very drinkable and go well with the traditional dishes of the area concerned.

On the Côte d'Azur, Bellet, one of the oldest vineyards in France, is widely known and much appreciated. It produces red, rosé and white wines, the white being dry and especially good with fish. In Cassis, people who are fond of *bouillabaisse* frequently complement it with the local wine which has a faintly greenish tinge and may not appeal to you when you try it for the first time. If you prefer something red and full of flavour, try Bandol which is extremely popular.

The vineyards in and around the Rhône Valley can be relied upon for some excellent wines such as Côtes-du-Rhône and Châteauneuf-du-Pape, so called because the grapes were grown originally on estates which were owned by the Popes at Avignon. Tavel, just north of Avignon, gives its name to a delightful dry rosé which is highly recommended by hotels and restaurants thereabouts. It is somewhat stronger than its counterpart from the Château la Guiranne in the Côte-de-Provence region near Toulon or Listel wines like the Domaine de Villeroy from the coastal area near Nîmes. The Château d'Ansouis takes as much pride in its history as it does in the vineyards surrounding the ancient castle north of Aix which has been in the Sabran family for more than 1000 years.

In the Hérault wine is produced at the rate of hundreds of millions of litres every year, much of which is exported, but enough is left to keep the locals and their visitors well supplied. Hotels and restaurants in the area round St-Jean-de-Fos have no hesitation in recommending Combaçal which is one of the Vins de Pays and very reasonably priced, as is the Château de Languedoc from areas nearby.

Further south in the Roussillon there are so many vineyards and so many different varieties of wine that a Route des Vins has been worked out. It takes in more than 100 cellars, not to mention historical sites and specially selected restaurants where local dishes are served with complementary wines, both frequently unknown outside the area but deserving of wider recognition. As the restrictions on drinking and driving apply here just as they do everywhere in France, it is a good idea to join one of the tours of the circuit which leave from Argèles each Wednesday and from Barcarès every Saturday and cost 150 francs inclusive of all expenses, with half-price tickets for children. However, if you prefer to explore on your own, try to include the Maury vineyards in the Agly valley, which produce red aperitif and dessert wines, and the coastal area from Collioure to Cerbère which is the home of Banyuls wines. The terraced vineyards were first cultivated by the Knights Templars, and when they produce a vintage of exceptional quality, it earns the title of Banyuls grand cru after having been matured for at last two and a half years.

Specialities

It is very seldom that you will be faced with anything other than excellent food in the South of France, although some of the older residents complain that the outbreak of supermarkets with their variety of deep-frozen dishes are having an effect on traditional cooking. Fortunately this effect is so limited at the moment that it is hardly worth bothering about. Small hotels, *logis* and *auberges*, not to mention little bistros and tucked-away restaurants, can be relied upon to produce simple but delicious menus, usually with wine to match. The more up-market you go, the more complicated the dishes become, until you reach the point where a master chef spends a great deal of time and energy inventing entirely new recipes to tempt the visitor who, probably quite incorrectly, insists that he or she has tried everything.

Anyone with an eye to economy would do well to choose a set menu, the cheapest usually having only three courses while the most expensive will run to five or six. The food will be just as good but, dish for dish, somewhat cheaper than the *à la carte*, although the latter may be dressed up a bit. For example, delicious oysters on the set menu often arrive tastefully decorated with prawns if you order them on their own.

Every region has its own specialities which can be either unique or simply

15

a variation on a recipe that is known and served from one end of the coast to the other. Oil is used extensively in cooking instead of butter, garlic and herbs play an important role without being too obtrusive, and the emphasis tends to be rather more on fish than meat except in country areas.

The famous *bouillabaisse*, which originated in Marseilles and is usually somewhere between a fish soup and a stew, is served everywhere but varies slightly according to the locality. The same goes for *bourride*, made with white fish and *aioli*, a distinctive garlic mayonnaise that is also used in a cod purée to produce *brandade de morue*. *Soupe de poisson* can vary considerably and is usually excellent, and the same goes for *pistou*, a thick vegetable soup. On the way to Spain you will find *l'ouillade*, a soup made from potato, cabbage, knuckle of pork and haricot beans.

Red mullet, known as *rouget*, is popular but rather over-blessed with bones, so you might prefer *loup au fenouil*, a dish of sea bass grilled with fennel. If you are staying in Nice, try sea dace cooked in champagne, a splendid turbot soufflé with crayfish sauce or an anchovy tart called *anchoiade*. The same name is given to anchovies prepared in the Catalan style throughout the Roussillon. Waterside restaurants in Marseille special-ise in the use of clams, mussels and sea urchins, and the city is also known for a kind of tripe that appears as *pieds et paquets*. When in Arles do not miss the famous local sausages that are rather like salami. Wood from the vines is widely used for barbecues. In Provence it gives an added flavour to lavender-fed lamb in dishes like *agneau de Sisteron*, while on the far side of the Camargue it is essential for *la cargolade*, which can be anything from grilled snails to sausages or lamb and is served with red wine. Wild boar is also grilled over vine wood or made into a stew that is extremely popular in areas bordering on the Cévennes. Other specialities in this part of the country include partridge going under the title of *perdreaux à la Catalane* and *boles de picoulat*, meatballs made from a mixture of beef and pork and accompanied by a rich sauce.

Apart from ices, which are many and surprisingly varied, the sweets are not particularly memorable, but the quality and variety of the fresh fruit more than compensates for this. Provence is justly proud of its succulent green figs, Cavaillon is famous for the sweet pink melons that find their way into every corner of Europe and in Avignon the local speciality is melon preserved in brandy. Peaches, apricots, cherries and grapes abound everywhere and Apt, in particular, produces mouthwatering crystallised fruit.

For snacks that you cannot resist between meals, try the diamond-shaped pieces of almond paste produced in Aix which are called *calissons*; crisp biscuits from Nîmes and St-Paul-de-Fenouillet; *panallets*, which are marzipan *petit fours* with Barbados nuts and are found in the Roussillon, together with *les tourons Catalans* that turn out to be honeycakes with hazel nuts, almonds and Barbados nuts or crystallised fruits. To round off the day there is nothing to beat *nougat* from Montelimar or a few chocolates from Tarascon.

A game of boules

Leisure activities

Whatever your favourite sport or pastime, you would be very unlucky not to find it in the South of France. On the other hand, there are only a few places with a range of attractions wide enough to cater for all tastes and all ages at the same time. It is no good looking for wide sandy beaches in the middle of St-Tropez, an all-night disco in Vallauris or a caravan site in Monte-Carlo. Casinos are easier to come by along the coast than they are up in the mountainous areas where the peace and quiet demanded by anglers would drive the average window-shopping enthusiast to distraction.

The majority of people head for the Mediterranean in search of sand, sea and sunshine, so it is as well to remember that most of the beaches between

17

Menton and Cannes consist largely of pebbles. After that the sand begins to assert itself, particularly when you get beyond Cap Camarat, south of St-Tropez, where there are some really beautiful places. However, the longest, widest and, at the moment, the least crowded beaches are to be found on the far side of the Rhône, stretching almost down to the Spanish border and providing safe bathing nearly all the way.

WATER SPORTS
Every holiday resort worthy of the name has at least one public swimming pool which may well be heated but in some cases may not be. Even large hotels with their own private beaches usually have a pool as well and so do a number of *auberges* and *logis* and a fair proportion of the bigger camping sites. Diving clubs and schools have been established wherever the conditions are right and you will find them in at least half the resorts along the Côte d'Azur and in the same proportion of *ports de plaisance* to the west of the Rhône from La Grande-Motte down to Cerbère. The same applies to water-skiing and windsurfing, and almost without exception if you choose a resort with a marina you will be able to join a sailing school and hire a boat. Charter companies operate in the larger centres, usually in the vicinity of the port where the authorities will give you the appropriate addresses and telephone numbers if you have not already obtained them from the local tourist office. Sailing and windsurfing are possible on most of the large inland lakes, although in many cases motorboats are frowned on or forbidden altogether.

Deep-sea fishermen are catered for in several places where there are resident fishing fleets, while in ports like Collioure and Banyuls-sur-Mer special trips are laid on every morning for anyone who wants to go out for a few hours before lunch. Anglers should have no difficulty in joining the local fishing clubs that can be found in almost every area. Permits are needed on the majority of lakes and rivers and these are supplied when you pay for your membership card and may entitle you to fish anywhere in the district, sometimes throughout the region and even, in some cases, anywhere in France. All the information you need is available from the Fédération Départementale des Sociétés de Pêche, 20 Boulevard Victor-Hugo, Nice (tel. 93–88.19.92).

SOCIAL PASTIMES
There are as many, if not more, tennis courts as there are swimming pools and here again quite a few hotels and camping sites have their own. Visitors are welcome to join the local club or hire a public court for an hour or two.

Golf courses are not quite so numerous but there is usually one within reach of the principal holiday resorts with such famous examples as the Monte-Carlo Golf Club and the Cannes Country Club at Mougins leading the field. They are rather more widely spaced beyond the Rhône but you can, for example, play at Nîmes and St-Cyprien Plage.

COUNTRY PURSUITS

The best area for pony trekking is, according to most people, the Camargue where parties are made up under the guidance of a *guardian*, but you will find riding schools and stables nearly everywhere. It goes without saying that inland resorts like Sospel, Fayence, St-Jean-du-Gard and Elne are ideal centres for anyone who wants a riding holiday, but if you are prepared to drive a mile or two into the country from most of the leading coastal resorts you will have no difficulty in hiring a horse for an hour or even a day.

Wherever you go in the South of France you are bound to see someone walking because there is no better way of getting to know an area than exploring it on foot. Along the coast there are, for example, paths leading from Cap-Martin to Monte-Carlo, Eze-Bord-de-Mer up to its parent hill village and along the cliffs west of Marseilles. The whole countryside is spider-webbed with bridle paths and mountain tracks, the vast majority signposted to make life easier. Vence is a typical example with some 40 different paths covering 160 kilometres (100 miles) through the valleys and up the mountainsides where the views are spectacular and the villages few and far between.

In the Roussillon there are any number of refuges, huts, lodgings and stopover places for long-distance hikers, some of them run by owners who live on the premises while others are no more than tiny stone cabins with no one about and no amenities at all. Quite a few are open throughout the year while others such as the chalet-hotel at Cortalets are closed during the winter, although in this case you can pay a deposit and take the keys if you are visiting the Taurinya district out of season. A list covering the Pyrenees, published every year, is obtainable from the Maison du Tourisme at Perpignan for 4F. Other information offices will give you details and maps of their own areas, but if you are out in the wilds the best plan is to ask the nearest Dutch tourist. They are the most determined walkers I have ever met and can usually be counted on to supply all the right answers.

SPECIALISED ACTIVITIES

If you are one of those people whose particular sport or hobby falls under an entirely different heading, you should still be able to find somewhere which has arranged things with you in mind. One such resort is La Grande-Motte where you can take up archery, play bowls, go canoeing or jogging, learn to dance or practise yoga while the rest of the family follow a more generally popular line. Much the same can be said of Bandol with the added attraction of a motor-racing circuit nearby. If it is gliding you are after, you will find it at Fayence, Banyuls offers parachute gliding and the Comité Départemental in Nice will point you in the right direction for caving, pot-holing and parachuting. All these and many other sports can be found elsewhere along the coast and the best people to pinpoint them for you are the local tourist offices. However, if you want to shoot wild sheep, wild goats or wild boar in the Pyrenees, you need to contact the Fédération Départementale de la Chasse, 3 Passage des Variétés, 66000 Perpignan (tel. 68–61.25.05).

The popular local game is *boules*, a form of bowls played on any more or less flat piece of ground, and in many village squares.

Weather

Generally speaking, you can expect good weather in the South of France but, like anywhere else, it can be horrible. The eastern end of the Côte d'Azur claims to have the warmest winters; Cannes, also sheltered by the mountains, is not far behind; while all the resorts from the Camargue onwards are reported to enjoy at least 320 days of sunshine every year. However, one must not forget the mistral which by common consent makes life a misery down and around the Rhône valley during the winter and early spring and which some people say spills over into the summer. When the Pyrenees are covered in snow, bitter winds sweeping down towards the sea are just as unpopular along the Vermilion Coast. Even quite hot days can be followed by cool evenings, especially up in the hills, so it is advisable to pack a sweater along with the beachwear, although with any luck you will not need it.

TEMPERATURE GUIDE

Average air °C	Jan	Feb	Mar	Apr	May	Jun	Jul	Aug	Sep	Oct	Nov	Dec
Riviera/Côte d'Azur	12.2	11.9	14.2	18.5	20.8	26.6	28.1	28.4	25.2	22.2	16.8	14.1
Provence	12.2	11.9	14.2	18.5	20.8	26.6	28.1	28.4	25.2	22.2	16.8	14.1
Languedoc-Roussillon	12.4	11.5	12.5	17.6	20.1	26.5	28.4	28.1	26.1	21.1	15.8	13.5

National holidays

There are eleven national holidays in France when banks, most museums and other public places are closed but shops and restaurants may well be open. New Year's Day, Easter Monday, Labour Day (1 May), VE Day (8 May), Ascension Day (six weeks after Easter), Whit Monday (ten days later), Bastille Day (14 July), Assumption Day (15 August), All Saints' Day (1 November), Remembrance Day (11 November) and Christmas Day.

Festivals

It would be almost impossible to count the number of festivals, carnivals, processions and other celebrations that take place in the South of France throughout the year. Some of them are extremely well known, others—and particularly those which are held in towns and villages off the beaten track— are seldom heard of outside the local community. The appropriate tourist offices will usually give you an idea of what is going on and tell you if they are tourist attractions or traditional events that have survived for hundreds of years. However, it is possible to list a few of the outstanding ones.

Agde holds colourful and entertaining water festivals on the first Saturday in July and the first Saturday in August.

Aix-en-Provence stages its famous International Music Festival from the middle of July to the first week in August.

Allauch attracts visitors to its Provençal Festival of St John the Baptist, which includes a blessing for the animals, on the Sunday following 24 June. There is also a Provençal Midnight Mass on Christmas Eve.

Arles celebrates with an Easter Festival which lasts all over the holiday and includes bull-fights, events featuring the cowboys of the Camargue, a mass and a blessing for the horses. There are performances in the Roman Theatre from late June to late July. Regular bull-fights are held from the beginning of July to the end of September and the year ends with the International Santon-makers' Show which opens in early December and lasts for about a month.

Avignon stages its month-long Festival of Dance and Drama from mid-July.

Béziers concentrates on bulls with events in the arena at the beginning of August and a grand finale on the 14th and 15th of the month.

21

Les Baux holds its age-old Shepherds' Festival and Midnight Mass on Christmas Eve.

Cannes, apart from all its other attractions, holds a Mimosa Festival in February, an International Antiques show in April and the famous Film Festival in May.

Cap d'Antibes honours its sailors with a festival and a procession of Our Lady of Safe Homecoming on either the first or second Sunday in July.

Carpentras is the venue for an evening procession which marks the Festival of Our Lady of Good Health in mid-July.

Céret boasts that some 400 dancers in national costume take part in its Festival of the Sardane, the traditional dance of the area, which ends before the last Sunday in August.

Collioure holds a procession of Penitents during Holy Week and celebrates its own saint's day with a festival in the middle of August.

La Grande-Motte goes to town at the beginning of July with several events including a Festival of Jazz.

Grasse predictably chose the rose for its May festival and jasmine for a second festival on the first Sunday in August.

Hyères, somewhat less predictably, devotes its attention to Experimental Cinema from late August to early September.

Juan-les-Pins, totally in character, is always crowded for the World Jazz Festival in July.

Marseilles stages a Santon Fair from the last Sunday in November until the first week in January when you can see all the little figures which originated as part of the Christmas Crib and now include typical characters like the fishwife, the baker, the policeman and even the local drunk all in national dress.

Martigues is well known for its Venetian Evening complete with a procession of decorated boats on the first Saturday in July.

Menton divides its attention between a Lemon Festival in the week before Shrove Tuesday and a Chamber Music Festival in August.

Monaco has endless celebrations and events throughout the year, three of which are the Feast of Ste-Dévote on 27 January, all the thrills of the Monaco Grand Prix in May and an International Fireworks Festival in July.

Montpellier holds a carnival in the spring and sets aside part of October for a wine festival and a week devoted to films.

Nice, apart from the famous Carnival in the weeks preceding Shrove Tuesday, has an International Book Fair in April, a May Festival of Folklore and a Jazz Festival in July.

22

Nîmes celebrates the Whitsun holiday with bull-fights and various other contests that last for four days and stages Spanish-type bull-fights from June to September.

Orange uses its magnificent Roman Theatre for an Arts Festival of drama, opera, ballet and symphony concerts from the middle of July to early in August.

Peille sets aside the first Sunday in September for a colourful folk festival.

Perpignan attracts large crowds on Good Friday when the Procession of Black Penitents takes place in the city. July and August attract music lovers to a series of concerts described as 'Music in the Plural'.

Roquebrune-Cap Martin have two most impressive religious processions during the year—the Procession of the Entombment of Christ on Good Friday and the Procession of the Passion on 5 August.

St-Tropez pulls out all the stops for its three-day Bravade starting on 16 May and the Spanish Bravade on 15 June.

Stes-Maries-de-la-Mer is the focal point for the annual Gypsy Pilgrimage on 24 and 25 May with a similar but rather less overwhelming version on the second last Sunday in October.

Sète stages a rally in January, a Theatre Festival in August and ends the month with a five-day fête in honour of St Louis, the patron saint of the town, in which anything goes from jousting on the water to fireworks after dark.

Tarascon recalls its legendary dragon during the Tarasque Festival and folk procession on the last Sunday in June and follows that with the arrival of the bulls on 14 July.

Toulon stages an International Dance Festival in July.

Vence has a busy time on Easter Sunday and Monday with an Episcopal Mass, Provençale dancing and a Battle of the Flowers.

Villeneuve-lès-Avignon celebrates the Feast of St Mark with a procession of vines decked out with ribbons towards the end of April.

Tourist Offices

Nearly every town has its own Office de Tourisme or Syndicat d'Initiative which is open from 9am until noon and from 2pm to 6pm on weekdays and usually on Saturdays and Sundays during the season. They will tell you what to see and how to get there, supply information on almost any subject you care to mention in relation to your holiday and sometimes help you with hotel bookings. It is a good plan to go in soon after you arrive so that you know exactly what the area has to offer, but if you are in a hurry and just have a single question it is probably easier to telephone instead.

Consulates

If you have any serious problems, and in the normal course of events there is no reason why you should, it is reassuring to know that you can contact the British Consulate at 24 Avenue du Prado, 13006 Marseilles (tel. 91–53.43.32). In addition there are consular representatives in both Nice and Perpignan. There are American Consulates at 13 Boulevard Paul Peytral 13286 Marseilles Cedex (tel. 91–54.92.00) and 31 rue Maréchal Joffre, 06000 Nice (tel. 93–54.92.00).

The people and language

The constant upheavals that have taken place in the South of France through the ages have left their mark on the people as surely as they have imprinted themselves on the towns and countryside. The inhabitants of the region tend to be small, somewhat stocky and dark, with expressive eyes that can blaze angrily at one moment and sparkle with pleasure the next. They are compassionate, hard-headed, artistic and industrious, and just as you think you have got to know them they show a totally unexpected facet of their character. They have less in common with their Teutonic countrymen to the north than they have with the people of northern Italy and Spain, with whom they share a common ancestry.

Even the language spoken in the South is at odds with the French dialects you come across in other places. Occitanian, or *langue d'oc* (*oc* meaning 'yes' in the South), as it is known, developed from the low Latin used in southern Gaul towards the end of the Roman Empire. Natives of northern Gaul spoke *langue d'oïl* (*oïl* being their word for 'yes'), which developed into modern French. The Southern dialect, *langue d'oc*, was spoken at the court of Richard the Lionheart, in Italy by people like Dante, by the troubadours and at the Papal court in Avignon. Inevitably it became known as Provençal. Four hundred years ago official French was imposed on the coastal regions, but in the middle of the last century the poet Frédéric Mistral and his friends made energetic efforts to prevent the local tongue dying out al-

24

together. Its name has been perpetuated in the region of Languedoc which separates Provence from the Roussillon where quite a few people still speak Catalan.

Today most people in the South find it easier and more convenient to stick to conventional French, albeit with an accent that is entirely their own. However, Provençal is still spoken in several areas, particularly the Comtat Venaissin and the region around Nîmes and Uzès, and local dialects are beginning to be taught in schools. Not only did Mistral succeed in preserving *langue d'oc*, but he also breathed new life into the ancient customs and traditions of the area. His Museon Arlaten in Arles set the pattern for an ever-growing number of displays that concentrate on the way of life, type of dress, variety of crafts and even the festivals of the past. All this combined with the *Trésor du Félibrige*, a massive dictionary of Provençal words and proverbs produced 100 years ago, and the plays and poems of the time add a fascinating dimension to the colourful history of the South of France.

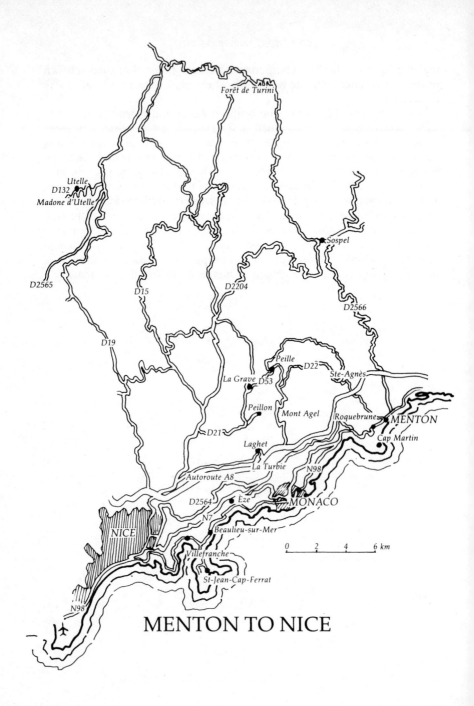

Chapter II

MENTON TO NICE

MENTON TO NICE

The shade of a street café

Menton

As a holiday resort Menton has been high on the British popularity list for well over 100 years. In fact, some of the early visitors were inclined to look on it in much the same way as they regarded Brighton and Bath. They called it 'Mentone', went out in droves to escape the English winter and some 5000 settled there permanently. The main attractions were the climate, which is almost perfect, the magnificent scenery and the old-world charm of the little fishing port. Inevitably these early tourists brought progress with them. The groves of tamarisk trees gave way to modern promenades, hotels appeared along the sea front and Augustus Hare, writing at the turn of the century, complained bitterly about all the new houses which he described as 'hideous and stuccoed villas in the worst taste'. It would be interesting to hear his reaction today: 20th-century Menton is not in the least like a fishing village, yet neither is it the epitome of high fashion as it was in his day. The villas, many of them standing in superb gardens, have mellowed with age and tourism has become a major industry. A statue of Dr Bennet, the

Englishman who started it all, stands in the Rue Partouneaux surrounded by the tangible results of a book he wrote in the 1850s drawing attention to the virtues of an obscure hamlet on the Gulf of Peace.

HISTORY

The history of Menton goes back a good deal further than the printed word—indeed, all the way to Adam and Eve if some romantically minded residents are correct. They say that Eve, not content with the apple and all the problems it caused, picked a lemon as she was leaving the Garden of Eden and planted it beside the Mediterranean. In no time at all the hills were covered with trees which still produce flowers and fruit all the year round.

For anyone more interested in history than legend, there certainly were people living on the Riviera in prehistoric days. The skull of the famous Grimaldi Man, found in les Rochers Rouges, a group of caves just across the Italian border, dates from 30 000 BC. It is to be supposed that the early inhabitants of the area went fishing and had little wars of their own but, even so, nothing much is known about Menton until the middle of the 13th century when its name appears for the first time. In 1346 the village was bought by the Princes of Monaco and for a long while afterwards was never quite sure if it belonged to France or Sardinia. The question was finally settled in 1860 and the people were able to give their full attention to the business of becoming a town and a holiday resort. The weather was a great help as Menton claims to be the warmest place on the Côte d'Azur during the winter, although Beaulieu disagrees. The rich, the famous and the gifted flooded in, preserving the *status quo* well into the present century, but Menton's troubles were not over.

The town was captured in 1940 by Mussolini who was determined to have at least a toehold in Hitler's occupied Europe and he held it until 1943. The Germans took it over after the collapse of Italy but were driven out as a result of the Allied landings the following year, waiting just long enough to blow up the harbour before leaving.

WHAT TO SEE

Although Menton is still a pretty resort, it has a slightly faded air of nostalgia about it. Many of the once-famous hotels that lined the sea front and attracted crowned heads and nobility from all over Europe have been pulled down or converted into holiday flats. Fortunately the powers that be resisted the impulse to replace them with garish modern equivalents, so it still retains a lot of atmosphere.

The **Promenade du Soleil,** festooned with palm trees, runs along beside the beach, changes both name and direction when it reaches the port and leads to the Quai Bonaparte. This wide thoroughfare was built by Napoleon on a series of arches round the edge of the bay to enable him to move his armies in and out of Italy in a hurry. Today it serves the same purpose for thousands of holidaymakers who do not mind crawling along, their cars nose to tail, drenched in the hot summer sunshine with the scent of citrus blossom obliterated by petrol and diesel fumes, as they make their way to the border.

The **Jean Cocteau Museum** is right on the front, close to the port. It is housed in a 17th-century bastion and, although small, has an interesting collection of drawings, paintings, pottery and stage sets as well as a tapestry or two. It is open from mid-June to mid-September between 10am and 6pm, closing at noon for a three-hour lunch break. During the rest of the year it takes only two hours for lunch and it is closed on Mondays, Tuesdays and holidays. The entrance fee is 3 francs but that includes a visit to the town hall. This is also a 17th-century building and the marriage hall was decorated by Cocteau, partly with pictures of local characters and partly with scenes from mythology. It keeps the same hours as the museum but closes on Saturdays and Sundays as well as holidays.

The **Quai Napoléon III,** right on the doorstep of the museum, provides what is probably the best view of the old town, rising steeply up the hillside behind the Quai Bonaparte. Although it is quite possible to drive up through an archway and into the Rue Longue, which used to be the main street, most people find it far more satisfactory to explore on foot.

The **Church of St-Michel** dates from the 17th century although much of the interior is more recent, having been badly damaged by an earthquake in 1887. It looks out over a really beautiful square, St-Michel Paris, reached from sea level after a steady climb up a wide, black and white pebbled stairway. It is extremely colourful both inside and out, which is only to be expected as it was modelled on the Church of the Annunciation in Genoa.

A few more steps separate St-Michel Parvis from the square in front of the **Chapel of the White Penitents** which is also highly decorated. Together the two squares form the setting for the annual Festival of Chamber Music, held every August. The open-air concerts are always in the evening when the churches are floodlit and banks of flaming torches greet the audience who converge on Menton from all over Europe. The old houses complete the picture and, according to experts, the acoustics are the next best thing to perfection.

Behind the squares is a positive rabbit warren of narrow, winding alleys, tiny stairways and little open spaces where you can stop to catch your breath and take your bearings. At one time they were filled with donkeys bringing olives down from groves high on the mountainside and doing a dozen other jobs for people who lived in the crowded, over-hanging houses. Although you would be lucky to meet a donkey nowadays, the atmosphere has hardly changed. It is one of the most fascinating of all the old quarters to be found in large towns along the Mediterranean and is certainly well worth a visit. Above it is the Old Cemetery, laid out on the site of an ancient castle in the 19th century and divided up between various nationalities. A corner of the English section has an excellent view over the town to the sea beyond.

Les Colombières is generally considered to be the most outstanding of all the beautiful villas along the Boulevard de Garavan. The gardens were designed in the Italian style by Ferdinand Bac and cover more than a dozen acres. He claimed that it took him a lifetime to plan them, although he managed to fit in a lot of writing and other creative work, to say nothing of a number of other gardens, at the same time. One can wander for hours under cypress and yew trees, discovering ornamental pools, fountains and statues as well as urns that cry out for great tumbling masses of geraniums. If you get tired there are strategically placed – if not always comfortable – benches where you can stop for a rest.

To complement his garden Monsieur Bac, who was alleged to be an illegitimate son of Napoleon III, designed and built a villa that owes as much to Greece as it does to Italy. It is a joyous conception that manages to include almost everything from a Salon des Muses to the Garden of Homer with a pool in the middle surrounded by a double row of columns. Many of the rooms are designed in the style of ancient Rome, the bedrooms coming complete with baths of the same era. You can look round any time between 9am and noon or 3pm and 8pm from January to the end of September at a cost of 8 F.

Just below Les Colombières is the old olive grove of Le Pian, a favourite meeting place for local people who are equally as proud of their olives as they are of their lemons. In contrast the **Tropical Gardens,** on the Chemin St-Jacques, are full of exotic flowers and shrubs, all set out in an orderly fashion as one would expect from the Natural History Museum in Paris who were responsible for arranging them in the grounds of the Villa Val Rahmeh. They are open from 10am to noon and from 2pm to 5pm from the beginning of February to the end of September, and close at 4pm during the winter as well as on Tuesdays and 1 May. Entrance costs 8 F.

Among other places to visit in the town are the **Palais Carnolès Museum,** devoted to paintings ranging from the early French and Italian schools through the 17th and 18th centuries to the present day (closed Mondays, Tuesdays and holidays, 3 F), and the **Municipal Museum** where, along with sections on local history, traditions and archaeological finds, you can see the skull of the Grimaldi Man. For a complete change of scene there is no better place than the **Biovès Garden** that bisects the town. Horticulture being what it is, Eve's original lemon has diversified into oranges, grapefruit, tangerines and other more exotic examples of the citrus family and many of them are to be found in this garden, interspersed with fountains and statues and edged with palms.

WHERE TO STAY
There are plenty of hotels to choose from in Menton whether you want a room overlooking the sea, something small and central or prefer to be up in the mountains behind.

The **Princess et Richmond,** on the Promenade du Soleil (tel. 93–35.80.20) is a road's width from the beach and costs up to 270 F. It also has a restaurant where you can get dinner or a light meal.

The **Auberge des Santons** (tel. 93–35.94.10) is a good restaurant where you can get a set menu for 95 to 250 F and also spend the night for around 190 F. It is close to the old L'Annonciade monastery where some people maintain that you can see the ghosts of 11th-century monks at the windows, probably objecting to all the reconstruction work that was done 600 years later! The auberge closes from mid-November to the middle of December, on Sunday evenings and Mondays except in July and August, and on holidays.

EATING OUT
Le Galion, Port de Garavan (tel: 93–35.89.73), specialises in Italian food, which is hardly surprising as the border is only just round the bend. The set menus range from 110 to 150 F and the restaurant is closed on Tuesdays and from the middle of October for two months.

L'Hacienda, on the road to Gorbio (tel. 93–35.84.44), prides itself on using mainly fresh produce from the farm and serves up delightful local dishes for anything from 140 to 200 F if you choose a set menu.

FESTIVALS
Apart from the famous Festival of Chamber Music in August, Menton goes

31

to town with a week-long Lemon Festival just before Easter with all the usual floats, flowers, fruit and eye-catching arrays of pretty girls.

ACTIVITIES

The beaches at Menton are generally sandy, not very wide and are usually crowded to capacity during the season with sun-worshippers, a breed of holidaymaker unheard of at the turn of the century. There are also swimming pools, at least one of which is heated, and you can join a sailing school, go water-skiing, windsurfing or skin-diving, hire a boat or a bicycle or play tennis. For enthusiastic hikers there are long walks into the mountains and along the valleys where it is said that you can find at least 1000 different kinds of wild flowers.

The marina, which is modern and efficient, shares the harbour with fishing boats and commercial craft and there are a few camping sites ranging from the organised variety with a shop and a beach nearby to the smaller type which have little in the way of facilities.

The nightlife is not really what you would call 'swinging', although there is a casino where the atmosphere is, admittedly, a trifle on the staid side, dinner-dances and cabarets in the summer and a cinema.

TOURIST INFORMATION

All the information you need is available from the tourist office in the Palais de l'Europe, overlooking the Biovès Garden (tel. 93–57.57.00), and it will also help you with hotel bookings.

Cap Martin and Roquebrune

Menton has expanded so much in recent years, moving sideways rather than inland because of the mountains behind, that Cap Martin and its protecting hill fortress of Roquebrune have, to all intents and purposes, become part of it. Not that this has made any difference to the fact that Cap Martin is both wooded and wealthy: it is not quite as exclusive as it was in the last century when a brace of empresses spent their winters there, but it still has some magnificent villas, hidden from view by olive and pine trees interspersed with clumps of cypress and mimosa.

ST MARTIN'S BASILICA

In the centre of Cap Martin are the ruins of **St Martin's Basilica,** part of a large religious building completed in the 11th century and destroyed by the

Saracens 300 years later. Opinion is divided as to whether it was a priory or a nunnery, but either way the story is the same. Apparently the Prior—or the Abbess, depending on the version—arranged for an alarm bell to be sounded at the first sign of a pirate so that the forces of Roquebrune could dash down to deal with them. One rather wonders what the sentry on look-out duty at the fortress above was supposed to be doing, but that is an academic question. Being of a rather doubting disposition, the head of the religious order decided to test the protectors and was gratified to find that the false alarm brought them rushing headlong down the hillside. Predictably their reaction was quite different. When at last the Saracens did arrive the people of Roquebrune stayed firmly in their beds, ignoring the bell and leaving the invaders to get on with the business of looting, burning and carrying off their prisoners. In spite of this I have to admit to a sneaking admiration for the pirates. It could not have been easy to creep ashore with their weapons between the great jagged black rocks surrounding the cape which still make swimming a fairly hazardous experience. The invaders might have been better advised to make for the shingle beach at Roquebrune and take a chance on the sentry.

THE FORTRESS AND KEEP

The fortress, dominated by its castle keep which is floodlit at night and can be seen for miles, is considered by many people to be the finest in the area. It certainly has been extremely well restored—the steep lanes and narrow covered stairways of the village are in excellent condition. There are many craft and souvenir shops where prices are about par for the course, and the medieval houses with their barred windows have a well-kept, 'on display' look about them.

Roquebrune, built by the Count of Ventimiglia at the end of the 10th century, is reputed to be the oldest feudal castle in France and as such it presents an interesting picture of life in the Middle Ages. For example, instead of the vast halls and spacious apartments we are used to seeing in romantic films about that period, the rooms are all amazingly small. The lord and his family made do with one bedroom, a living room and a small kitchen where the bread was baked. On official occasions they spilled over into the ceremonial hall below but even there they and their guests must have been decidedly cramped. The head of the household would sit on the baronial throne, keeping one eye on any prisoner who happened to be occupying the cell in the wall and the other on the family's water supply. Stored in a special tank topped up by the rain, it could make quite a difference between victory and defeat in the event of a siege. His armed guard had their own living space with its attendant prison area.

Everyone else lived outside the keep, protected by the castle walls with their fortified gateways and imposing battlements. These did a sterling job against the Saracens but were quite useless when it came to the plague. As a result, during the unhealthy summer of 1467 the villagers made a vow to hold a religious procession every year on 5 August if God protected them against the epidemic. Apparently their prayers were answered and for more than 500 years their descendents have re-enacted scenes from the Passion. They take the form of a series of tableaux which have remained unchanged down the centuries, starting with the Judas kiss and ending with the Crucifixion. A group of people dressed as disciples, holy women and a cross-section of Roman soldiers carry the statue of Jesus along streets decked out with religious symbols and lit by hundreds of minute lights made from cotton wicks saturated in olive oil and floating in snail shells.

You can wander round the village any time you like and inspect an olive tree which is said to have grown there for 1000 years, making it one of the oldest trees in the world, but the keep is a different matter. It is open from 9am to noon and between 2pm and 7pm from the beginning of April to the end of September. Thereafter it opens at 10am and closes at 4pm and on Fridays as well as on 1 May and for the first three weeks in November. The entrance fee is 5 F.

EXPLORING THE AREA

Roquebrune and Cap Martin are not the best of places to choose if you just want to swim or lie on the beach—that is, unless you enjoy the feeling of gravel underfoot and pitting your strength against the sea. It can be extremely turbulent, even for people who know the area well like the famous architect Le Corbusier, who was drowned there in 1965. However, there are no such hazards for visitors who enjoy simply walking. There is a most attractive footpath leading from the Avenue Winston-Churchill (the British political leader was one of the resort's most famous visitors) round the coast to Monte-Carlo Beach. And while on the subject of personalities, the Dutch painter Hans van Meegeren, who made a name and a fortune for himself copying Old Masters, perfected the art of forgery when he retired there in the 1930s.

The mountains which run right down to the sea along this part of the Mediterranean are justly famous for their outstanding views, wild countryside and isolated hill villages. There appears to be no end to the number of places waiting to be explored whether you choose to do it the hard way—on foot or by bicycle—or, as most tourists prefer, by driving from one focal point to another. The majority of the small but heavily fortified villages were either Saracen strongholds or built by the local tribes to keep out their enemies. The inhabitants grew their crops and grazed their animals outside the walls but huddled inside to sleep or to present a united front in the face of danger. They are perched like eagles' nests in the most inaccessible places and it is difficult to see how any attacker, having scrambled up hundreds of feet of rock and scrubland, could have had enough puff left to start a battle.

Ste-Agnès

One of the highest and most memorable of all these villages near the coast is Ste-Agnès, straddling a peak some 762 metres (2500ft) above sea level. Anyone who gets dizzy looking out of a high-rise flat might think seriously about driving up the tortuous route linking it directly with Menton. The alternatives are to go another way round or to settle for one of the many organised trips instead. The road, which is fairly narrow, winds remorselessly in a series of tight curves that would be the envy of an agitated boa constrictor. The surface is generally good but there are very few places to stop along the way. Most of the ones that look promising turn out to be private property, a drive leading to a nearby house or the entrance to a terraced vineyard or olive grove. Drivers who take a chance on parking, even if there is apparently no one around for miles, could find their popularity at a very low ebb indeed. Half an hour spent picking flowers or doing a little gentle mountaineering could result in a confrontation with an irate owner.

During the early part of the drive one gets an ant's-eye view of the autoroute into Italy, soaring hundreds of feet above on its massive concrete stilts. An impressive number of curves later, as the houses dwindle and the Mediterranean unfolds into a breathtaking panorama of mountains, coastline and blue water, the aspect changes completely. Now it is a case of looking down on a toy-size autoroute with smaller-than-matchbox cars, buses and heavy vehicles beetling backwards and forwards. With an occasional pause to look out across the deep valley, where wolves could be found not so very long ago, the drive to Ste-Agnès takes the better part of an hour. It is a sobering thought to realise that any self-respecting crow could have covered the distance in a matter of minutes.

The car park at Ste-Agnès is outside the walls, up against a rock face punctuated by heavy wooden doors that are kept locked and the odd gun emplacement dated 1932/1938. The road meanders on up a fairly gentle incline to the village with its cobbled streets, craft and souvenir shops and superlative views. The dedicated walker can carry on up a goat track to the ruined Saracen castle 92 metres (300ft) or so above. It was the home of a chieftain called Haroun who terrorised the district until he was fortunately converted to Christianity by Agnès, a young girl he had captured in a not-so-idle moment. There used to be an annual procession, led by the lord of the manor in ceremonial dress, to present a gilded apple filled with gold pieces to the local clergy. They in turn used it to help the poor and needy but the leaders of the Revolution frowned on that sort of thing and the practice was tactfully discontinued.

EATING OUT

Le St-Yves is a delightful little *auberge* with a handful of rooms, a good restaurant and an exceptional view (tel. 93–35.91.45). The same goes for the **Logis Sarrasin,** although it does not offer its guests a bed for the night (tel. 93–35.86.89). They are both rather basic and very much in keeping with their surroundings.

Sospel

Beyond Ste-Agnès the road continues on its winding way to Sospel, a popular summer resort in a valley on the road from Nice to Turin. It has plenty to offer in the way of historic buildings and modern amenities. On the one hand there is a splendid medieval bridge, its twin arches linked by a toll-gate in the middle which had to be rebuilt after it was destroyed in the last war. The 17th-century **Church of St-Michel,** sometimes described as a cathedral although it was demoted years ago, is quite ornate and justifiably enthused over by the local people, some of whom live in the picturesque old houses along the river bank. On the other hand there are some very modern buildings, a few hotels and restaurants, none of which is very expensive, and a choice of well-equipped camping sites. Visitors can ride, play tennis, swim or fish, go for long walks or watch a game of boules, especially when the championships are under way in July.

Sospel is also a particularly good centre for excursions—northwards, for instance, to the beautiful **Forest of Turini** with its acres of beech, oak, maple, chestnut and pine trees or further afield to Utelle.

Utelle

In this case the attraction is not so much the village with its usual blending of the old and the ancient as the **Madone d'Utelle** 6½ kilometres (4 miles) away. It is a lonely little sanctuary at the end of a winding mountain road, founded in the 9th century but largely re-created 200 years ago. It is, and always has been, a focal point for pilgrims who collect the key from one or other of the restaurants in the village. A short distance away there is a domed viewing table to help you appreciate one of the most outstanding views to be found anywhere in the Alpes Maritime.

Peille, Peillon and Laghet

A shorter trip from Ste-Agnès is along a winding and sometimes extremely narrow road to Peille, one of the many medieval hill villages that are being bought up rapidly to provide second homes. From there it twists its way cheerfully on to La Grave, where there is a huge cement factory and no incentive to stop for a stroll or a picnic, before heading for Peillon. This is interesting because it is a good example of how old houses are being converted to modern living standards, it will give you a chance to visit the Paillon Gorges and provide you with an excellent lunch at the **Auberge de la Madone** (tel. 93–79.91.17). The cooking is traditional and the best set menu costs 127 F. The *auberge* also has comfortable rooms for up to 320 F, offers pension terms but closes on Wednesdays and from the middle of October for two months.

If you have both the time and the inclination, you might stop briefly at Laghet where the **Sanctuary of Notre-Dame** and the museum next door share an incredible collection of ex-votos. These can be anything in the art line, were offered by people to fulfil a vow and are frequently intriguing and sometimes amusing. In the 17th century Laghet was a great place for pilgrims and its reputation for miracles grew so fast that the Bishop of Nice eventually refused to believe them and closed the church. After a fairly lengthy and probably partisan investigation he was persuaded to open it again and the statue of the Virgin was solemnly crowned. Local nobility as well as the rank and file of the population returned in droves. King Charles

Emmanuel II attributed the recovery of his child to the intervention of the Virgin and presented her with a baby exactly like his own but made of gold. This and all the other treasures in the shrine were carried off by the French in 1792, although the statue escaped because someone was quick enough to hide it until the danger had passed.

La Turbie

From Laghet it is only a few minutes journey by car to La Turbie, the last stop before Monaco.

Personally I found the famous **Trophée des Alpes** a trifle disappointing. Most drawings and even the occasional photograph suggest that it is a grim and largely ruined monument brooding over a windswept mountaintop where it was built by Augustus 2000 years ago. However, that has not been in any way true since an American admirer, Mr Edward Tuck, decided to rebuild it shortly before the last war. He could not do much about the stones that generations of villagers had appropriated to build their houses or even about the statue of Augustus which used to be its crowning glory, but he could, and did, restore 30 metres (100ft) of its estimated 45 metres (150ft). The enormous square base is dutifully inscribed and the whole freshly minted Trophy can be seen from a long way off, fingering the sky with a handful of gleaming columns rising above the housetops.

Near the Trophy, also by courtesy of Mr Tuck, is a small museum which has a model of the site as it was, or at any rate is thought to have been, when the Senate decided to commemorate Augustus and his victory over the local tribes with something fairly permanent. It suffered various indignities like being turned into a fort and blown up by the French in 1705, so it is rather surprising that enough remained to rebuild it at all. It is open from 9am to 12.30pm and from 2pm to 7pm between the beginning of April and the end of September. The hours are 9am to noon and 2pm to 5.30pm during the rest of the year but it is closed on public holidays. Entrance costs 7 F for adults and 1 F for children.

The **Church of St-Michel-Archange,** built in the 18th century, is almost next door and on the other side are the terraces from which you can look down on Monaco and follow the coast round past Cap Martin and into Italy. Inland there is an uninterrupted view of Mont Agel with its observatory and famous 18-hole golf course, the pride of the Monte-Carlo Golf Club and reputed to be one of the best on the Côte d'Azur.

Monaco

To me the most amazing thing about Monaco is that it exists at all. Who would have thought that a tract of rocky coastline the size of a postage stamp with no particular claim to fame could have become an international byword for wealth and pleasure in a little over 100 years?

HISTORY
In Roman times the natural harbour was known as the Port of Hercules but the cliffs behind were so forbidding that no one used it except to put in briefly to escape a storm. The Genoese got hold of it in 1197 and built a fort a decade or so later. This was taken through trickery by the Grimaldis in 1297 who were so pleased with themselves that they recorded the event on their coat-of-arms. With the help of a succession of protecting powers they have held on to it ever since, although there was a slight hiccup during the French Revolution.

The old town of Monaco, from the Tropical Gardens

At one time the family owned a considerable amount of real estate in the area but gradually they lost it or sold it off, as they did with Menton, in an

39

attempt to balance the budget. Things had become critical by the reign of Prince Charles III so he decided to gamble on a casino. Casinos were banned in France at the time but there was nothing to stop Monaco following the lead set by Germany. After a few false starts in the late 1850s, the project took off. A rather bleak area which supported nothing but heather, rosemary and a few olive trees blossomed into the suburb of Monte-Carlo, named after the far-sighted Prince. The opening in 1865 was helped along by the arrival of the railway from Nice. Money started flooding in, to a large extent from the pockets of the rich and famous wintering on the Riviera and anxious to try their luck at the new game of roulette as well as some of the better-known ways of making and losing a fortune. Magnificent hotels were built to receive them, the Opera House became justly famous, the ballet flourished and most of the important buildings already in existence, like the palace and the cathedral, were face-lifted into the 19th century. When Prince Albert succeeded his father, he had both the time and the money to spend on oceanography and, although there were those who said he should do less gadding about, his voyages of discovery provided the basis for one of the foremost oceanographical museums in the world. His great grandson, Prince Rainier III succeeded to the throne in 1949 and seven years later married the beautiful American film star Grace Kelly, who died so tragically in a motor accident a few years ago. Their son, Prince Albert, is Heir Apparent to the title which can be traced back more than 700 years.

WHAT TO SEE

Looking at Monaco a couple of decades ago one would have said that it was so built up and built over that little could be done to change it. One would have been wrong. As the revenue from gambling became less spectacular, a wise administration turned its attention to the business world, taking adequate measures to ensure that the country did not become a tax haven. Land was reclaimed to provide new homes, offices and space for profitable light industry. Everything flourished, including the tourist trade.

The **Prince's Palace,** parts of which date from the 13th century, rises up out of the rock with all the appropriate battlements to protect it. The guard is changed in the Place du Palais every day just before noon, watched by an admiring crowd, many of whom join one of the guided tours round the state apartments, resplendent with furniture, carpets and family portraits. The tours take place from the beginning of July to the end of September from 9.30am to 12.30pm and from 2pm to 6.30pm and cost 10F with half-price tickets for children.

The **Musée Napoléon,** sited in one wing of the palace, divides its attention between the Bonaparte family and the history of Monaco. There are clothes and trinkets, uniforms and flags, coins and medals and, probably to emphasise its American connections, a piece of rock brought back from the moon. It is open from 9.30am to noon and 2pm to 6pm from July to September; from 10am to 11.30am and 2pm to 5.30pm during the rest of the year and is closed on Mondays in the winter and from New Year's Day to the middle of February. The entrance fee is 8 F.

The **Oceanography Museum,** in the Avenue St-Martin, was founded in 1910 by Prince Albert I and includes an institute for scientific research which is going from strength to strength under the direction of Jacques Cousteau, one of the great names in underwater exploration. The exhibits range from scientific instruments and reproductions of the sea bed to items made from shark-skin or decorated with mother-of-pearl. In the vast aquarium, which is one of the best in Europe, there are fish of every description, while the skeletons of larger marine mammals stand about in the oceanic zoology hall. The museum is open from 9am to 7pm in the summer but stays open until 9pm during July and August. It opens half an hour later in the winter and costs 27 F, with children getting in for half-price.

Among the other museums are the **National Museum,** on the Avenue Princess-Grace, which has one of the finest collections of dolls and mechanical toys in existence. There are guided tours between 10am and 12.30pm and from 2.30pm to 6.30pm when some of the animated figures may be put through their paces. The museum is closed on some holidays and costs 12 F. Close to the palace is the **Historial des Princes de Monaco,** generally referred to as the Waxworks Museum, which traces the history of the Grimaldi family with a series of life-size figures. You can see them for 10 F at any time between 9.30am and 6.30pm, although they take a two-month holiday from the beginning of December.

The **Tropical Gardens,** at the western end of the principality, are full of cacti from the very large to the very small and include a balloon-shaped, prickly specimen called 'mother-in-law's cushion' as well as exotic and often brightly coloured plants from as far afield as Mexico and southern Africa. The **Grottes de l'Observatoire** alongside are full of stalactites and stalagmites and are thought to have been inhabited some 200 000 years ago. Bones and tools found inside are on show in the **Museum of Prehistoric Anthropology** which is also on the site. The gardens themselves are open from 9am to 7pm during the season, but close at sunset during the rest of the year as well as being closed on 1 May and 19 November. The entrance fee of 17 F, (half-price for children), includes a guided tour of the caves and entry to the museum which keeps the same hours but closes at 5.30pm out of season regardless of when the sun sets.

There are not many outstanding churches to visit in Monaco. The **Cathedral,** near the palace, was built on the ruins of an old church at the end of the 19th century. The **Miséricorde Chapel,** dating from 1646, has a statue of Christ which is carried in procession through the streets of the old town on Good Friday, and in January a small ship is burned in the square outside the **Ste-Dévote Church** near the harbour followed by a procession the next day. This is all in honour of a legend. Apparently the body of Ste-Dévote, who was murdered in Corsica in the 3rd century, was guided into the harbour by a dove. At some time during the Middle Ages thieves stole the relics and tried to get away by sea but they were caught and their boat was burned—hence the ceremony in memory of the country's patron saint.

Nobody could possibly visit Monaco without going to the **Casino,** an extremely ornate building designed by Charles Garnier who was responsible for the Paris Opera House. It is surrounded by formal gardens and includes a theatre, the famous gaming rooms and a night club as well as a tea room where you can take the weight off your feet. It is open from 10am to 4am but closes on 1 May. You have to be over 21 and have your passport or identity papers to get an entry card for the public or private gaming rooms and it will cost you 20 F.

WHERE TO STAY

The size of your bank account will decide where you stay in Monaco. Famous hotels like the **Paris** and the **Hermitage** will cost you well over 1000 F a night and **Loews**, with its own casino, is in the same category. If you want to come down-market it will be necessary to search for a bed-and-breakfast establishment or, better still, settle for a hotel just outside.

The **Olympia**, in Beausoleil, 17 bis Boulevard Général-Leclerc (tel. 93–78.12.70), would be a modest choice at 145 F a night but it has no restaurant.

EATING OUT

The restaurants in Monaco are also predictably expensive but you can get a set menu for upwards of 200 F at most of the best hotels. The **Paris**, like the restaurant **Dominique Le Stanc** in the Boulevard Moulins, will set you back at least 300 F. Instead, try the sea food at **La Calanque**, 33 Avenue St-

Charles (tel. 93–50.63.19), where you pay 195 F for the smallest set menu. It is closed on Sundays and from the middle of March to the middle of April.

FESTIVALS
Something is happening in Monaco all the year round and you would be most unlikely to pick a time when there was not a festival or a local celebration of some kind. The year starts off with the Monte-Carlo Rally and the Festival of Ste-Dévote. February brings a Television Festival, followed by the Tennis Championships in April. The Monaco Grand Prix turns the town upside down in May and the summer is given over to the arts and music with innumerable firework displays. The Monegasques hold their National Fête in November and the year ends with the International Circus Festival in December.

ACTIVITIES
The famous marina, a wide blue expanse of water into which some of the world's most extrovert boat owners have poured millions of pounds in the shape of sleek yachts and floating gin palaces, takes up a good bit of the foreshore. However, not all the craft are in the millionaire category and quite a few are available for charter. For anything in the way of sailing lessons or deep-sea fishing it is necessary to contact the Yacht Club de Monaco, Quai Antoine-Ier (tel. 93–30.23.96).

Whatever other sports you have in mind, Monaco can meet your requirements. Golfers can play 18 holes on the slopes of Mont Agel by contacting the Monte-Carlo Golf Club (tel. 93–41.09.11) and there are tennis and squash courts at the Monte-Carlo Country Club just off the road to Menton (tel. 93–78.20.45). You can water-ski, windsurf or skin-dive, hire a bicycle or take long walks into the mountains. The only thing you cannot do is find a camping site because caravans are forbidden in Monaco.

There are quite a few beaches in the principality but only one of them is free and the majority are closed during the winter. Instead you can swim in any of a number of pools, indoor as well as outdoor, heated and unheated, including some belonging to the bigger hotels where you also have to pay.

TOURIST INFORMATION
The information office, grandly titled Direction Tourisme et Congrès, at 2a Boulevard Moulins (tel. 93–30.87.01), is one of the most efficient to be found anywhere and will provide facts and figures to keep even the most enquiring mind occupied for days on end. It was riveting to discover that Monaco could not declare war on Germany in 1939 because it had overlooked the small matter of signing a peace treaty at the end of the First

World War. And there is a certain charm in the observation that the army, numbering less than 100, is about the same size as the National Orchestra. One writer at the end of the last century said he had been told by an official that the strength had been doubled to 24 as a result of a recent war, so it has increased considerably since then. The fact that it is not equipped to launch an attack or to defend its homeland is neither here nor there. The boundaries are invisible to everyone except the initiated. The line to the east dividing Monte-Carlo from Roquebrune–Cap Martin runs at such an angle that the famous beach is in 'foreign territory', while Beausoleil, which looks like a suburb and contains most of the markets and less expensive houses, is in reality a French town.

On the western side of Cap d'Ail, and beyond a rather incongruous Bailey Bridge, the never-ending line of houses and hotels melts into Èze, or rather Èze-Bord-de-Mer as the village proper is well over 300 metres (1000ft) up and you have to crick your neck to look at it. The beach is pebbly and the railway runs along the side of it, making access almost impossible if it were not for the specially constructed crossing points.

Èze

Not a great many people would think of walking up to the village of Èze, although some say that they have done it along a bridle path through pine and olive trees and enjoyed the experience. For the majority it is possible to drive up and park, provided there is anywhere available that is not strictly out of bounds. Either way it is the usual 'pedestrians only' rule inside the protecting walls.

Èze, by common consent, is among the best-known and therefore most frequently visited attractions of its kind. The restoration has been completed with the utmost attention to detail. There is nothing to recall the Greeks or the Romans, but you can see the remains of a 14th-century castle that was destroyed in 1706 on the orders of Louis XIV. However, he ignored the White Penitents' Chapel, built at about the same time, which is open from 8am until 7pm all the year round. The main church was rebuilt in the 18th century and has a magnificent view over the tropical gardens towards Corsica which is said to be visible on a clear morning. The village is highly commercialised and caters for tourists on the lookout for pictures, pottery and other souvenirs. Out of season it is most entertaining to wander along the tiny narrow streets and alleys where several artists live and sell their wares, but when the holidays are in full swing it is a question of brute force over politeness.

The **Château Èza** (tel. 93–41.12.24) is one of the most expensive hotels on the Côte d'Azur, charging up to 2200 F a night and 60 F for a continental breakfast in your room, but you can get a set menu for 120 F. It is closed from the middle of November until the middle of February.

Just outside the entrance to the village in the Avenue des Jardins Exotique is a shop called Anicroche which no one could overlook. It does not go in much for jewellery or wrought-iron work, which are considered to be the leading local products, but it does offer a selection of scents, soaps, sweets and crystallised fruits as well as paintings by local artists and a nice line in rough clay plaques. However, the items that really attract the eye and bring the money rolling in are the *petits villages provençaux*. They are tableaux of any little hill village you care to mention, made up of tiny individual china houses, drinking fountains, bell towers and so on which all fit together in groups of any size, preferably in front of a large piece of rock. They range from 30 F to 160 F and more and the idea is to buy as many pieces as you like or, more to the point, as many as you can afford and re-create the Provençal village of your choice on a convenient shelf at home. If you have any money left over, you might call in at the Fragonard factory nearby to look round and choose a bottle of scent.

Back at sea level from where, at night, the floodlit village seems to float in the air, looking rather like the little crown that Queen Victoria used to wear, the next stop westwards is Beaulieu-sur-Mer. Once again it is difficult to tell where one resort ends and the next begins. New houses are going up all along the sides of the wide tree-covered ravine, served by a narrow road with a good surface. As in so many other places it is possible to rent a furnished villa or an apartment but a good deal more difficult to find anywhere to rest your caravan.

Beaulieu-sur-Mer

Although Beaulieu could no longer be described as glamorous, there is still a great deal to recommend it. For one thing it claims to be as warm as, if not warmer than, Menton in winter: for another it has a large and well-run marina with some quite impressive boats tied up alongside. You can hire a motorboat, join a sailing school, water-ski or skin-dive, but there are no public swimming pools and the beach is shingle. After dark the casino takes care of gamblers without making too much noise about it.

There are some splendid houses about, the most impressive of which is the **Villa Kerylos,** constructed in the style of ancient Greece. It was built by the archaeologist Theodore Reinach, sumptuously furnished and left to the French Institute in 1928. It is open from 3pm to 7pm in the summer, from 2pm to 6pm in the winter, is closed on Mondays and throughout November and costs 10 F.

WHERE TO STAY

Among the many hotels, some of them in the very expensive bracket, is **La Réserve,** built 100 years ago by Gordon Bennett who owned the *New York Herald* and was responsible for sending Stanley dashing off to Africa in search of David Livingstone. It will set you back 1520 F a night.

The Frisia, on the Boulevard Maréchal-Leclerc (tel. 93–01.01.04), is comfortable and reasonable at 350 F but there is no restaurant and it closes from the end of October until just before Christmas.

EATING OUT

Les Agaves, 4 Avenue Marechal-Foch (tel. 93–01.12.09), is small and was aptly described by a close friend as 'very Tunbridge Wells'. It charges 150 F for a set menu with a cheaper one on weekdays and closes on Wednesdays and from the middle of November for a month.

Villefranche

If Beaulieu is booked up, out of your price range or not as lively as you had hoped in spite of its night club and cinema, try your luck at Villefranche. It is an old fishing port on the other side of St-Jean-Cap-Ferrat, tucked into one of the loveliest bays anywhere along the coast. Its water is so deep that the French navy developed the habit of anchoring in the roads, and so did the Americans until France pulled out of NATO and they had to find somewhere else. The old town, huddled in the shadow of the citadel, has the usual mixture of alleys and stairways, some of them covered like the appropriately named Rue Obscure where it is so dark that you can hardly see a thing. Brightly coloured houses line the waterfront with a plethora of open-air cafes and restaurants.

At the entrance to the little port is the ancient **Chapel of St-Pierre** which dates from the 14th century. At one time it was a sanctuary for fishermen who gratefully stored their nets in it, but in the mid-fifties the nets were moved out and Jean Cocteau moved in to decorate the walls and ceilings. The effect is most attractive if a little unexpected, mixing, as it does, gypsies and fisherfolk, angels and scenes from the life of St Peter. It is open from 9am to noon and from 2.30pm to 7pm in the high season, closes at 6pm in the spring and autumn, opens from 9.30am to noon and 2pm to 4.30pm in the winter and is closed on Fridays, at Christmas and from the middle of November for a month. The entrance fee is 4F.

St-Jean-Cap-Ferrat

The peninsula with all its coves, palms and pine trees is almost entirely in private hands. A case in point is the Villa Mauresque where Somerset Maugham used to live, bitterly resenting any tourists who included him in their list of sights to be seen.

The **Ephrussi de Rothschild Foundation,** standing in its magnificent gardens, has been a museum since the Baroness died in 1934, leaving it to the Académie des Beaux Arts. The contents were also included in her bequest, a perfectly logical decision when you realise that the house was designed to set off her extremely valuable collection rather than the other way round. As there seems to have been very little that did not interest the Baroness, the variety of items is astonishing. Superb furniture, carpets, tapestries and pictures vie for attention with treasures from the Far East, fine examples of Sèvres and Dresden china and displays of costumes worn at the time of Louis XVI and Marie Antoinette. There are guided tours of the mansion between 3pm and 7pm in the high summer and between 2pm and 6pm from the beginning of September to the end of June. It is closed on Mondays, 1 January, 1 May, Christmas Day and for all of November. entrance costs 15F.

A small private zoo occupies the space where King Leopold of the Belgians once had a lake and is a thoroughly enjoyable place to spend an hour or two between 9am and 7pm from mid-June to mid-September and 9.30am to 6pm for the rest of the year. It costs 17F for adults and 10F for children.

There are several hotels and restaurants on the cape, most of them quite reasonably priced. The small fishing village of St-Jean is now a delightful holiday resort with facilities for sailing, water-skiing and hiring a small boat, but there are no camping sites, the beaches are more often shingle than sand and it has neither a cinema nor a casino. For anyone who wants to live it up in the evenings, Nice is only 6 kilometres ($3\frac{1}{2}$ miles) away.

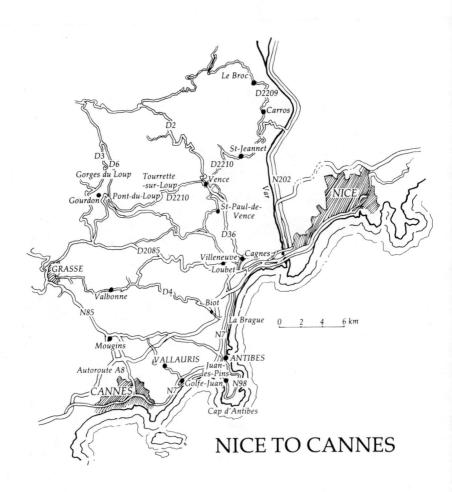

Le Broc

D2209

Carros

D2

St-Jeannet

D3
D6
Gorges du Loup
Tourrette
-sur-Loup
D2210
Vence

N202

NICE

Var

Gourdon Pont-du-Loup D2210
St-Paul-de-
Vence

D36

D2085
Villeneuve
-Loubet
Cagnes

GRASSE

Valbonne
D4
Biot

N85
La Brague

0   2   4   6 km

Mougins
N7

VALLAURIS ANTIBES

Autoroute A8
Juan-
les-Pins
Golfe-Juan N98
N7
CANNES

Cap d'Antibes

NICE TO CANNES

Chapter III

NICE TO CANNES

Château Grimaldi containing the
Picasso Museum and Cathedral, Antibes

Nice

More has probably been written on Nice than any other place on the Côte
d'Azur with the possible exception of Monte-Carlo, and it is interesting to
find how few writers seem to agree about it. One describes it as fascinating
and stimulating, another dismisses it as a commercial city with tourist over-
tones. An author in the 19th century went so far as to say that it was the
home of the millionaire and the working man and everyone else would do
better to stay away. Very few took his advice, of course, and soon it was forgotten altogether.

HISTORY
Nice first saw the light of day in about 350 BC when it was founded by the
Greeks from Marseilles and named Nikea after their goddess of victory.
When the Romans took it over some 200 years later, they established their
own town at Cimiez on the hill behind which still shows traces of Roman
habitation. Among other things they built a set of remarkably fine baths that

51

are divided into cold, warm and hot rooms for important members of the community, a different section for the general public and yet another reserved for women only. The arena was fairly small by Roman standards, although it comes in handy for modern spectacles, and not far away it is just possible to identify the site where the temple of Apollo used to stand. As was usually the case, the town was eventually destroyed by the barbarians.

It took quite a while before things began to improve and even then it was trade that flourished rather than art and architecture. Nice had been doing very nicely as part of Provence for 400 years when Queen Jeanne was murdered in 1382 and the Count of Savoy moved in. The inhabitants must have approved because as he rode past cherubs were hoisted into the air waving palm leaves. Once things had returned to normal, the people had time to devote to peaceful occupations and an interesting school of painting grew up led by the Brea family, much of whose work can still be seen in the area.

They were, however, turbulent times and the lack of interesting old buildings has been laid firmly at the door of the Duke of Berwick. He was an illegitimate son of James II who made a name for himself as a victorious commander in the French army during the reign of Louis XIV. In the course of a fairly destructive career he attacked Nice and made a thorough job of blowing up the château built by the Dukes of Savoy on the site of the old Greek acropolis. In the years that followed, control of the port was tossed backwards and forwards between France and Savoy like a ping-pong ball. By the time its future was finally settled under the Treaty of Turin in 1860, it had been taken over peacefully by British tourists and transformed into a highly desirable holiday resort. Queen Victoria wintered there and is said to have found it very much to her liking.

WHAT TO SEE
Nice is a town which exists in its own right regardless of holiday makers, being one of the largest and most cosmopolitan in France. It is the capital of the Côte d'Azur, an administrative centre as well as a university town, supports and is supported by a wealth of light industry, has excellent road and rail services and an extremely busy international airport.

The **Promenade des Anglais,** one of the most famous streets in the world, runs in a gentle, palm-shaded curve along the Baie des Anges. It was built with the help of the British community after a severe winter in the early 1800s had left a lot of people without either work or money. It runs from Cap de Nice, round Port Lympia, along the front and down towards Antibes.

On the way it passes the **Château,** the name still given to the rocky hill where the acropolis stood which is now a public garden. With commendable foresight the authorities have installed a lift, so there is no need to attempt the long climb to the top unless you are doing it for its own sake.

The **Naval Museum** makes a good stopping place on the way. It is at the top of the Bellanda Tower where Berlioz once lived, is guarded by two ancient cannons and is full of model ships, aids to navigation and exhibits tracing the history of Nice through the ages. It is open from 10am to 12.30pm and from 2.30pm to 7pm but closes two hours early in the winter. It is also closed on Tuesdays, holidays and from mid-November for a month. The museum is free but the lift, which operates throughout the year, costs 2.60 F.

Further along the Promenade, which at this stage has the sub-title Quai des États-Unis, you skirt the edge of the old town, pass a couple of small galleries and come eventually to the **Masséna Museum.** It contains a bit of everything from carpets and furniture, paintings and statues to folklore and reminders of famous citizens. Naturally the Massénas, including the famous Marshal, get a fair crack of the whip and so does Garibaldi who was born near the Customs House. Napoleon also counts because he lived in Nice on two different occasions, on one of which he was arrested but talked his way out of trouble fairly speedily. A gold-embroidered cloak worn by Josephine is included for good measure.

Next door to the museum is the incredible **Hôtel Negresco,** a great white palace of a place decorated with lights that vaguely call to mind Harrods at Christmas. It has been classified as a National Monument and the magnetic attraction it exerted on the high and the mighty after its opening in 1912 has not diminished in the least. When Giscard d'Estaing was President he chose to stay there for his meeting with more than two dozen African heads of state. They, in turn, are reported to have been suitably impressed by the grandeur of its public rooms and the old-world elegance of the suites allotted to them.

The old quarter is divided roughly into two sections, the more ancient presenting the familiar pattern of shadowed streets and tall houses in contrast to the grid system which became popular in the 17th century. The **Palais Lascaris** is an ornate example of the kind of mansion that was all the rage in Genoa at that time. The grand staircase is particularly impressive and so, in a different way, are the tools of the apothecary which are housed on the ground floor in a reconstructed pharmacy from Besançon. It is open from 9.30am to noon and 2.30pm to 6.30pm between July and September but closes on Mondays and holidays. During the rest of the year it closes at 6pm on Mondays, Tuesdays and holidays.

Among the many churches are the **Cathedral of Ste-Réparate** which dates from the 17th century, the **Church of St-Martin and St-Augustin** where Luther once celebrated mass and where Garibaldi was christened, the **Church of St-Jacques** and two small chapels. The **Miséricorde**, belonging to the Black Penitents, is a fine example of Italian Baroque and is only open for guided tours but you can see the amazingly ornate **St-Giaume Chapel** at any time and would be unlucky not to find the altar dedicated to Ste Rita banked with flowers and lit by dozens of candles.

The **Russian Orthodox Cathedral** on the Boulevard du Tsarevitch, built in 1903, could easily have emigrated from Moscow or St Petersburg and owes its existence to the Tsar. It is open from 9am to noon and 2.30pm to 6pm in the summer, opens later and closes earlier in the winter as well as on Sundays and orthodox holidays and costs 5 F.

Museums are to be found everywhere and for devotees of Chagall an obvious choice would be the **Marc Chagall Museum** on the Avenue Docteur Ménard. It was built especially to house a large proportion of his works and was opened by the grand old man himself in 1973. Its main items are the 17 large canvases which make up his 'Biblical Message' and took 13 years to complete. There is a story told of one visitor who, after subjecting them to a long silent scrutiny, observed to her companion that it was a good thing he had lived long enough to complete them. 'Yes,' agreed the other; 'when did he die?' A voice from behind chipped in, 'Madam, I have not yet had that pleasure.' It was the artist on one of his periodical visits to the museum which were only discontinued shortly before his death in 1985. It is open from 10.30am to about 3pm, is closed on Tuesdays, and costs 8 F except on Sundays when the fee is 4 F and on Wednesdays when entrance is free.

The **Matisse Museum** on the Avenue des Arènes-de-Cimiez includes examples of the work of Henri Matisse from 1890 to the *Blue Nude* painted two years before his death in 1954. It is a treasure trove of paintings, drawings and sculptures as well as furniture, personal souvenirs, his private art collection and sketches and models for the Chapelle du Rosaire in Vence which he decorated as a present for the nuns who nursed him through a serious illness. It is open from 10am to noon and from 2.30pm to 6.30pm in the summer but curtails the hours somewhat during the winter.

The **Chéret Museum** in the Avenue des Baumettes includes any number of art treasures; the **Malacology Gallery** is worth visiting for its collection of rare molluscs in ever size, shape and colour and is to be found in the **Natural History Museum**; while the **Terra Amata Museum,** a short walk from Port Lympia, concentrates on very ancient history indeed and stands on the site of one of the first human settlements in Europe.

Although Nice is the oldest of all the European coastal resorts, it is not an ideal place to go if you want to spend all your time on the beach. There is only a narrow strip and what there is of it is shingle and extremely crowded. Rather, it is a place to explore thoroughly, to shop, preferably with a fair amount of money to spend, and to sample the local dishes.

The Cours Saleya, which was originally the main street, used to be the home of the world-famous wholesale flower market but this has now moved out near the airport. The retail one, not far from the fish market in the Place St-François, is colourful and wonderfully scented but, sadly, is only a pale shadow of its former self.

Port Lympia started to take shape in the middle of the 18th century and has been modernised and extended considerably since then. Today it is a busy harbour dealing with merchantmen and fishing boats, private yachts and ferries including regular services to Corsica and boat trips along the Riviera.

WHERE TO STAY

It would be very strange if Nice did not have an enormous number of hotels and it is said that something like 20 000 rooms can be found for visitors. These establishments range from a good half-dozen in the luxury class to a variety in the average and modest categories.

La Pérouse, 11 Quai Rauba-Cape u (tel. 93–62.34.63), is one of the more unusual ones. It is built into the side of the Château hill, is partly surrounded with gardens and you can get to it the easy way by lift. There is no restaurant but you can have a snack at lunchtime beside the swimming pool. A room with a wonderful view costs 800 F.

The **Windsor,** 11 Rue Dalpozzo (tel. 93–88.59.35), is only a stone's throw from the Promenade des Anglais and also has a swimming pool but no restaurant. The price of a room is up to 340 F.

EATING OUT

Whatever you want to eat, you are bound to find it in Nice whether you are wandering round the old town, exploring further afield or lounging on the beach. A popular choice is *bouillabaisse*, a sort of fish soup-cum-stew in which, apart from the obligatory saffron, the ingredients tend to vary slightly. Surprisingly it can be quite pricy and sometimes has to be ordered in advance. Other local specialities include *salade niçoise*, stuffed vegetables and vegetable pies and a particularly delectable fritter made with marrow flowers.

La Merenda, 4 Rue Terrasse, about a block from the fashionable Place Masséna, specialises in local dishes and provides a good set menu at 85 F. It is closed in August and on Saturday nights, Sundays and Mondays.

Le Gourmet Lorrain, 7 Avenue Santa-Fior (tel. 93–84.90.78), is a restaurant which also provides rooms for visitors at around 170 F a night. It has an excellent menu from 70 F upwards, a comprehensive wine list and includes among its specialities *filet d'autruche*. The ostrich meat is imported and it would be interesting to know if it is considered a delicacy by the breeders back home. The restaurant is closed in August and on Sunday evenings and Mondays.

FESTIVALS

Nice really goes to town where festivals are concerned. Apart from the famous carnival before Easter, with its processions, floats, fireworks and masked balls, there is an occasion to highlight almost any interest you care to mention. Twice a year, in spring and autumn, the Nice Philharmonic puts on a special music festival at the Opera House. The Jazz Parade attracts both leading performers and enormous crowds in July and there are special times set aside for festivals of dancing, films, folklore, crafts, theatrical productions and sacred music. In August the wine festival is celebrated with enormous enthusiasm. Even dogs have their day, and so do book lovers and people who enjoy tennis tournaments, athletic meetings and horse racing which takes place on the course at Cagnes.

TOURIST INFORMATION

As the country's leading tourist centre Nice obviously provides far too much work for one information office, so you can take your pick from one in the Avenue Thiers (tel. 93–87.07.07), another in the Palais des Congrès on the Esplanade Kennedy (tel. 93–92.80.80), a third at 5 Avenue Gustave-v (tel. 93–87.60.60), or pop into the one at the airport when you are out that way.

EXCURSIONS

As a change from life in the city there are a considerable number of places to visit inland. For such trips you can use public buses, most of which are frequent, regular, clean and comfortable. They have come a long way since the days when you could find yourself sitting next to a farmer's wife clutching a piglet or two live hens. If you are without a car, it is not difficult or too expensive to hire one. Alternatively you could opt for the train, especially a delightful narrow-gauge railway that links the city with Digne, an attractive spa town about 160 kilometres (100 miles) away. During the summer it is pulled by a self-important steam engine and you can get all the details of times and fares from the offices of the Chemins de Fer de Provence (tel. 93–72.34.62)

St-Jeannet, Carros and Le Broc

There is some magnificent country to the north-west, reached by any of a number of minor roads that start from the far side of the airport. Once you have shaken off the flat, urbanised and frankly ugly stretch along the lower reaches of the Var, the possibilities are endless. Stop for a cool drink or a good lunch at St-Jeannet, once associated with the Knights of St John, where the women used to have a formidable reputation for sorcery. Now it is better known for the quality of the local wine and the view from the Baou St-Jeannet, but only after a good hour's climb up a mule track to the top of the cliff.

Further north you come to Carros, a typical hill village with a view, a windmill and an ancient castle to recommend it. Beyond le Broc life becomes a series of ups and downs as wooded valleys rub shoulders with mountaintops not infrequently capped by a deserted village. These are all very similar, built with local stone and merging into the background so that it is sometimes difficult to tell if they are rocky outcrops or crumbling walls and terraces. At times the roads can be very narrow but this hardly matters because, except in high summer, there is unlikely to be much traffic about. Every now and again you come across a cleft in the rock with crystal water pouring out of it. These make idyllic places for a picnic, especially if there is also a clear if rather cold pool suitable for bathing.

Vence

When meadows, pine forests and lonely stretches begin to pall, there is always Vence. Like so many places which have become popular tourist centres, the town has had a somewhat chequered career. The Romans drove out the local tribes who were there first, only to be ousted in their turn. With the arrival of Christianity the settlement grew in importance; two of its early bishops were made saints and a third was sent to Rome in the 16th century as Pope Paul III. Not unusually, there was constant friction between the church and the local barons who resented anyone's influence other than their own, but eventually the church got the upper hand.

Another famous churchman connected with Vence was Bishop Godeau. In his youth he had been a court favourite and was known as the wittiest man in France in the early 17th century. Suddenly he gave up royalty for religion, took holy orders and was appointed Bishop of Grasse and Vence. Unlike Bath and Wells the two congregations would not agree to a communal link with heaven, so he chose Vence and immediately set about restoring the ancient cathedral in the centre of the somewhat egg-shaped town. He also encouraged the villagers to take up pottery, tanning and scent making to earn some urgently needed money.

WHAT TO SEE

The **Cathedral,** built on the remains of a Roman temple and a 5th-century church, is still one of the major sights together with the old houses, where local arts and crafts are sold, and the Place du Peyra, an enchanting little square on the site of the old Roman forum. The fountain, in the shape of a large urn, is punctured round the bottom so that the water can spurt out; nearby it is possible to have a candlelit dinner out in the open, surrounded by the ancient stone walls.

By far the most outstanding attraction in Vence is the **Rosaire Chapel,** decorated by Matisse and considered by him to be his masterpiece. The whole interior of the little tiled building is white and the tiled walls are decorated with black line drawings of religious figures. They are simple to the point of being primitive and have no features at all. The altar is stark and made of sandstone. Light pours in through long stained-glass windows, dappling the floor with geometric patterns that look vaguely like yellow plants and angular green leaves against a blue background. The effect would be arresting under any circumstances, but as the work of a man who was an agnostic and near the end of his long life it is unforgettable. The chapel is open from 10am to 11.30am and from 2.30pm to 5.30pm on Tuesdays and Thursdays unless they happen to be public holidays. It is also said to be open at other times by appointment, but this can be misleading. At least one group of visitors who thought the necessary arrangements had been made were given the brush-off by a disdainful young woman in the tourist office, so it is better to contact Foyer Lacordaire, Avenue H. Matisse (tel. 93–58.03.26). The telephone number of the **tourist office** in the Place du Grand Jardin is 93–58.06.38.

WHERE TO STAY AND EATING OUT

For an amount that feels not too far short of the National Debt you can stay at the **Château du Domaine St-Martin** (tel. 93–58.02.02.), which stands in its own park just outside the town with its own ruined castle for company. Tiny modern villas are provided for guests who demand even greater privacy and the heart-shaped pool is said to have been built for Harry Truman. It costs about 1550 F for a room and you can get a cheap set menu for 280 F except on Sundays and public holidays.

A good alternative without any of the frills would be the **Auberge des Seigneurs** in the Place du Frêne (tel. 93–58.04.24) which is an excellent restaurant with a few rooms for guests. You can stay there for around 200 F and eat well at about 129 F, although it is closed on Mondays and from mid-October to the beginning of December.

Anyone with a preference for camping and caravanning would enjoy the **Domaine de la Bergerie** on the Route de la Sine (tel. 93–58.09.36). It has a restaurant, a shop, provides take-away meals and you can swim, ride and play tennis nearby. Dogs are allowed, but only on a leash.

Hikers, whether they favour long distances or rambles of a mile or two, will find the paths well signposted. They weave their way along the valleys and up the wooded mountainsides, linking vantage points which lesser mortals could well dismiss as being inaccessible.

St-Paul-de-Vence

St-Paul-de-Vence, within walking distance if you are that way inclined, is a very pretty town filled with little squares and fountains linked by paved lanes and alleys that are always full of people. There are several reminders of its days as a frontier post when hundreds of houses were pulled down to make way for the ramparts that still stand today. The shops, filled with antiques and examples of local craftsmanship, charge top prices but their turnover is considerable, especially at L'Herbier de Provence with its tempting array of oils, herbs and scented soaps.

The church, which was built at the end of the 12th century and has been restored a couple of times since then, is extremely attractive inside. Among its treasures are a picture of St Catherine of Alexandria looking very

Fountain at Saint-Paul-de-Vence

militant, which is thought to have been painted by Tintoretto, and a beautiful enamel Virgin and Child.

On the outskirts of the town is the amazing **Maeght Foundation,** an oustandingly modern building which is all pink and white and has a faintly eastern look about it. The museum was created in 1964 and is considered to be one of the most important collections of modern art in France. It also has a library and a cinema, gives concerts and ballet performances and has dotted the park with statues, ceramics and other examples of 20th-century art. It is open from 10am to 12.30pm and from 3pm to 7pm in the summer but closes at 6pm from the beginning of November to the end of May. The price of entry is 12 F.

St-Paul also has a famous hotel, **La Colombe d'Or,** which is not very big but extremely expensive and has a collection of pictures that more than one museum might envy. After the First World War the late Paul Roux, who owned it, befriended several up-and-coming artists as well as some who had already arrived. Often, if they were hard up, he would waive the cash that was owing and accept settlement in kind. It is a tribute to his judgement, and probably his business acumen as well, that people are willing to book a room in order to look round.

The **tourist office** is in the Grande Rue (tel. 93–32.86.95). It is closed in November.

Tourrette-sur-Loup and Gourdon

The countryside around has, unfortunately, broken out into a rash of not-very-attractive modern houses, but it is worth pressing on to Tourrette-sur-Loup. If possible, park in the large main square marked out for the purpose and walk through one of the two ancient gateways, linked in an arc by the Grande Rue that runs through part of the old town. On every side there are craftsmen hard at work. Some specialise in painted silk, others in puppets; in one cellar you catch a glimpse of jewellery being made while, round the corner, a boutique specialising in knitted goods spills out into the open with its own version of the poncho in delicately shaded, subtle colours. The pottery is attractive but not unique and the same goes for items in olive wood. Restaurants are tucked away at intervals in cellars or up short flights of stone steps and some look dark enough to be mildly depressing. Apart from the old towers, which account for the name, there is a 15th-century church with the remains of a pagan shrine behind the high altar.

The **Gorges du Loup,** not far away, are at their best after heavy rain when the waterfalls spill over in cascades of white foam. For part of the way the road runs along the bottom, tunnelling through the rock when it cannot get round it, and then climbs up in a series of hairpin bends to Gourdon nearly 460 metres (1500ft) above. It is one of the most spectacular mountain villages in Provence, but through becoming commercialised has lost some of its atmosphere.

The old houses, which have been carefully restored, are full of people making glass and pottery, carving all sorts of items out of olive wood, distilling lavender or getting honey ready for sale. The castle, built on the foundations of a Saracen fort in the 13th century, contains two museums, one devoted to art and the other to history. You can see an interesting collection of armour and several items of furniture including a secretaire that once belonged to Marie Antoinette. The castle is open from 11am to 1pm and from 2pm to 7pm in the summer and from 2pm to 6pm in the winter and is closed on Tuesdays out of season. It costs 6F for a guided tour of one museum and 9F if you want to see them both.

Grasse

Around the 12th century Grasse was a minute republic, earning its living by tanning hides largely imported from Italy. It also did a roaring trade in soaps and oils and in this way laid the foundations for what was to become the perfume capital of the world. When scented gloves came into vogue in the 16th century, Catherine de Medici saw the advantages of combining a countryside where everything grew in profusion with the talents of local craftsmen who produced some of the best leatherwork of the time. Many of the townspeople were initiated into the art of scent making by experts from Italy and in due course the hillsides became a mass of flowers. Wild lavender and aromatic herbs grew side by side with orange blossom, jasmine and roses to be followed by dozens of other flowers including mimosa. The methods employed by the ancient Greeks and Romans were updated, new and exotic ingredients were added to existing formulae and the process of absorbing the perfume in grease and washing it out again with alcohol was streamlined to meet more modern needs.

WHAT TO SEE

Some of the scent factories are open to the public and it is fascinating to see how things are done. During a tour of **Fragonard,** for instance, guides explain the three principal methods used for different types of flowers and draw attention to a few of the additives, not all of which are pleasant. A fragrance designed to make the wearer irresistible could owe part of its success to a bilious whale. Equally fascinating is the **Fragonard Museum** where the whole history of perfume is on display. Although some factories make a little scent of their own which can be bought on the premises, the bulk of the essence is shipped off to leading perfume houses in many parts of the world. They, in their turn, mix and blend it to their own specifications, bottle it in exotic shapes and several sizes and launch it on to the market, often at an exorbitant price per ounce.

Apart from perfume Grasse has other things to offer, which is fortunate for anyone who is not interested in the subject or who has no sense of smell.

The **Museum of Provençal Art and History,** on the Rue Mirabeau, has an astonishingly varied collection of items. Historical documents and some beautiful china compete for attention with *papier mâché* boxes lined with a sort of orange peel called bergamot. The Roman section is fairly predictable, but when you get round to the articles that were used in the home or out in the fields the whole thing comes alive. The museum is open from 10am to noon and from 2pm to 6pm but closes at 5pm in the winter. It is also closed on the second and third Sundays of the month, on Mondays, holidays and during November. A ticket costs 4.50 F but if you buy one for 7 F it also takes you into the Fragonard Museum which keeps the same hours.

The **Cathedral of Notre-Dame-du-Puy,** with its heavy columns, rough walls and narrow vaulted nave, is most impressive. It contains some interesting pictures, including one of the few religious paintings by Fragonard who was not exactly renowned for his piety and devotion.

The **Marine Museum,** with some splendid models of 18th-century warships and a section devoted to more modern craft, can be found at the Hôtel de Pontèves on the Boulevard du Jeu-de-Ballon. It may seem a bit out of place up in the mountains but it is all in honour of Amiral de Grasse, a French naval hero whose exploits helped America to win the War of Independence. He was born in 1722 at le Bar-sur-Loup, a small village near the gorges which is famous for its 18th-century church and a rather horrible picture called *Danse Macabre.* The painting shows a group of lords and ladies dancing happily, unaware that Death is picking off his victims with a bow and arrow. Each has a tiny personal devil ready to pull the soul from the body when it is dead. After they have been weighed in the heavenly scales and found wanting, the miserable little creatures are shovelled into the jaws of hell. The message is: 'Repent before it is too late,' which could have been a general warning or perhaps connected with the plague. But to return to Amiral Grasse's museum: it is open between 2.30pm and 6pm from the beginning of June to the middle of September, and closes at 5.30pm during the rest of the year as well as on Sundays, Mondays and holidays and for all of November. A ticket costs 3F.

The **Place aux Aires** is an attractive square in the old quarter surrounded by arcades and, beyond them, by little streets that have been taken over to a large extent by refugees from Algeria. Further away, outside the town proper, is a delightful little garden where Pauline Borghese, Bonaparte's sister, used to spend a lot of time thinking over the trouble she was having with her husband and her brother and wondering, perhaps, if fame was really worth it.

WHERE TO STAY AND EATING OUT

There are very few hotels in Grasse and not a great many good restaurants, so many people tend to look for something they like on one of the main roads out of town. Not that this will get you into the country, for Grasse has sprawled out to such an extent in every direction that it is as easy to get lost driving in the suburbs as it is on foot in the medieval part. If you head for Châteauneuf-de-Grasse you will find the **Auberge des Santons** on the Route de Vence (tel. 93–42.40.97) where the rooms cost up to 175F and you can sample some excellent home cooking for anything from 56 to 120 F but it is closed from mid-October until the beginning of February.

Alternatively head for Opio where the **Tour d'Opio**, 14 Route de Cannes (tel. 93–77.24.50), charges 170 F a night and 85 to 100 F for the set menus. You can swim and play tennis and arrange pension terms. The *auberge* is closed on Sunday nights and Mondays and the restaurant from just before Christmas to the beginning of February.

The **tourist information office** is in the Place Foux (tel. 93–36.03.56).

Villeneuve-Loubet

The road to Villeneuve-Loubet has been built up, if not every inch of the way at least every mile, but it is worth taking to inspect the Baie des Anges Marina. This complex provides a foretaste of things to come as you drive along the coast and it can be seen from quite a distance. From Nice, looking across the water, the four large buildings appear to be roughly in the shape of pyramids with rather jagged edges but when you drive up alongside them they resemble nothing so much as the bridge section of some gigantic ocean liner. Each one curves gently in a shallow arc on either end of which are half-covered balconies, stepped back to allow the sun to get to the garden terrace of the flat below. A lot of apartments have been sold but it is also possible to rent them and, as an added incentive, there are boutiques and restaurants attached. The marina itself can accommodate more than 500 boats, and when you get tired of watching the owners painting and varnishing you can swim in the sea or the swimming pool, go sailing, water-skiing or windsurfing. Provision is also made for visitors who would rather play tennis or spend their time deep-sea fishing.

Unless you are interested in urban development, in which case there is more than enough to see, Villeneuve-Loubet has only one other claim to fame. It is the birthplace of Auguste Escoffier, regarded by many as the most famous of all French chefs. Anyone who eats a peach Melba has him to thank for it. The house he was born in has, as one might expect, been turned into the **Auguste Escoffier Foundation** and a dedicated gastronome could spend the better part of a morning there without getting bored. Quite what one would do these days with an icing sugar palace or pagoda is debatable, but they are most entertaining to look at. Hostesses could pick up a few tips from any of over 1000 menus, some of them dating from 1820. However, the number of ingredients and the time taken to prepare them would make even Mrs Beaton look like an exponent of convenience foods. If you really want to know what goes into *bouillabaisse* and how to make it, there are pictures that take you every step of the way. However, Escoffier was not from Marseilles, where the dish originated, and every chef and cook claims, loudly and at some length, to have the only correct recipe. It is also fascinating to compare the utensils of the last century with the labour-saving devices of today. Escoffier's house is open from 2pm to 6pm, closes on Mondays, holidays and in November, and costs 10F to visit.

Cagnes

Sharing the concrete jungle of tall buildings, looped highways and large supermarkets is Cagnes. Its castle bears witness to a more elegant past when the Grimaldis lived there in an atmosphere of wealth and intrigue. They lost it at the time of the Revolution but the inner courtyard with its ancient pepper tree, the marble columns and painted ceilings all survived. On the ground floor is a section known as the **Museum of the Olive Tree** which traces the history of the olive industry, exploring all its facets from cultivation to culmination in the form of products like inlaid boxes and oil. From the top of the tower there is a view of the hills behind, still covered with olive and orange trees and flowers destined for the perfume factories at Grasse. It is open from 10am to noon and 2pm to 6pm in the summer, closes at 5pm during the rest of the year and on Tuesdays, 1 January, 1 May, and from 1 October to 15 November. The entrance fee is 2F.

Olive trees also grow in profusion in the garden of **Les Collettes,** an unpretentious villa where Renoir spent the last years of his life. His studio remains almost exactly as it was with his easel and brushes and the wheelchair that he used when rheumatoid arthritis made it impossible for him to get about any other way. A large picture of him in this chair in the studio can give visitors an uneasy feeling that they are intruding and should wait for an invitation before looking round. The museum is open from 2.30pm to 6.30pm from mid-April to mid-October and from 2pm to 5pm during the rest of the year, but is closed on Tuesdays, holidays and from 15 October to 15 November. The price of entry is 2F.

Biot

Beyond the racecourse which is close to the sea at Cros-de-Cagnes there are a number of roads to choose from and, with the help of a good map, it is easy to chop and change to get the best out of the area. For example, you can head for Biot where an imposing modern building is devoted to the works of Fernand Léger, one of the pioneers of cubism. The **Fernand Léger Museum** was given to the nation by his widow Nadia after his death in 1955 and includes more than 300 examples of his progress from impressionism to machinery. The building, situated just outside the village, is open from 10am to 6pm with the usual two hours off for lunch, closes an hour early in winter and on Tuesdays and 1 May. Tickets cost 8 F.

Since ancient times the rich clay deposits have made Biot a natural centre for craftsmen and, because they concentrate on useful articles in preference to the gaudier souvenirs, visitors tend to leave with something they will still appreciate when they get it home. The same goes for the glassworks, opened in 1957, where you can see the whole process of glass making from start to finish. They are open from 9am to 8pm on weekdays and 3pm to 7pm on Sundays in the summer, from 8am to noon and 2pm to 6pm during the week throughout the winter when they close on Sunday mornings; and they are also closed on 1 January, 1 May and Christmas Day.

It is pleasant to wander round the village itself where a series of arrows point the way past the 16th-century gates and ramparts, past the little church and into the Place des Arcades. You can get an excellent meal at the **Auberge du Jarrier** (tel. 93–65.11.68) for anything from 150 to 250 F but as it closes at different times during the year it might be as well to ring in advance.

There are quite a few caravan sites round about, the most up-market being **L'Eden,** Chemin du Val de Pome (tel. 93–33.43.27), where you will find every creature comfort on the premises or within easy reach.

Valbonne

An interesting comparison can be made with Valbonne which also has its engaging side but probably attracts more people on a long-term basis as a result of the International Scientific Park of Sophie Antipolis. As the name suggests, it was designed especially to cater for research and advanced technology. The buildings are extremely modern but for some reason the residential quarter is based on a typical Provençal village and without the authentic atmosphere the experiment does not quite come off.

La Brague

For holidaymakers the coast road has rather more variety. At La Brague, below Biot, you will find Marineland, widely publicised as the first marine zoo in Europe. It is open all the year round and crowded to bursting point during the summer. Anyone whose idea of entertainment includes performing seals, a killer whale, dolphins and sea lions, to mention but a few, will have nothing to complain about. Performances are given from 2.30pm to sunset and there is an aquarium and a special play area for children where the noise can be deafening. The price of entry is 30F with half-price tickets for children.

Antibes

Throughout its history Antibes has tended to bustle, first as a Greek trading post in the 4th century BC, then as a fortress town between France and Savoy, and eventually as a commercial centre and a holiday playground. The only building that still remains is **Fort Carré**, where Napoleon was once imprisoned, apart from the much older **Grimaldi Castle**, built in the 12th century but almost entirely rebuilt 400 years later. Although it contains some interesting items like a picture of the Virgin with the earliest-known view of Antibes in the background, it is more famous as the home of the **Picasso Museum.**

When he returned to the Mediterranean from Paris after the war, Picasso could not find anywhere to work so he was offered part of the castle as a studio. No doubt inspired by his surroundings, he set to work at a tremendous pace, producing his interpretation of mythology with the accent on satyrs and sirens augmented by some highly imaginative birds and animals. When he moved to Vallauris he showed his appreciation by leaving the whole lot behind on permanent loan and later added a good many ceramics by way of contrast. Françoise Gilot was his model at the time and there is a delightful picture of their daughter Paloma with her doll.

The Archaeological Collection, also housed in the castle, is just as fascinating in a totally different way. The exhibits range over about 4000 years, some having been dredged up from the harbour or recovered from ancient wrecks while others were uncovered when the foundations for new buildings were being laid. The castle is open from 10am to noon and from 3pm to

67

6pm; in the summer it stays open until 7pm but it closes on Tuesdays, 1 May and for all of November. The entry fee, which covers everything including the Picasso Museum, is 10 F.

The beaches at Antibes are divided between sand and shingle but it is difficult to see which is which because they are usually covered with sun umbrellas, mattresses, canvas chairs and beds, to say nothing of bodies in various shades ranging from white, through lobster to mahogany. People who prefer to be on the water rather than in it can join a sailing school, hire a boat or go water-skiing. The tennis courts and golf course are open to visitors and those with a preference for riding can chose between a horse and a bicycle. All this, added to a long list of camping sites and a modern yacht marina, means that it is hard to get away from the constant activity. At night there are open-air bars and dance floors, a cinema and a casino. Fruit, fish and vegetables are on sale in the Place Masséna where the market is not so much quaint as functional.

Antibes goes in for small hotels and apartments rather than lush establishments which come into their own at Cap d'Antibes. One that is comfortable, has its own garden and is close to the sea is the **Mas Djoliba**, 29 Avenue du Provence (tel. 93–34.02.48), where the rooms cost up to 350 F. No lunches are served but the set menus at dinner are between 60 and 110 F.

Restaurants are a different matter: there are plenty of them and a reasonable percentage are very good. You might try the **Oasis** in the Boulevard President-Wilson (tel. 93–34.02.35) where the set menu costs 120 F. This establishment does not serve dinner in the winter and the restaurant closes for the first two weeks in May and during November.

The **tourist office** for all enquiries is in the Place du Général-de-Gaulle (tel. 93–33.95.64).

Cap d'Antibes

Cap d'Antibes, to the south, is altogether a quieter, more restrained sort of place. Like so many wooded peninsulas along the coast it is liberally sprinkled with expensive villas only just visible through palm trees, lush vegetation and rainbow-coloured banks of exotic flowers. Not unnaturally, it has a reputation for being a rich man's playground, and with some justification. The famous **Hôtel du Cap d'Antibes,** standing back from the road in splendid gardens that run down to the sea, has had more than its share of celebrated visitors. Numbered among them are such diverse personalities as John Kennedy and Haile Selassie, literary giants led by Bernard Shaw and a host of others who were, or wanted to be, somebody. If you are thinking of joining that happy brigade, it will cost you 1650 F for a room, more for an apartment, of course, and you can eat at the **Pavillon Eden Roc** for a mere 270 F upwards.

However, you do not have to be rich to stay at Cap d'Antibes. There are some quite modest hotels and restaurants and, for relaxation, a choice between the Botanical Gardens (open from 8am until 12.30pm and from 2pm to 5.30pm but closed on Saturdays, Sundays and holidays) and excellent sandy beaches, some of which are free.

The **Naval and Napoleonic Museum** is housed in a former battery and concentrates mainly on Napoleon. He and his family lived in Antibes when he was in charge of the coastal defences and later, as an emperor in exile, he landed at Golfe-Juan further round the coast on his way back from Elba to Waterloo. The museum is open from 10am to noon and 3pm to 7pm between mid-June and mid-September, but closes an hour early in winter as well as on Tuesdays, 1 January, 1 May, Christmas Day and from the beginning of November to the middle of December. Entrance costs 8 F.

A short walk up to the Plateau de la Garoupe brings you to the lighthouse where you can join a conducted tour any time between 9am and noon and 2pm and 6pm, but only until 4.30pm in the winter. Beside it is the **Sanctuaire de la Garoupe** which really should not be missed. In the early days it was a sailors' chapel and the ex-votos are concerned mainly with vows made by seamen in times of stress. A survivor from the Battle of Trafalgar offered a picture of the action as he saw it and an ex-convict gave graphic thanks for his escape from Toulon jail. However, some of the deliveries depicted are more mundane and a good deal more recent. A fall with no bones broken deserved to be recorded and so did a motor accident with the car upside down in the ditch and the family giving thanks to Our Lady of La Garde for their escape. Fortunately she was still keeping an eye on them and may well have had to intervene again because they elected to show their gratitude by kneeling in the middle of the road.

Notre-Dame-de-Bon-Port is the patron saint of sailors and every July, on either the first or second Sunday of the month, her statue is taken from the sanctuary to the cathedral in Antibes and brought back in procession by local seamen.

Juan-les-Pins

Juan-les-Pins is a product of the 1920s when an American millionaire called Frank Jay Gould turned a stretch of beach into a Mecca for the young. It is noisy, exuberant and flashy, specialising mainly in pizza bars, discos and anything-but-chic boutiques. On the other hand, people who go there will not have a word said against it. They enthuse over all the sports that are available, pointing out that there are clubs you can join for sailing, water-skiing and skin-diving; that you can play tennis or golf, hire a horse, a boat or a bicycle, swim in a heated swimming pool and walk for ages along clearly marked paths. The harbour is geared for fishermen as well as private craft and at night there is a casino if you do not want to go to the cinema.

Some of the hotels are very much in the luxury class but there are others all the way down the scale which are very reasonable. The best restaurants, with a couple of exceptions, are to be found in the large hotels, but the whole place teems with cafes and little bistros. Everywhere is full during July for the Jazz Festival but anyone going there in the winter will have the resort practically to themselves. Predictably there are fêtes and concerts right through the season and the best way to find out about them is to contact the **tourist office** right on the front (tel. 93–61.04.98).

Golfe-Juan

Anyone who likes to take their holidays a bit more quietly would probably prefer Golfe-Juan, just round the corner. It is a popular resort with a long sandy beach, a selection of fairly ordinary hotels, some good restaurants and a general air of well-being. There is a harbour for fishing and pleasure boats and it has all the same sports facilities as Juan-les-Pins apart from golf, so anyone who feels like playing 18 holes would have to try to arrange it next door. The same goes for a visit to the cinema or a flutter at the casino. The American navy used to anchor in the roadstead before France left NATO, but apart from that and Napoleon's landing in 1815 nothing very exciting seems to have happened at Golfe-Juan which, come to think of it, makes it practically unique.

Vallauris

The same cannot be said for Vallauris, about 3 kilometres (less than 2 miles) inland and surrounded by hills covered with mimosa, vineyards and orange trees. Although it was a pottery centre in Roman times, razed to the ground in 1390 and rebuilt some 200 years later, it remained a fairly nondescript little place until Picasso discovered it. Single-handed he revived the fortunes of the potteries which were plodding along without much success and seemed to be in danger of expiring altogether.

On a visit to the Madoura pottery Picasso began, rather absent-mindedly, to experiment with bits of clay. The shapes he made were fired after he had gone and this so delighted him when he saw them later that he moved into a house near the town and got down to work in earnest. All the ceramics he produced as well as those he simply decorated were copied, as arranged, by the Madoura pottery and in next to no time the industry was on its feet and thriving. Colonies of artists descended on the town, new potteries opened up and weaving and glassware joined in the bonanza. Today the Avenue Georges-Clemenceau and the streets round it are full of studios and shops where, as well as far too many things that leave a lot to be desired, you can buy beautiful ceramics that could well become collectors' items eventually.

Most of Picasso's original work went into the museum at Antibes but Vallauris has two masterpieces of which it is extremely proud. One is a bronze statue of a man holding a sheep which he created in Paris and presented to the town when he became an honorary citizen. It stands in the Place Paul-Isnard in the centre of Vallauris where you can admire it first and shop at the market afterwards. The second is a chapel, once part of a priory, which he decorated in 1952 and called the Temple of Peace. The whole interior is covered with plywood panels, fitting together perfectly to create a single picture. Like *Guernica* it is an indictment of war and a plea for peace. On one side a violent mêlée of figures, germs and weapons is painted in garish colours while on the other everything is peaceful with dancing girls, a musician and a juggler. Pegasus is shown pulling a plough, and four figures representing the nations of the world clasp hands in a gesture of unity. The chapel stands on the same square, is open from 10am to noon and from 2pm until 6pm. It closes an hour earlier from October to the end of April as well as on holidays and throughout November. The entrance fee is 5 F.

Mougins

Picasso spent about ten years in Vallauris and then moved to Mougins, a delightful and much-restored hilltop village a short distance away where he remained for the rest of his life. His house, the mas of Notre-Dame-de-Vie, is hidden by trees and shrubs and stands opposite an ancient hermitage that is reached by way of a track leading off the D3. The chapel dates from the 17th century and was a sanctuary of grace where still-born babies were brought in the belief that they would revive just long enough to be baptised. It is open only for mass at 9am on Sundays and the house is not open to the public at any time.

Mougins itself has the remains of some ramparts, a fortified gate and a White Penitents' Chapel which is now the town hall and looks out on to the fountain in the Place de la Mairie. An ideal place to stay is the **Mas Candille** (tel. 93–90.00.85), an old farmhouse outside the village with its own gardens and a swimming pool. It is extremely good value at 440F a night and has an excellent restaurant where the cheapest set menu is 195F and worth every centime. The hotel closes from early November until after Christmas.

There are a number of restaurants in the village, ranging from the good to the outstanding with prices to match, which is only what you would expect when you realise that the whole place has been promoted from antiquity to become a fashionable suburb of Cannes.

CANNES TO TOULON

Chapter IV

CANNES TO TOULON

Cannes

Cannes

It is more than a trifle disconcerting to realise that Cannes is a relatively modern town with a history going back less than 200 years. It was a non-descript fishing village when Lord Brougham, a British ex-chancellor, was forced to stop there on his way to Italy in 1834 because an outbreak of cholera had closed the frontier. He found he liked it so much that he built himself a villa. For the next 34 years society followed in his wake whenever he set out to winter in the South of France. The Prince of Wales and the Tsar both turned up in Cannes and, when elegant hotels appeared all along the sea front, the most fashionable place to be seen was walking along the Boulevard de La Croisette. Lord Brougham was also responsible for the harbour in the sense that he put up the idea to King Louis-Philippe who in turn put up the necessary funds.

Cannes continued to be a popular holiday resort among the rich and titled until well into the 20th century, but when summer holidays became more popular than winter ones and venues were being sought for conventions, film festivals and trade fairs the character of the town began to change. The palm trees remain, visitors still stroll along the Croisette in front of the hotels and the beach is just as inviting as before although only a small part of it is available if you are not prepared to pay.

The summer casino, described by one gambler of my acquaintance as 'a folly not far short of the Brighton Pavilion' has a dance floor and a swimming pool apart from the usual gaming rooms. It is still considered to be smart and sophisticated and expects its visitors to dress and behave accordingly. The Jackpot Disco is both cheerful and lively but less unrestrained than its larger and noisier competitors.

La Castre Museum is worth a visit if you are interested in things like Japanese armour, Chinese porcelain and the early civilisations of South America and the Pacific. It is housed in one of the few local antiquities, the remains of a refuge built by the monks of St-Honorat to protect local fishermen from the barbarians in the 11th century. Together with a 17th-century church, an ancient watch tower and the remnants of a defensive wall, it marks the site of Canois, the original fishing village which took its name from the reeds that grew in the marshes thereabouts. The museum is open from 1 April to the end of September between 10am and noon and from 2pm to 6pm. It closes an hour early in winter and on Mondays, holidays and from the beginning of November to mid-December. A ticket costs 3 F.

WHERE TO STAY

As you would expect, Cannes has an abundance of hotels, some of them extremely expensive and others quite reasonable. Many of the luxurious ones, like the **Carlton** and the **Majestic**, are strung out along the Boulevard de la Croisette and will set you back about 1450 F a night, but of course they do have excellent restaurants and all the amenities you could wish to find.

The **Hôtel Ruc**, 15 Boulevard de Strasbourg (tel. 93–38.64.32), was built fairly recently in the style of the 18th century and is elegant without being too expensive. It is within easy reach of the sea, close to swimming pools, tennis courts and an ice rink and has a terrace where you can sit out in the sun. It closes from the beginning of November until Christmas and charges 390 F including breakfast.

Les Roches Fleuries, 92 Rue Georges-Clemenceau (tel. 93–39.28.78), is a more modest establishment with some rooms looking across to the sea which is almost but not quite on the doorstep. You can stay there for 206 F at any time except from the middle of November until just after Christmas.

El **Puerto,** 45 Avenue du Petit Juas (tel. 93–68.39.75), is a good deal further from the beach but it is quiet and central and has a restaurant, closed on Mondays, with a set menu for 90 F. A room costs 280 F and the hotel is closed from the beginning of October until the middle of December.

There are several camping sites within easy reach of Cannes, three of which are inside the city boundaries.

Ranch Camping, Chemin St-Joseph, Rocheville (tel. 93–46.00.11), would be a good choice. It is quite close to the sea and provides meals and snacks as well as all the usual facilities, but it will almost certainly be full during the season so it is necessary to book well in advance.

EATING OUT

Restaurants in Cannes range from the outstandingly good to the perfectly acceptable and there is no need to walk more than a block or two from the sea front to find an excellent choice of dishes.

La Poêle d'Or, 23 Rue des États-Unis (tel. 93–39.77.65), is one that should not be missed and although it offers a set menu for 120 F the specialities like *bourride* are irresistible. Because it is fairly small and has a lot of regular clients, it is wise to book a table rather than leaving things to chance. It closes on Mondays and throughout November.

Au Mal Assis, 15 Quai St-Pierre (tel. 93–39.13.38), is one of the least expensive good restaurants on the quay with a set menu for 65 F. It closes from about the second week in October until just before Christmas.

FESTIVALS

The Cannes Film Festival in May is undoubtedly the best-known and most crowded event of the year, but for anyone who takes their pleasures a trifle less obviously there is an attractive Mimosa Festival in February and a Royal Regatta in September which lasts for about two weeks.

BOATING

Although Cannes has something for everyone, and keeps most of its offers open throughout the year, it is equally preoccupied with boats and boating. All along the Jetée Albert-Edouard, named after the Prince of Wales, private yachts are tied up side by side with hardly enough space to swing a fender between them. Sightseers, who normally have not the slightest interest in nautical matters, walk up and down inspecting the craft which include some of the most luxurious yachts afloat. If you want to charter a boat there are any number of firms ready and willing to meet your requirements and you will find several of them on the Quai St-Pierre beside the old harbour.

Once aboard you will need something to eat and some of the best small shops specialising in food are to be found in the Rue Meynadier about two minutes' walk away. It covers only three or four blocks, but if you stop to buy one of literally hundreds of different sorts of cheese, visit the cellars where they are matured, select a cut of meat for dinner, choose a pasta for lunch and a mouth-watering sweet to follow, you will find it takes a long while to get from one end to the other. The Forville Market nearby, open in the mornings, is a good place to get the rest of your supplies at quite acceptable prices.

OTHER ACTIVITIES

For golfers there are at least three courses within easy reach of the town: the golf Club de Cannes-Mandelieu, the Club de Biot and the Club de Valbonne. It is possible to hire cars, motorcycles and bicycles, and you will find a rowing club near the Palm Beach Casino.

TOURIST INFORMATION

For details of these activities and anything else you want to know about, including hotels, call in at the tourist office at the railway station or ring 93–99.19.77.

EXCURSIONS

If you have come in by plane or train and decided against hiring a car, there are plenty of ways of getting about. Apart from all the buses that trundle round the town there are regular services both inland and along the coast. Coaches leave from their base near the Town Hall for places like Grasse, St Raphael and Vallauris, or you can take an excursion, lasting for a few hours or a full day, to visit the Gorges du Verdon, Pont du Loup or coastal resorts ranging from Villefranche to St-Tropez. During the season it is wise to book for these excursions through a travel agent or in the Square Merimée (tel. 39.79.41). From the Gare Maritime opposite boats leave regularly throughout the year for the Iles de Lérins which are so close that you almost feel you could swim out and save the fare.

Les Iles de Lérins

The two islands have quite enough history between them to compensate for the newness of Cannes. The first settlers were the Greeks, closely followed by the Romans. Then, in about AD 400, St Honorat founded a monastery on the smaller of the two which is called after him. It grew steadily in wealth and importance until, in the seventh century, it was among the most powerful monasteries in Christendom. Its possessions included scores of castles and priories on the mainland and, in fact, it owned Cannes for another thousand years. The monks built up one of the finest libraries in Europe and provided training for thousands of young men. Hundreds of them went on to become bishops, including one who founded the monastery at Jarrow and instructed the Venerable Bede. Rather fewer became saints, but one who did was St Patrick who spent several years on the Ile St-Honorat. Anyway, all good things come to an end and there were only four monks left when the monastery was closed by the Pope in 1788. During the last century it was bought by the Cistercians who rebuilt much of the abbey and are still there. Nobody else lives on St-Honorat but visitors are allowed ashore and, after being reminded that they are on holy ground, can wander round the deserted keep with its cloisters, marble cistern and small chapel overlooking the sea.

Ste-Marguerite, the larger of the two islands, is believed to share its name with St-Honorat's sister, said to have been the Mother Superior at the island nunnery. According to legend, he would visit her once a year when there was blossom on an almond tree near the beach. However, if she wanted to see him more frequently she would say a short prayer, the tree would burst into flower and he would be left to wonder where on earth the last few months had gone! Excavations have turned up the remains of houses, complete with wall paintings and mosaics dating back to 300 BC. They are in the vicinity of the fort which was built by Richelieu in the 1600s and was used as a state prison. The inmates included the Man in the Iron Mask and Marshal Bazaine who lost face and the confidence of his country when he surrendered Metz to the Prussians in 1870. There is also a statue to six Huguenot pastors who were kept there in solitary confinement. Looking at the cells, the visitor is not surprised to learn that only one of them was still sane when he died. The **Fort-Royal** opens when the boats arrive and cost 25 centimes. The **Musée de la Mer** charges 3F and is open from 9.30am to noon and from 2pm to 6.30pm from July to September, but opens at 10.30am and closes at 5pm during the rest of the year, and is closed on Mondays and throughout November and December.

There are some very attractive walks on the island taking in the Pond of Bateguier, with its bird sanctuary, and several coastal inlets shaded by pine trees where it is possible to swim, dive, sunbathe and fish. The journey time to the islands depends on where you are coming from, as does the cost of the fare, but you should think in terms of around 25 F for the latter. For more precise information you can ring 93–39.11.82.

La Napoule

La Napoule, back on the mainland, is a suburb of Mandelieu and, quite frankly, is the only one worth visiting from the tourist point of view. Taken in tandem they have a small airport, an excellent golf course, provision for all the usual sports and several acres devoted to yacht marinas. The architecture is predominantly modern and even the old château was practically rebuilt at the beginning of this century by Henry Clews, an American sculptor with a mind of his own. The extraordinary versions of wildlife that he created to decorate the main gate give an indication of the sort of things to be found inside. There are guided tours of the **museum** at 3pm costing 8 F but the château is closed in January, June, July and December as well as at other unspecified times, so if you want to see it you would be wise to ring 93–49.95.05.

Behind the town hills covered with mimosa and dotted with attractive little villages make a pleasing area to explore, although fishermen head straight for the **Lac de St-Cassien** where most water sports are encouraged apart from motorboating.

The **Massif de l'Esterel** is a weird, lonely place as befits one of the oldest land masses in Europe. It consists of volcanic rock, mainly red but occasionally green, yellow, purple or blue, which has been worn down over millions of years into harsh crags and deep ravines. The forests of pine and cork oak have been largely destroyed by forest fires although the wild lavender, gorse and other shrubs have survived. The road running along the northern side follows roughly the same route as the Via Aurelia, built by Augustus to ensure a direct link with Rome. For nearly 2000 years it was the only through road anywhere near the coast and the wild mountain country to the south became the haunt of ex-convicts, highwaymen and other criminals. Fortunately that belongs to the past and climbers anxious to clamber up to the **Pic de l'Ours** can do so quite safely provided they take care along the rough roads on the way.

However great the temptation to use up all your available time in the Massif de l'Esterel and rejoin the coast further west, try to resist it. The cliff road is just as memorable and should really not be missed.

Théoule-sur-Mer

Théoule-sur-Mer could not be described as isolated but it makes an ideal starting point or a perfect break for lunch. There is a small restaurant beside the bay where you can practically dangle your feet in the water, but I would head for **Chez Aristide** (Avenue de Lérins, tel. 93–49.96.13) which advertises *bouillabaisse* in glowing terms. One American all the way from Honolulu is on record as saying that it is the best be found on the Riviera and you can order it at 160 F for two people or a rather richer version for 220 F. The *Menu Langouste* is excellent value at 250 F but you can eat more cheaply if you feel so inclined. The prices are inclusive except for drinks and coffee.

Port-la-Galère, Miramar and Le Trayas

Beyond Théoule-sur-Mer the coastline takes on a reddish hue which deepens rapidly to become something approximating a ruby glow. Great outcrops of bare red rock tower over tree-covered slopes which are already disappearing under a blanket of new villas, some in quite amazing shapes. Port-la-Galère, where there is a new development including a modern hotel, looks for all the world as though ancient cave dwellers had returned to update their village with panes of glass and a coat of paint. At Miramar one building, tucked away among the others, closely resembles a fistful of bathyscopes tossed aside and forgotten by some petulant giant child. On the road down to Le Trayas you may well see a visitor from North Africa, resplendent in flowing white robes, selling bead necklaces and skin bags to passing motorists. Like their ancestors before them they have obviously discovered that rich pickings are to be had along the coast but luckily their methods are much more·peaceful.

Anthéor and Agay

On the far side of the perfectly named Cap Roux and the Pointe de l'Observatoire, where the view is exceptional and the cliffs rise straight out of the sea, the resort of Anthéor crouches below three blood-red peaks. Then the coastline swings round to enclose an almost-circular bay which had considerable appeal for the Greeks and Romans as a deep-water anchorage. Judging by the variety of things brought up from the sea bed, more than one ship must have foundered or been attacked and sunk there. The beach is long and sandy as it sweeps up to Agay. This fishing-port-cum-holiday-resort has rather more hotels than the ones mentioned earlier. Like Miramar it has a small marina and there are sites for people who bring their own tents and caravans.

St-Raphaël

St-Raphaël, at the other end of a stretch of coast where the Americans landed in 1944, has never been anything except a holiday resort. The Romans built villas there overlooking the water but they have long since disappeared. For the next few centuries the Saracens made life impossible for everyone else but eventually they were driven off and the monks built a village and a church which they placed for safekeeping in the hands of the Templars. The population consisted mainly of fishermen but they were so badly affected by marsh fever that no attempt was made to develop the town any further. However, Napoleon drew attention to it when he landed there from Egypt in 1799 and again 15 years later when he sailed into exile on Elba.

It was left to the journalist Alphonse Karr to put St-Raphaël back on the map in 1864. He found it so attractive after Paris that he decided to settle there and persuaded several friends to visit him. One was Gounod who took advantage of the peace and quiet to compose *Romeo and Juliet*. Perhaps because it never became really fashionable the port quickly developed into a family resort and is an ideal place to relax on the beach, play golf at Valescure where there is a famous 18-hole course and try your luck at the casino.

The **Museum of Underwater Archaeology** in the Rue des Templiers encourages local diving clubs to bring their finds in for inspection. The result is that it has a sizable collection of ancient flasks, bottles and other similar objects as well as two 18th-century cannon which are kept in the garden. It is open from 10am to noon and 3pm to 6pm between mid-June and mid-September except on Tuesdays, from 11am to noon and 2pm to 5pm except on Sundays for the rest of the year and costs 3F. The same ticket will take you into 800-year-old **St-Raphaël Church** which is open and closed at the same times.

There are several hotels in the medium price range and a sprinkling of good restaurants in and around the old town and the port area as well as a variety of camping sites and provisions for every kind of water sport. The information office is only a short step from the railway station (tel. 94–95.16.87).

Fréjus

Fréjus is completely different. To start with, the town is about a mile from the sea, although it was once an important naval base founded by Julius Caesar in 49 BC and developed by Augustus. As well as building galleys and providing land for veteran soldiers, it was large enough to take the battle fleet captured from Antony and Cleopatra at Actium. Part of one of the twin towers that used to guard the canal entrance is still standing but not much else is left. The buildings were destroyed, the harbour silted up and eventually the whole site was filled in to provide land for development. However, part of the arena escaped and now that modern seating has been added it is used for bull-fights and the occasional pop concert. The theatre, on the other hand, is in ruins, although you can see where the stage was and make out the remains of the orchestra pit.

The **Episcopal Quarter**, as it is called, includes the cathedral, built on the site of a temple to Jupiter, the Bishop's Palace and a 5th-century baptistry which is thought to be one of the oldest in France. Only adults were baptised in those days and they were immersed in the font before having their feet washed in an earthenware basin set in to the floor close by. The cloisters are most attractive with thin marble pillars, a well and a rose garden. Unfortunately many of the panels, decorated with strange little animals, that covered the ceiling disappeared during the Revolution. There are guided tours between 9.30am and 6pm in the summer, with two hours off for lunch at noon, but only until 4.30pm during the rest of the year. It is closed on Tuesdays and some holidays and costs 5 F.

Fréjus makes little attempt to cater for tourists, leaving that to Fréjus Plage where there are plenty of beaches that link up eventually with those of St-Raphaël. On the other side of the River Argens, to the south, the coast is a mass of tiny resorts, most of them with their own little bays, attendant hotels, inexpensive restaurants and camping sites.

As opposed to the somewhat uniform attractions of sea and sand, the

83

countryside behind Fréjus is full of interest. You might like to compare the deserted mosque, a replica of the famous one at Djenne in the Sudan and painted to look like the original, with an exotic Buddhist pagoda built in memory of Vietnamese soldiers who died fighting for France in the First World War. Then again, you might prefer the **Parc Zoologique** and the **Safari de l'Esterel** where you can drive throught the part devoted to ferocious animals before walking round to look at the birds and smaller creatures that are kept there.

One thing that is unique is the remains of the **Malpasset barrage** a few miles to the north. After heavy rains at the end of 1959 the dam burst, sending a wide torrent of water surging down the valley to the sea. Hundreds of people were killed, houses and farms were washed away and a completely new reservoir system had to be built at the Lac de St-Cassien. Below the old barrage it is still possible to see giant lumps of reinforced concrete strewn among the trees that have grown up in the past 25 years and enormous pipes twisted into grotesque shapes lying in the undergrowth. The road is narrow and very bumpy but there is space to leave the car at the far end and walk the rest of the way.

St-Paul-en-Forêt, Tourrettes and Fayence

Most of the country thereabouts is taken up with forests and woodland without a great many roads or villages to be found. St-Paul-en-Forêt is about the biggest and has a delightfully quiet camping site with bungalows and caravans to let. South of the D562 linking Draguignan with Grasse it is worth stopping at **La Bégude** for lunch. The **Restaurant aux Grillades,** standing slightly back from the road, has comprehensive set menus for about 70 F, the local wines are very pleasant and the service is excellent.

Still heading almost due north, you will see the twin villages of Tourrettes and Fayence standing out on their respective hilltops, the latter being the larger of the two. The old town below the 18th-century church is beautifully preserved and the narrow streets with their resident craftsmen, including weavers and coppersmiths, look neat and prosperous. The only trouble is that quite heavy vehicles are allowed through and when they are on the move everything else comes to a standstill. Meeting headlight to headlight means that someone has to reverse in to one of the little squares and even there it requires a certain amount of juggling to sort things out. The locals are apparently resigned to it: they stand or sit about in tiny bars, not even glancing outside to see what all the fracas is about. Pedestrians caught up in the mêlée retreat under one of the small stone arches, sit on the steps leading to the house and wait patiently for a return to normality.

St-Cézaire and Mons

From Fayence the road writhes up into the mountains, presenting a new and more glorious view at every turn. Before long the village can be seen as one of many dotted about the landscape as it sweeps erratically down to the sea. The limestone caves of St-Cézaire make a welcome detour if you enjoy climbing about among superb stalactites and stalagmites in the bowels of the earth. Mons is another village built of rock on rock and is typically isolated and rather forbidding when seen from outside the protecting walls. Inside there are fountains and little squares interlaced with alleys that go back to the Middle Ages and a restaurant at the **Auberge Provençale** where you can have lunch for less than 70 F except on Wednesdays or during November.

It is really no distance from Mons to the Route Napoleon through some fairly arid country set about with white rocks. At the Col de Valferrière, where the two roads meet, you may well be able to buy scent from a wayside stall that advertises its presence with large flagons of jewel-coloured liquid rather like the ones that used to appear in the windows of chemist shops some years ago.

The main thought that struck me bowling along the highway was that I was glad I had not done it with Napoleon. The idea of marching up and down all those mountains, where the valleys far below look vividly green and the rocky summits a bit overpowering, is enough to put anyone off walking for life. The feeling of desolation is increased by the sight of little ruined houses, many of them no more than stone boxes without a roof and with weeds growing up where the floor used to be.

Castellane

Eventually from high on the mountain tops you catch your first glimpse of a citadel-shaped rock below, crowned with a tiny chapel. Beyond is a stretch of river and, bright red against the green grass, a couple of tennis courts. The effect is rather claustrophobic, as though one or other of the peaks is bound to topple over and smother the whole lot. Contrary to expectations the valley widens and so does the river, the rock begins to tower up over the road until it reaches its true height of 200 metres (600ft) and the town appears at the other end of a bridge.

Castellane combines all the virtues and all the vices of a tourist centre allied to a market town. Out of season it is quiet and most enjoyable, but when the summer crowds start arriving it becomes decidedly noisy. The swimming pool, though large, does not seem large enough, there is a queue for the tennis courts and kayaks dispute their rights with fishermen all along the river banks. Life centres on the main square where there are several small hotels, a few shops, a rather ordinary fountain and plenty of parking space. On Sundays one or two stalls are added where you can get bread and wine, while women wander about with large baskets of flowers.

The **Church of St-Victor** dates from the 12th century, with the side aisles added later, and some way behind it is an ancient tower which is all that is left of the original ramparts. Just before nightfall, as it catches the last rays of the sun, the effect of the light on the old stones is spectacular. The **Chapel of Notre-Dame** on top of the rock, although less than 300 years old, has become a place of pilgrimage and if you want to look at the ex-votos inside remember to collect the key from the Presbytery next to the parish church before starting the half-hour climb. The key for the church of St-Victor is kept at the tourist office in the Rue Nationale (tel. 92–83.61.14).

The old town is small and runs true to type with winding streets, little squares and rather sombre houses. One of them, which was a sub-prefecture at the time, played host to Napoleon when he stopped along the route for a short rest from marching. It is rather dour and uninviting, just the thing for a little corporal but a bit basic for an emperor. Perhaps it might not seem quite so bad if the historic atmosphere had not been totally ruined by a green and glassy pizza bar opposite.

Ma Petite Auberge on the main square (tel. 92–83.62.06) is a pleasant little hotel in the rural style where you can eat well in the dining room or out on the terrace under the trees. The rooms cost up to 220F and there are set menus from 55 to 85F. The restaurant is closed on Wednesdays except during the season and the hotel is open from March to the beginning of November.

Many people bring their own tents and caravans, taking advantage of a site on the outskirts of the town and of the fact that it is a first-class place for walking, riding and sightseeing in the area. A good way of spending a lazy day is to go up to the Castillon Lake which is large, artificial and could have been designed for picnics and bathing. Later you might like to explore some of the little roads that run between orchards and fields tufted with lavender that smells wonderful when it is in bloom and gives the local lamb its delicious flavour.

Canyon du Verdon

Another trip that needs a full day, although it can be done in less, is to the famous **Canyon du Verdon,** said to be one of the finest in Europe. It is rather like *bouillabaisse* in that everyone has a pet version of the best way to 'do' it and will defend his or her route with remarkable fervour. The road from Castellane to Pont-de-Soleils follows the course of the river which is fast-flowing and where it is possible to stop and clamber down the steep banks, although notices at frequent intervals warn that this is dangerous.

Anyone who prefers to be on the inside and not on the outside of a road above a precipice would then be wise to continue on the northern side of the gorges. The route serpentines its way along the cliffs, hemmed in by mountains and some magnificent rock formations. A lot of these have variegated strata and at least one looks like a softly draped curtain striped with pale gold. There are very few places to stop and when the road narrows and turns inwards through an arch in the overhanging rock it is as well to sound your horn in case there is a caravan or a madcap driver coming the other way. Sometimes it does not look as though two vehicles could pass each other safely but experience shows that there is just enough room.

At one point the road drops back to the level of the water and you imagine, quite incorrectly, that you have been through the canyon. There is a camping site, a large area of grass and, round a sharpish bend, the **Relais des Gorges du Verdon** with a restaurant, chalets and caravans under the trees. Then it is onwards and upwards again with the scenery becoming even wilder and more impressive as the canyon drops away to its full 760 metres (2500ft). Any feeling that you are a lone explorer is quickly dispelled by groups of cyclists taking the gradients in their stride, coachloads of tourists and shrubs along the verges trimmed down to neat squares like a series of small box hedges. Finally, when you least expect it, you catch a glimpse of the Lac de Ste-Croix, a vast man-made area of water that looks as though someone has spread out an enormous piece of emerald-green velvet in the sun to dry.

Moustiers-Ste-Marie

Before turning back along the south side of the canyon it would be a mistake to miss Moustiers-Ste-Marie, a most incredible place built into a ravine several hundred feet deep. A small bridge connects the two sides of the village at a point where a torrent of water gushes out of the rock. Above the cluster of houses the chapel of Notre-Dame-de-Beauvoir appears to cling to the cliff face. It was founded in AD 470 but has been reconstructed and added to at least twice since then. However, the thing which really captures the imagination is an iron chain nearly 215 metres (700ft) long strung across the top of the ravine from one mountain peak to the other. A giant star, said to be gold but looking very tarnished indeed, is suspended from the centre. Legend would have us believe that it was put there by a knight on his return from the crusades to fulfil a vow he made when he was taken prisoner. If he was ingenious enough to get it up there one would imagine that he could have outwitted Saladin without too much trouble.

There is no room in the village for many hotels and restaurants but you will find an old church as well as the chapel and a pottery museum. Moustiers has been famous for its white-glazed earthenware since the 17th century when it was one of the leading pottery centres. The industry sickened and died 100 years ago but it was revived in the 1920s and is now very much back in business. The **Musée de la Faience** is open from 9am to noon and 2pm to 7pm from 1 June to the end of August. In April, May, September and October it closes an hour early and is shut on Tuesdays and during the winter.

The hotel **Le Relais** (tel. 92–74.66.10) is small and basic and charges 160F for a room and between 62 and 100F for its menus. It is open from mid-March to the end of November. **Les Santons** in the Place de l'Église (tel. 92–74.66.48) is a good place to eat and is not expensive at 180F for the best set menu but it closes on Tuesdays except in the high season as well as during January and February. As befits a popular tourist centre the town now has a leisure park down in the valley with a camping site and a few facilities for sport but no sophisticated entertainments.

It is a short double-back from Moustiers to the Lac de Ste-Croix which is a good place for people who want to sail, fish, swim or simply picnic on the beach, and it is not difficult to find somewhere for a tent or a caravan in the vicinity. If you do not enjoy sand in your sandwiches there is a pleasant little hotel at Aiguines on the edge of the plateau above the Canyon du Verdon.

However, if you just want a glass of something stop at a small cafe on the road through the village overlooking a fountain where dogs and children take turns to drink the water without apparently suffering any ill effects at all.

The road along the south side of the gorges is less wild and tortuous than the northern route with plenty of places to stop along the way. As its name, Corniche Sublime, implies there are some superb viewing points where you can look right down to the water below. There is a restaurant about half-way along and two tunnels with windows cut out of the rock walls before the road drops down slightly to a single-span bridge, swings back for one last look at the gorges and then turns away in the direction of Comps-sur-Artuby.

For anyone who is really experienced and adventurous it is possible to explore the canyon on foot or by canoe but this, as you may imagine, can be dangerous. It is essential to get expert advice, collect a detailed map (two are on sale locally), and load up with a torch, warm clothes and something to eat before setting out.

Draguignan

South of Comps-sur-Artuby, which is mildly interesting, the road crosses a large military area and can sometimes be closed if the army feels so inclined. It is the direct but far-from-straight route to Draguignan, an old market town at the bottom of a valley which can get uncomfortably hot and oppressive in the summer. The old quarter has an attractive network of little streets reserved for pedestrians only, two original gateways and a comparatively recent clock tower that stands on the site of a Roman fort. The **museum** and **library** are housed in a 17th-century convent that became the summer residence of the Bishop of Fréjus about 100 years later. The former is concerned with furniture, porcelain and pictures for the most part, leaving the library to gloat over a large collection of rare books including the works of Aristotle printed in Venice in 1497. There are plenty of gardens but not many hotels and restaurants, a large sports centre and, on the outskirts, an Allied War Cemetery with the graves of men killed in 1944 after the paratroop landings.

The Massif des Maures, to the south, is another old land mass covered with forests of cork oak and chestnut trees. Not many people bother to explore here, so if you like solitude, wild flowers and little-used roads twisting up and down between the mountains, it is exactly the place for you.

However, if you are longing for a breath of sea air the direct road will take you straight to Ste-Maxime.

Ste-Maxime

This is another fishing port which has successfully turned itself into a fashionable holiday resort. There is nothing very historical to interest the tourist but you cannot fault amenities which bring back the visitors year after year. The long sandy beach is crowded during the summer and you can sail, hire a boat, dive, play tennis or golf and ride a horse or a bicycle. The marina is on the small side but very efficient and the evening entertainments include both a cinema and a casino. Anyone with a weakness for old musical instruments would thoroughly enjoy the **museum** in St-Donat Park. There is everything from musical boxes to barrel organs and 1878 phonographs to a talking doll that dates from round about the same time. There are guided tours from the beginning of May to the end of September between 10am and noon and from 2.30pm to 6.30pm. The museum closes on Tuesdays and for the whole winter. The entrance fee is 7F.

WHERE TO STAY AND EATING OUT
Naturally there are a lot of hotels and restaurants, ranging from the fairly expensive to the modest seaside variety. The **Hôtel Calidianus**, in the Boulevard Jean-Moulin (tel. 94–96.23.21) is fairly typical and quieter than most where you can swim, play tennis and pay only about 290F for a room.

The promenade is littered with cafes and restaurants which tend to fill up quickly in the summer. Both **La Gruppi** on the Avenue Charles-de-Gaulle (tel. 94–96.03.81) and the **Hermitage** close to the port (tel. 94–96.17.77) specialise in sea food but the former is slightly more expensive at 140F against 120F for the cheapest set menus.

Port Grimaud

If you try to imagine a small section of Venice where all the houses are typically Provençal, painted in clear pastel shades, many with roses round the door, you will begin to get some idea of the appearance of Port Grimaud. The houses are all joined together in batches, rather on the lines of London terraces, although every one is different. Their front doors open on to small squares and each has a private mooring alongside the patio. Each group is on a tiny island which is linked to its neighbours with little bridges and is surrounded by canals.

As the idea was to create a genuine village and not simply an architectural talking point there are also shops and cafes, estate agents and firms specialising in boats and boating. It is possible to rent a house with its attendant mooring and, if necessary, charter a boat. The main square has a delightful tiled fountain and provides an ideal meeting place for residents and visitors. There are two beaches at the entrance to the Grand Canal, one inside the harbour and the other on the sea front. Parking spaces are available for visitors who want to wander about and pleasure boats run sightseeing cruises along the waterways.

The **Giraglia** (tel. 94–56.31.33) is an elegant hotel built in the same style as the rest of the port with its own private beach and swimming pool. It is in the top income bracket at 990 F and has an excellent restaurant where you will not get away for less than 185 F. The restaurant is closed on Monday evenings and on Tuesdays from the beginning of January to the end of March and the hotel itself is closed from the beginning of October until Christmas.

Not far from the port Les Prairies de la Mer have a large camping site. It is well shaded and provides all the creature comforts anyone could want including mobile homes to rent. There is a sandy beach, places to eat and shop, a resident hairdresser and facilities for all kinds of water sports. Naturally it gets booked up a long time in advance, particularly for July and August, so it is essential to let them know early if you are hoping to stay there (tel. 94–56.25.29).

If you have something to celebrate and enjoy eating in unusual surroundings try the **Port Diffa** at La Foux on the way to St-Tropez (tel. 94–56.29.07). It is a little bit of Morocco where everything is authentic from the furnishings to the food and you can even have a set menu for 112 F. It closes from the first week in November until just after Christmas.

St-Tropez

It is said that St-Tropez is all things to all men, and all women too, for that matter. Some find it rather unattractive because of its reputation as a swinging centre for eccentrics and extroverts, others enjoy the atmosphere of the old port which appealed to writers and artists long before the film world discovered it. Between the two are the endless tourists who converge on it during the summer simply because, like Everest, it is there. Without a doubt the town is highly commercialised, the folk festivals are not so much parades as free-for-alls with everyone welcome to join in and the restaurants maintain that they sell thousands of lunches every day.

The yacht marina is famous for the number of celebrities who keep their boats there and the size of the gaping crowds who saunter past trying to see and identify them, usually at the top of their voices. But although many well-known people still live or spend their holidays in St-Tropez, it is very seldom that one runs across them. They are usually sunning themselves beside their private swimming pools while look-alikes have a splendid time pulling the wool over inquisitive eyes.

One visitor who looked in at the turn of the century said the streets were dirty and dark and it was not at all a suitable place for a winter residence. To a certain extent the last observation is true because the town is the only resort on the Riviera that faces north and so catches the full force of the mistral. Consequently most places close down at the end of the season but if you can stand the wind it is not a bad time to look round. Regardless of these drawbacks—some would say because of them—the little town is a fascinating place which cannot even make up its mind about the origin of its name. It might be derived from Torpes, the name of a Roman officer turned Christian, who was martyred and whose body was cast adrift in a small boat; it was washed up in the bay and buried locally but when the town came under attack someone removed it to a place of safety and it has never been seen since. The legend persisted through centuries of attack and counter-attack and is now the basis for a festival in May.

It was not until the end of the 19th century that St-Tropez was invaded by writers and artists from Paris who shared it with kindred spirits from Britain and America until the Germans arrived in the Second World War. When they in their turn were driven out they blew up the port before surrendering and most of the quayside houses that look so attractive today are actually copies of the originals. The last big invasion was in the 1950s, led by Roger Vadim and Brigitte Bardot who made a film there and put the resort firmly on the tourist map.

The **Annonciade Museum** and the 400-year-old **Citadel** are the two main places of interest. The former, with its collection of pictures, few if any dating back more than 100 years, is open from 10am to noon and 3pm to 7pm between May and September, changing the afternoon hours to 2pm to 6pm during the rest of the year. It is closed on Tuesdays, some holidays and in November and charges 8 F. The Citadel includes an interesting Maritime Museum and is open from 10am to 6pm between mid-June and mid-September, 10am to 5pm for the rest of the year, closes on Thursdays and some holidays and from mid-November to mid-December. Entrance costs 7 F.

WHERE TO STAY AND EATING OUT

There are a great many hotels and restaurants of every description in the town and in the surrounding area. An expensive choice would be the **Byblos**, Avenue Paul-Signac (tel. 94–97.00.04), at up to 1500 F a night. It is predictably luxurious and certainly worth the money if you can afford the price. The restaurant ranks among the best on the Côte d'Azur but you won't get away for less than 185 F. The hotel is closed from the beginning of November to the end of March.

The tourist office is on the Avenue Général Leclerc (tel. 94–97.41.21).

Because St-Tropez has no beaches of its own it has adopted those on either side but neither compares with the magnificent sweep of sand that runs from the Plage des Salins southwards towards Cap Camarat. Anyone who would have appreciated it in the days before it was 'discovered' will be sadly disappointed because it has become one enormous recreation centre with a gigantic caravan park. Admittedly it is divided into sections, each with a different name and slightly different things to offer, but basically it is a question of degree. Tahiti was the first beach to be developed and over-exposed. As the crowds moved in the select few moved out to set up their own little conclaves further down the coast. Mobile homes and caravans by the hundred were positioned along Pampelonne Beach. At Toison d'Or you can have a mobile home with a bath or shower but you have to go to Kon-Tiki if you just want a caravan unadorned.

At Kon-Tiki the caravans are all set out in straight lines, nose to tail, with narrow roads in front and thin bamboo hedges planted immediately behind. Of course, you can take your own caravan, and for visitors who wish to do this a site of slightly larger dimensions is provided so that you can get it in. Everyone who rents a mobile home or caravan has to join the Pam Beach Club and carry a membership card—actually quite useful, because the club provides tennis courts free and arranges special rates if you want to hire a horse, a boat or a windsurfer and it also provides instructors if you do not know what to do next. Both sites belong to Les Prairies de la Mer at Port Grimaud and are just as full in the summer so it is essential to book well in advance.

Cogolin

A short detour on the N98 will take you to Cogolin. Most of the bamboo furniture you find in this part of the world comes from Cogolin which positively bristles with cottage industries. A lot of residents spend their time making carpets and visitors are welcome at the workshops if they go round with a guide any weekday morning between 8.30 and noon or in the afternoon between 2 and 6. The entrance to Les Tapis et Tissus de Cogolin is at 98 Boulevard Louis-Blanc; the workshops are closed at weekends and on holidays.

Other craftsmen turn out briar pipes or keep an eye on silkworms while others use the reeds that grow in the marshes for anything from furniture to clarinets and fishing rods. The only trouble with Cogolin is the noise. Loudspeakers are positioned at all-too-frequent intervals along the main roads, making sure that you do not miss a note of whatever piece of music is being played.

Ramatuelle, Gassin, La Croix-Valmer and Gigaro

The village of Ramatuelle, which gave its name to the whole peninsula, was a Moorish fortress until the French drove the Moors out about 100 years before William the Conqueror landed in Britain. It is an attractive little place and surprisingly unspoiled considering that it is only a short drive from the coast. Its main attractions are an ancient elm tree in the Place de l'Ormeau and three ruined windmills on a hilltop nearby. For excellent food drop in at the **Auberge des Vieux Moulins** (tel. 94–97.17.22), where you can eat for 160F and choose a room for 400F. It is closed from mid-September until the third week in May and no food is available on Wednesdays during May or June.

The companion village of Gassin was another Moorish stronghold with equally good views across wooded country to the sea. All around is a network of tiny roads some of which have not been maintained very well. On a signpost at one intersection some wag—or desperate motorist—had sprayed the word 'autoroute' in blue paint. It was without doubt the worst road we found anywhere along the coast. There are not many places to leave a car in Gassin and all the houses and housing estates make it a poor choice for rambling or pulling on to the grass verge for an al fresco lunch.

La Croix-Valmer is where Constantine the Great is supposed to have had a vision when he was on his way to Italy. A stone cross marks the spot where he is believed to have seen a much larger cross in the sky with a message that he would be victorious if he confronted the pagans in the name of Christianity. You can stop here for lunch or carry on to Gigaro where the beaches are not very crowded and you may find a stretch of sand to yourself.

Cavalaire-sur-Mer

Cavalaire-sur-Mer, about the same distance from la Croix-Valmer as Gigaro but in the opposite direction, is a popular resort with woods of mimosa, oak and pine at the back door and miles of silver sand in front. Chandlers cater for the needs of visiting yachtsmen and little shops along the main street sell everything from beachwear to buckets and spades.

La Pergola, in the Avenue du Port, is a hotel with plenty of atmosphere. The dining room, which is rather like a series of white caves, opens on to a terrace with tables set out under orange trees, while the lounge could easily be part of a private house. The focal point is a fireplace where logs burn brightly at the slightest hint of cold weather and the chairs drawn up round it are large, comfortable and made from bamboo. It will cost you 210 F and the hotel is closed from November until just before Christmas. The restaurant serves very appetising dishes with a set menu for 145 F and is closed on Sunday nights and on Monday at lunchtime during the winter. Tel. 94-64.06.86.

Le Lavandou, Bormes-les-Mimosas and Cabasson

The Corniche des Maures follows the coastline westwards from Cavalaire-sur-Mer through a number of rapidly growing seaside towns and it is only a matter of time before they all join hands in an imitation of the eastern Côte d'Azur. The old fishing port of Le Lavandou, which took its name from the lavender fields along the river banks, has all but disappeared under a sea of modern glass and concrete. It has a smallish marina and an energetic fishing fleet, plenty of sea bathing and all the usual water sports. When you get tired of them you can visit Bormes-les-Mimosas, a pastel-coloured hill village to the north, or Cabasson on the far side of Cap Bénat. The coast here is very rocky and you cannot wander about at will because a good deal of the

Bormes-les-Mimosas

peninsula is closed to the public. The army has exclusive rights to some parts and the old fortress of Brégançon is strictly private because it is an official summer residence of the Presidents of France.

Collobrières and La-Garde-Freinet

A pleasant afternoon drive would be up into the Massif des Maures, calling at Collobrières, a delightful village on a river in the heart of the cork oak forests. A small road which has definitely seen better days leads up to the **Chartreuse-de-la-Verne**, a ruined monastery which has been partly restored to give an idea of what life was like for the monks who lived there before it was abandoned during the Revolution. Like La-Garde-Freinet, which has a ruined Saracen castle, Collobrières is very much involved in the production of cork but it also finds time to provide grapes for the local rosé wine and specialises in *marrons glacés* from the chestnut trees that grow extensively in the mountains.

Le Thoronet

A small winding road takes you northwards past La Sauvette, the highest point in the Massif des Maures, and deposits you on the main road to

Toulon. If you have more time to spare, another minor road a little further on leads directly to Le Thoronet and the famous abbey of the same name. The first thing that strikes you is the colour of the countryside because everything, including the trees, is tinged with red. This is as a result of bauxite being mined extensively in the area and notices at regular intervals warn of the dangers that lie just off the beaten track. Presumably they are necessary, but it is difficult to imagine that anyone would want to walk or picnic in bright red dust that stains wherever it clings.

It is a good thing that there are plenty of signs pointing the way to the **Abbey of Le Thoronet** as otherwise it would be quite easy to drive past without even seeing it. The whole monastery is below the level of the road and only the top of the church spire stands out above the trees. It is one of three Cistercian houses that were built in Provence during the 12th century, the others being at Sénanque and Silvacane, and is generally considered to be the most beautiful of them all. From the outside this is a little difficult to believe because it is squarely built of local stone without any form of decoration and does not even have a main door in the façade. The fact that it is equally simple and austere inside has led more than one person to describe it as sublime. Fortunately all attempts to dress it up in the 18th century have either faded or been removed, leaving the high vaulted nave and narrow side aisles to tell their own story. The cloisters are equally uncluttered and functional with a washing room complete with a basin and a decidedly primitive method for bringing in water. The chapterhouse was added a while later and the tour ends with a visit to the dormitory which now has glass in the windows but even that does not make it the least bit cosy.

Before leaving, have a look at the small niche outside in the south wall. It was where local people could leave their dead for burial and is said to be one of the very few still existing in Provence. The whole abbey is in an excellent state of repair, thanks to the State which bought it in the 19th century and has maintained it ever since. It is open from 10am until noon and from 2pm to 6pm between May and September, closes at 5pm in March, April and October and at 4pm from November to February. It is closed on 1 January, 1 May, 1 and 11 November and on Christmas Day. Entrance costs 8 F.

Lorgues

After this, provided you are in the mood for some more sightseeing, continue on to Lorgues which has an extremely attractive main square shaded by splendid plane trees. The old part of the town is the usual mixture of small streets, stairways and the odd fountain all tucked away behind ancient fortified gateways. The **Auberge Josse,** on the Route Carcès (tel. 94–73.73.55), serves a delectable lunch for between 75 and 100F but is closed between Christmas and February and on Wednesdays out of season. Anyone with a weakness for angels should look in at the church where the altar is decorated with them.

The Cistercian Abbey, Le Thoronet

Carcès

Alternatively, leave the Abbey of Le Thoronet in the opposite direction and head for Carcès where the town has little to tempt you out of the car but the lake is only a short drive away. This is another man-made reservoir that looks as though nature intended it to be there. The water follows the original line of the river between wooded hills that have a vague resemblance to the Fal above Carrick Roads. The trees grow right down to the edge and there are some good places to stop along the eastern bank but rather fewer on the opposite side. It is a great haunt for fishermen and is crowded during the season with families enjoying a lazy day walking under the trees or lying in the sun. Apart from a small *auberge*, an equally modest restaurant and a few little boats, the whole place appears to be uninhabited and is delightfully quiet.

Cotignac

The same unhurried atmosphere is to be found at Cotignac which is reached through miles of vineyards and specialises in the production of wine and honey. The village is dominated by the ruins of a castle and has an open-air theatre at the bottom of a cliff which is honeycombed with caves and tunnels. A path leads up to one cave which local people insist was once the home of some very early inhabitants. If it is true, they could not have found a better place to keep an eye open for their enemies because it has a commanding view over the countryside.

Hyères

For those who prefer to follow the coastline the best bet would be to carry on to Hyères on the N98. There is not much to see along the way if you discount a large salt works, a market garden centre, an airport and some quite pedestrian beach resorts. However, Hyères is a name to conjure with, once you remember how to pronounce it.

It is the most southerly of all the holiday towns along the Riviera and was fashionable 200 years ago as an inland resort. The Greeks originally set up their trading station at what is now Ayguade Ceinturon and the Romans followed suit with a town of their own. Everything thrived and it became a favourite port with crusaders on their way to and from the Holy Land. St Louis landed there on his way home in 1254 but even that was not enough to ensure its survival. The townspeople packed their bags and moved up the hillside where the castle offered some measure of protection from enemy attacks. Once the hill town was established, the harbour was allowed to silt up and nobody bothered about things like beaches until well into the present century.

The castle was destroyed in 1620 but enough is still standing to make the long walk up through **St-Bernard Park** worth the effort. There is not a great deal left of the medieval town either apart from the **Massillon Gate**, a church or two and a tower which was built by the Knights Templars in the 12th century but now watches over nothing more dangerous than the morning market. As time went by, Hyères began to expand back towards the coast, broad avenues appeared planted with date palms and visitors increased in both quality and quantity. Among them was Robert Louis Stevenson who insisted that it was the only place in the South of France which he had enjoyed. Tolstoy apparently enjoyed it too but he said less about it. Then, through no apparent fault of its own, the town lost its popularity; it retained its capacity for survival, however. By developing the salt marshes, stepping up the production and sale of early fruit and vegetables and increasing its output of wine, Hyères lessened its dependence on the tourist trade. At one time its publicity included the fascinating information that the town offered 'mild gaiety for young ladies' and that is probably not too far from the truth today.

The Giens peninsula, which is actually an island attached to the mainland by two long sandbanks, has a village, a camping site without much to offer in the way of extras apart from skin diving, some good views and a jumping-off place for people who want to visit the Iles d'Or. It is the best choice for anyone prone to seasickness as the crossing takes only about a quarter of an hour.

Les Iles d'Or

The Iles d'Hyères, to give them their correct name, were probably rechristened because of their strange metallic sheen which some people used to think was caused by the presence of gold but which, in fact, is caused by mica. There are three islands altogether, the closest and largest being the Ile de Porquerolles. It boasts one small and comparatively recent village with a yacht harbour and a couple of hotels but no caravan site because cars are not allowed on the island. The beaches are sandy and there is plenty of space where you can picnic without being disturbed. The lighthouse is closed to the public but it has an excellent view and anyone too lazy to walk that far can hire a bicycle.

The Ile du Levant, which is nearly the same size, is very rocky and there are only two inlets where it is possible to get ashore. The greater part belongs to the French navy and probably no one would bother to go there if it were not for the nudist colony centred on the village of Héliopolis. In spite of the fact that people are tossing off their clothes in all sorts of places along the coast this out-of-the-way area is very popular with sun-worshippers. Visitors are tolerated but cameras are not.

Port-Cros is the wildest and most beautiful of the three islands, covered with thick vegetation and kept green by a series of natural springs. There is a minute port and the staff who run the island as a nature reserve lay on guided tours for people who are seriously interested. They also take scuba divers along an underwater path to see marine life in its natural environment. On the other hand, there is little to attract the casual tourist because there are not many beaches and nothing in the way of organised entertainment.

There are regular boat services to the islands which take anything from 15 minutes to two hours depending on your starting point and are priced accordingly. You can get full details from Cie Iles d'Or, 15 Quai Gabriel-Péri, Le Lavandou (tel. 94–71.01.02) or from Transrade, Quai Stalingrad, Toulon (tel. 94–92.96.82).

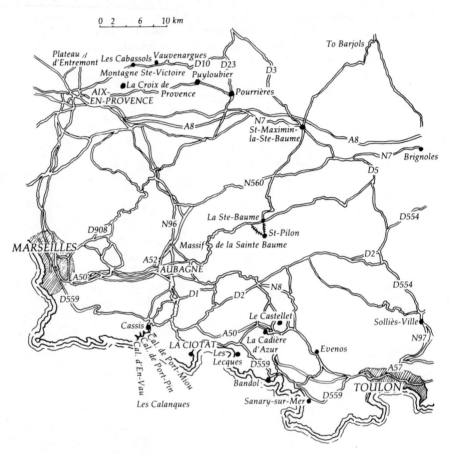

TOULON TO
MARSEILLES

Chapter V

TOULON TO MARSEILLES

Water jousting at La Ciotat

There are some places in the world that should, if possible, be seen for the first time from a particular vantage point. For instance, Cape Town from the sea with Table Mountain in the background or Niagara Falls from the Canadian side of the river. The most impressive view of Toulon is from **Mont Faron**, the high limestone ridge that rises sharply just at the back of the town. You can get there by funicular or by a winding road that climbs steeply through pine woods, runs along the ridge and then drops down again into the built-up area over 600 metres (2000ft) below.

The view from the top is magnificent, taking in the coast as far as Bandol to the west, the Iles d'Or to the south-east and in the far distance the peaks of the Alpes Provençales. Immediately below is Toulon itself with the old quarter clustering up against the harbour, surrounded by the more modern section with its commercial buildings and naval installations. This gives way eventually to the suburbs that insinuate themselves up into the mountains. The focal point is the large, natural harbour with its two sets of protecting arms. This has the advantage of being a very safe anchorage and the disadvantage of being quite easy to blockade. Sixty French warships were scuttled there in 1942 to keep them out of German hands, but the navy was back in a couple of years and now shares the port facilities with commerce and industry. From the mountain top it looks rather like one of those plotting tables used by chiefs of staff during the war, although in this case the ships move about under their own power.

When you get tired of looking at the view, Mont Faron has other things to offer. Anyone who has been fascinated by the total recall of the D-Day landings in the museum at Arromanches should find the **Mémorial National du Débarquement** just as absorbing. It gives the whole history of the Allied invasion of Provence in 1944, bringing the turbulent background to the area right up to date. It is open from 9am to 11.30am and 2.15pm to 6.45pm in summer, reduces the afternoon visiting hours to 4pm to 5.30pm out of season, and a visit there costs 8 F. At the other end of the ridge you will find a small zoo with the usual wild animals and some much tamer ones that are being bred in captivity. It costs 16 F (7 F for children) and is open from 10am to noon and 2pm to 7pm in summer but 2pm to 5pm in winter. There is nothing to prevent you exploring on foot provided you pay attention to the notices warning people away from military installations, and if you take a camera be careful not to use it anywhere near the prohibited areas or you could find yourself answering some rather awkward questions.

Toulon

At first glance Toulon does not really stand out as a popular holiday resort and it is doubtful if it would be high on anyone's list of favourite places to stay. However, it improves enormously on acquaintance, is not as expensive as other big towns along the Riviera and has a history which is just as interesting as theirs.

HISTORY
Somewhat surprisingly, there is very little evidence of Roman occupation apart from traces of the ancient dye works on the site of the present arsenal. The town was famous for the royal purple colour it produced from pointed conches that are found along that part of the coast. It was some considerable time before the emperors would allow anyone else to use it and even then the money it realised went straight into the royal coffers. Not a great deal happened during the next few centuries apart from the usual comings and goings of the Saracens and little local rivalries.

Although part of the old port dates from the 16th century, it took Louis XIV to realise the potential value of Toulon as a naval base and provide it with everything necessary to maintain the greater part of his fleet. Because the ships needed crews and they were hard to come by, thousands of prisoners, slaves and convicts were rounded up and transported to the town in chains. There they were joined by an occasional soldier of fortune, shackled firmly to both the galleys and the oars and encouraged to show a bit more effort by an overseer with a rawhide whip. More fortunate citizens would amuse themselves by jeering at any new arrivals as they shuffled past and some visitors would actually go down to the quay to see them hunched together on the seats where they ate, slept, lived and frequently died. This state of affairs persisted into the middle of the 18th century when the galleys were phased out and prisons took their place.

In the early stages of the Revolution, Toulon remained faithful to the King and invited Britain and Spain to send in warships to protect the town. The British built a fortress on the site of the present Fort Carré but were driven out by a certain Captain Bonaparte who was immediately promoted. Sir Sidney Smith destroyed the dockyard before his troops were evacuated and the Republican forces retaliated by killing 6000 royalists and refugees they found there and renaming the battered area Port-la-Montagne. The name did not stick and the town soon reverted to its previous title and function as the most important naval base in France. The port was badly damaged again by Allied bombs in the last war and the Germans blew up what was left of the harbour installations before they surrendered in 1944.

WHAT TO SEE

With the return of peace the old Quai Cronstadt, named in honour of a visit by the Russian navy 50 years before, was rebuilt and rechristened Quai Stalingrad. It is full of shops and cafes and makes a good starting point for an inspection of the old town immediately behind. Unfortunately there is not a great deal to see behind the façade of modern buildings that line the waterfront.

The **Naval Museum,** at the end of the Quai Stalingrad, includes model ships, statues of famous 17th-century admirals and numerous paintings and other reminders of the good old days. It spills over into a tower which was once part of the harbour defences and is open from 10am to noon and 1.30pm to 6pm but is closed on Tuesdays and on public holidays apart from Easter and Whitsun.

The **Cathedral of Ste-Marie-de-la-Seds,** about a block from the

Cours Lafayette, was founded in the 11th century but has been completely modernised and is extremely dark and gloomy.

The **Museum of Art and Archaeology** and the **Museum of Natural History** are to be found near the Jardin Alexandre Ier, a fairish walk away. There are some prehistoric exhibits, Roman remains, an Oriental gallery and paintings covering the past 700 years. They are both closed on public holidays. The former opens from 10am to noon and from 2pm to 6pm but you can get into the Natural History Museum only between 9.30am and 11.45am and again from 2pm until 5.15pm.

The morning market in the Cours Lafayette and the covered fish market near the quay are both quite atmospheric and some of the little alleyways are fun to explore, but on the whole the old quarter is less attractive than its counterparts in other towns along the coast. There are quite a few guided tours round the harbour and out into the Roads; however, as nearly all the buildings are modern the only advantage, apart from a breath of sea air, is to get a sailor's-eye view of the port and the hills behind.

WHERE TO STAY

There are not a great many hotels in Toulon and most of those that do exist are small.

The **Frantel,** on the slopes of Mont Faron near the funicular (tel. 94–24.41.57), has a magnificent view, is modern and comfortable and is about the biggest of them all. A room costs 410 F and you can get a good meal in the restaurant for around 140 F upwards, although it is closed for Saturday lunch and all day Sunday from October to May.

EATING OUT

Apart from all the little cafes along the Quai Stalingrad, there are several places to eat in the old town behind. One excellent restaurant is the **Madeleine,** 7 Rue des Tombades (tel. 94–92.67.85), a few minutes' walk from the cathedral. The specialities are in a class of their own but you can get a very good menu for 75 F. It is closed on Tuesday evenings and on Wednesdays.

FESTIVALS

Toulon does itself quite proud where festivals are concerned. There is a parade of flowers in April, circus performers hold their celebrations at the height of the summer when there is also an international dance festival and the November Fair is concerned almost entirely with *santons*, the little traditional figures, sometimes animated, which are mainly designed for

106

the Christmas crib but also recall local types in much the same way as the 'Cries of London' do in Britain.

INFORMATION
The tourist office is at 8 Avenue Colbert (tel. 94–22.08.22) and, apart from being a mine of information, will help you with hotels.

The countryside behind Toulon is fairly wild and mountainous with several places of interest within easy reach. They range from the deserted village of **Evenos** with its ruined castle to **Solliès-Ville** where you will find one of the oldest church organs in France.

Brignoles

From Solliès-Ville, one could take the scenic route north and branch off on the N7 to Brignoles which has been busy producing marble since the Romans were there. It has now added wine and bauxite to its other major industries and consequently is pink-tinged, expanding and industrial. Visitors usually do the round of the old quarter at some speed because, apart from a small church and a local museum, there is practically nothing to see. In the Middle Ages the village was famous for its plums, but during the League troubles in the 16th century thousands of trees were destroyed and today you are much more likely to be offered a home-grown peach. Although it is not what you would call an ideal holiday centre, there is a camping site, and an angling club will advise on the best places to fish.

St-Maximin-la-Ste-Baume

Unlike Brignoles the town is small and full of life without being industrialised. It also has a very fine abbey and a splendid legend to go with it.

The story tells how St Mary Magdalene arrived in the Camargue with a boatload of other saints including St Maximin. The two of them set out to convert the heathen and when he stopped at Aix, where he was eventually murdered, she set up home in a cave and spent the rest of her life there. They were both buried in the church crypt and the town took his name once the Romans were no longer in any position to object. Then the Saracens arrived, and the villagers, who had been converted to Christianity, hid the

Saints' relics so well that for the next 500 years no one knew where to look for them. At the end of the 13th century the King's brother, Charles of Anjou, made a thorough search of all the likely places and came across two graves, both of which were said to be intact. He immediately arranged to build a church on the spot and established a Dominican monastery to watch over it.

The monks were thrown out during the Revolution but fortunately another brother was on hand to help. Lucien Bonaparte, in charge of military stores, used the building as a warehouse and managed to save the organ by instructing a member of his staff to brush up his musical talents and play the *Marseillaise* on it loudly and frequently. Although work on the church went on for about 500 years, it was never finished and fortunately no one has tried to add the missing pieces, such as the belfry. It is surprisingly light inside and there are also switches you can turn on to see some of its greatest treasures, amongst them a magnificently embroidered cope which was worn by the Bishop of Toulouse at the end of the 13th century. Most pilgrims go straight to the crypt, once the burial vault of a Roman villa, which contains what they believe to be the skull of St Mary Magdalene. There are also four Roman sarcophagi that may or may not contain the remains of other saints but are certainly among the oldest Christian relics in France. The cloisters, built at the same time as the church, are also very fine, and the pilgrim hostelry that was added later now does duty as the town hall. The cloisters are open from 9am to 11.30am and 2.30pm to 6pm and 5 F is charged to visitors.

The **Massif de la Ste-Baume**, to the south of St-Maximin, takes its name from the Provençal word *baoumo* meaning cave and referring of course, to the one where St Mary Magdalene is thought to have lived. It is to be found about an hour's walk from the pilgrim hostel, high up in the limestone cliff overlooking a forest of giant beech trees. Inevitably time has changed many things; an altar has been added, some relics have been returned from the abbey, a statue of the saint reclines on a ledge out of reach and a midnight mass is celebrated there every July as it has been since the Middle Ages. Close by is **St-Pilon**, the highest point of the Massif, where legend has it that St Mary Magdalene was carried several times a day by angels so that she could listen to the heavenly choir. Anyone with a map and tough walking shoes would enjoy exploring the whole area, but that does not mean to say that it is closed to everyone else. Minor roads, although not as many as one might expect, wander off into the forests, some going nowhere in particular but producing an occasional view, a less welcome bauxite mine, the odd ruin and greenery ranging from the holly and the ivy to limes, maples and yew trees.

Le Castellet

A good place to make for is Le Castellet, an ancient stronghold which used to belong to the Lords of Les Baux. It has been well preserved and restored, so much so that an occasional film director has disrupted the life of the village to add an authentic touch to his latest period piece. Some of the houses go back 300–400 years but most of the inhabited ones have been skilfully modernised inside to provide homes for the craftsmen who live there. They turn out pottery, woven materials and leather goods which are less expensive in the workshops than they are in the boutiques of the larger towns. Add a castle partly built in the 11th century, a 12th-century church and some ramparts and you have all the ingredients for an enjoyable visit.

Castel Lumière, in the village (tel. 94–90.62.20), serves exceptionally good meals for as little as 130F, although it is well worth ordering something more expensive as you sit on the patio looking at the view. The restaurant is closed on Tuesdays and for most of November.

La Cadière-d'Azur

The companion village of La Cadière-d'Azur, on the other side of the motorway, has been even less affected by the passage of time. It has an old gate but nothing which could possibly be mistaken for a castle or an ancient fort, so tourists tend to pass it by. However, the pottery and the cloth are well up to standard, the atmosphere is peaceful and quite unspoiled and the Hôtel Bérard has delightful rooms and excellent menus. You can stay there for 350F a night and sample local dishes or meat roasted over an open fire for anything from 270F upwards. It is closed from late October until the beginning of December (tel. 94–29.31.43).

Sanary-sur-Mer and Bandol

Once back on the coast you might decide to take your family to the zoo which is half-way between Sanary and Bandol, cheek by jowl with the motorway, and concentrates on little cuddly animals rather than the large dangerous kind. The birds deserve special mention and so do the enclosing gardens with their collection of exotic plants. It is open from 8am until noon and between 2pm and 7pm, but opens two hours later on Sundays and holidays and closes at 6pm out of season. During the winter it is also closed on Sunday mornings and on Tuesdays. It costs 12 F for adults and 6 F for children.

Both Sanary-sur-Mer and Bandol are popular seaside resorts but the former does not make a great to-do about it. There is a beach with plenty of sand but some shingle, and an attractive little harbour full of private boats as well as local fishermen. You can sail, skin-dive and play tennis, stay in a modest hotel and find at least one first-class restaurant.

Bandol, on the other hand, sings its own praises from the rooftops with some justification. It is fairly sophisticated with a harbour that treats yachtsmen and fishing boats quite impartially, has a sailing school and a diving club. There are tennis courts, bicycles for hire, and a casino where you can lose the shirt you took off earlier in the day. Palm trees like feather dusters line the main promenades and you would be hard put to find a notice recalling the Romans, the Saracens or even Napoleon, although there is a quay named after General de Gaulle.

The town's two outstanding attractions both belong to Paul Ricard, the man whose *pastis* has made him a millionaire. The first is a motor-racing circuit near le Castelet which is named after him and where there are events nearly every weekend and quite a few major races each year. The other is the Île de Bendor, a rocky uninhabited bit of real estate about a mile from the coast which he bought and turned into a tourist centre. Whatever you think should be included on an island like this, Paul Ricard thought of it first: a Provençal village with craftsmen hard at work, a marina, an art gallery and a conference centre where you can learn just about anything from art to yoga and probably zoology to complete the alphabet. Logically he also included the Universal Wines and Spirits Exhibition which is open from 10am to 12.30pm and from 2pm to 6pm, is closed on Wednesdays, and includes thousands of bottles, displays of glasses and decanters and liquor from nearly 50 different countries.

The nearby Ile des Embiez has also been developed by Ricard as a centre for powerboating. All types of craft put in to the marina and any necessary repairs can be carried out while the crews visit the aquarium or the marine research centre.

WHERE TO STAY AND EATING OUT
Apart from a hotel on the Île de Bendor, there is a tremendous range to choose from in Bandol, starting at 1550F a night and dropping to about 120F.

La **Ker Mocotte,** Rue Raimu (tel. 94–29.46.53), has a private beach, which can be a great advantage at the height of the season, and a pleasant restaurant. It charges 246F for a room, while dinner, which is for residents only, starts at 86F with wine at comparable prices. Dogs are not allowed in the bedrooms. The hotel closes from November to February.

Le Lotus (tel. 94–29.49.03) in the Place Lucien-Artaud, close to the casino, offers a choice of French, Chinese and Vietnamese dishes with set menus for 75 to 87F. It is closed on Wednesdays.

Les Lecques

Further round the coast to the west, Les Lecques is a family resort with a good beach and a few Roman connections. It is supposed to have been a trading post founded by the Greeks after one of their ships went aground there. The original harbour and nearly all the town have disappeared but the **museum,** on the site of a Roman villa, contains enough evidence to show that there is some substance to the story. It is open between 3pm and 7pm from June to September, from 2pm to 5pm during the rest of the year, and is closed on Tuesdays. Entrance costs 5F.

La Ciotat

La Ciotat, a little further on, has been a port right through the ages, suffering all the common problems of invasion, occupation and devastation. At one time it had quite a respectable merchant fleet and the shipyards can still handle fairly large vessels although, since the slump in world shipping, there has not been all that much work about. Fishermen and privately owned boats keep the old harbour busy while holidaymakers are inclined to gravitate towards La Ciotat Plage where the beaches are highly recommended by families who, according to the hotel owners, keep coming back year after year. Places for tents and caravans are at a premium during the season and requests for horses and bicycles should be made well in advance.

For any details you need you will find the **tourist office** at 2 Quai Ganteaume (tel. 42–08.61.32).

111

Cassis

A narrow winding road that follows the rugged coastline some of the way, passing Cap Canaille where the cliffs are the highest in France, and a straighter road that ignores the sea altogether both lead to Cassis. It is a charming little fishing port which is largely unspoiled by its popularity if you ignore the flats and villas that have been built as holiday homes. Most of the area round the port has been reserved for pedestrians—not a moment too soon judging from the crowds who pour in at the weekends and throughout the season.

In essence Cassis is rather like St-Tropez. The town is popular with artists as it has been for a great many years; wealthy people from Marseilles have holiday villas there; the shops are filled with attractive goods at a little-above-average prices; and there are some first-rate hotels and restaurants. The casino, only about ten years old and a splendid mixture of marble floors, sculptures and oriental gardens, boasts that it is far more active than its counterparts elsewhere along the coast. Discos cater energetically for younger visitors who also tend to take over the smallish gardens along the Quai St-Pierre. There are beaches with a choice of sand or shingle, but as they shelve quite steeply it would be as well to keep an eye on any young children playing close to the water.

Most of the better hotels and restaurants are to be found to the west of the harbour on the way to Port Miou but there are also plenty of places to eat along the Quai des Baux. Fish naturally figures largely on the menus and complements the local wine which is slightly greenish and not to everybody's taste.

St Pierre is the patron saint of fishermen and Cassis celebrates his feast day on 29 June but also finds a lot of other things to celebrate throughout the summer. All the details are available from the **tourist office** in the Place Baragnon (tel. 42–01.71.17).

Apart from a small museum there is nothing of particular interest to see in the town but the *calanques* more than make up for the absence of old buildings and ancient alleyways. They are a series of deep creeks, rather like miniature Norwegian fiords, which eat their way in to the cliffs to the west. For anyone who enjoys walking, paths lead past the quarries, which incidentally supplied hard white stone for the Suez Canal, to both Port-Pin and En-Vau, but for the less energetic the obvious thing is to take a boat. Regular trips leave from the Quai St-Pierre, take anything up to two hours and cost 18 F.

Aubagne

North of Cassis a positive 'spaghetti junction' of autoroutes, main highways and secondary roads threatens to overwhelm the old town of Aubagne. Founded in the Middle Ages, it used to be famous for the production of *santons*. These figures are still turned out in their thousands and are snapped up by tourists as souvenirs. The modern ones, which can be most attractive, give a clear picture of the various old-world occupations and details of the clothes worn in former times. However, it is most disconcerting to find that all the faces look exactly the same. It is rather like finding Alec Guinness in a rural French version of *Kind Hearts and Coronets*. *Santons* are still produced in Aubagne and there are a number of other industries, but the town is better known nowadays as the home of the French Foreign Legion. The regiment moved there when Algeria became independent in 1962 and its exploits over the past 150 years are faithfully recorded in a small museum that captures much of the romance and a good deal of the reality Hollywood overlooked. The museum is open from 10am to noon and between 3pm and 7pm from June to September, although it closes on Mondays and Saturday mornings. For the rest of the year you can get in on Wednesdays and Sundays from 10am to noon and 2pm to 6pm and on Saturday afternoons, at a cost of 2F.

Instead of taking any of the main roads to the north, try one of the less crowded minor variety that goes to Allauch, although there is nothing to stop for apart from some old windmills, a ruined castle and an excellent view over Marseilles. From there it is an easy drive through rather nondescript country to Aix-en-Provence.

Aix-en-Provence

The majority of people find Aix totally enchanting with so much to see and do that there is always the temptation to stay on indefinitely. One is inclined to describe it as a 'little' town because the old part only measures about 915 metres (1000 yards) across in any direction and the fact that it is completely enclosed by highrise flats, industrial sites, supermarkets and all the other paraphernalia of progress is neither here nor there. It is actually the largest centre for prepared almonds anywhere in Europe and the shops are filled with small diamond-shaped blocks of almond paste which are iced, sometimes wrapped and boxed and go by the name of *calisson*.

HISTORY

Aix was founded by the Romans in 122 BC who called it Aquae Sextiae after a combination of the warm springs and the Consul Sextius who decided to build a town round them. It grew in importance and for a short period was the local capital, but when the Romans left it went into a steady decline that lasted until the early Middle Ages. However, the Counts of Provence, who also had a liking for thermal springs, returned it to favour in the 12th century and by the time Good King René appeared on the scene 300 years later it was famous for its music and poetry and was firmly re-established as the capital of the region. He was a man of many talents who had studied a wide range of subjects and was interested in everything from maths to music and agriculture to the arts. Somewhat carelessly he lost both his Italian kingdom and the duchy of Anjou, but instead of going to war over it he settled down to enjoy life as the ruler of Provence. A statue of him in the Cours Mirabeau shows a rather kindly man with a crown and sceptre clutching a well-worn bunch of muscat grapes which he introduced from Sicily.

After King René died in 1480, Aix continued to be an important cultural and administrative centre but without quite the same degree of independence from France. The university, founded in 1409, continued to flourish, parliament was established there in 1501, buildings went up at a tremendous rate and in 1789 Count Mirabeau sat for Aix in the States General. However, things did not go entirely according to plan and gradually its position was usurped by Marseilles.

WHAT TO SEE

Aix today is a highly civilised town in every sense of the word, with a reputation for being both stylish and self-possessed. Most of the outstanding places of interest date from the 16th and 17th centuries but there are still a few reminders of its golden age.

The **Cathedral of St-Sauveur** on the Rue de la Roque began life in the 5th century and was added to, improved and embellished almost without ceasing for the next 1200 years. Two of its most important treasures are the magnificent carvings on the west door and the famous *Burning Bush*, painted for King René in 1475. They are both kept under lock and key but the sacristan is only too pleased to open them up and explain their significance. It is not so easy to see the set of Brussels tapestries which were woven for Canterbury Cathedral in the early 16th century, sold by Cromwell and eventually bought by a local canon for what would now be described as 'a song'.

All the statues except one were destroyed during the Revolution and had to be replaced later. Only the Virgin escaped and that was because someone pulled a cap of Liberty over her head to show that she was supporting the right side.

The **Tapestry Museum,** housed next door in the Archbishop's Palace, includes several tapestries collected during the 17th and 18th centuries which show scenes from the life of Don Quixote. These escaped destruction because, either by accident or design, they spent the dangerous years safely hidden in the roof. The museum is open from 10am to noon and again from 2.30pm to 6.30pm in the summer but reduces the afternoon hours to 2pm to 5pm from October to June; it closes on Tuesdays, some holidays and for the whole of January. The entrance fee is 6 F.

The **Museum of Old Aix** is a stone's throw away at 17 Rue Gaston-de-Saporta. It has an astonishingly fine collection of *santons*, mechanical dolls and cardboard puppets, including a set piece showing the Corpus Christi procession as it was in the last century. The figures were originally intended to provide colour and animation during traditional festivals but are now considered too fragile to be allowed out of doors. The museum is open from 10am to noon and from 2pm to 6pm, closes an hour early on winter afternoons and is shut all day Monday and throughout February. It also charges 6 F.

Another stone thrown in the same direction would probably land in the Place de l'Hôtel-de-Ville where you will find a flower market surrounded by parked cars and several vans bringing in replacement pots of plants and bunches of greenery. It is all so crowded that you have to stand on a few toes to see the post office, which was once the old grain market, with its imposing 18th-century sculpture of the goddess Cybele dangling her foot in the air as she tries to seduce a very masculine River Rhône. At right angles to it is the town hall which houses the Saint-John Perse Collection, and beyond it an ancient clock tower with four wooden statues representing the four seasons. They are attached to a revolving base so that only the appropriate one can be seen at any time of the year.

Among the many other places of interest is the **Granet Museum** in the Place St-Jean, with one of the best art collections in Provence. It keeps the same hours as the Museum of Old Aix but is closed on Tuesdays and some holidays and charges 10 F.

The **Pavillon de Vendôme,** 34 Rue Célony, is a heavy square mansion looking out over small formal gardens devoid of flowers which used to be the summer home of the cardinal 300 years ago. Two weary-looking atlantes hold up the balcony and inside a grand double staircase links rooms filled with furniture and pictures of roughly the same period. It opens and closes in unison with the Tapestry Museum but closes at Easter, 1 May, 1 and 11 November and on Christmas Day. Entrance costs 8 F.

Of more recent date is the **Atelier Cézanne** on the Avenue Paul-Cézanne. Although he was born in Aix and lived there for the latter part of his life, the painter always kept his home and his studio separate. Every day he would go out to the little house in the suburbs, well away from the old town, where his studio on the first floor has been maintained very much as he left it 80 years ago. As in Renoir's studio, the easel and palette stand ready, his hat and coat hang in the corner, there are bottles and glasses on the table and other personal effects lying about. Some people find the atmosphere a little disquieting as though the man who liked painting skulls might have left something of that side of his personality behind as well. The studio is open from 10am to noon and 2.30pm to 6pm, but closes at 5pm in winter and on Tuesdays and holidays. The charge is 5 F.

The **Cours Mirabeau,** built along the line of the old ramparts, is a wide, straight avenue shaded by four rows of giant plane trees with fountains at intervals down the middle. On one side banks and offices have taken over the large stone mansions without detracting from them very much but cafes, restaurants and ice-cream parlours have done their best to turn the pavement opposite into a relaxation centre for students and visitors. Sometimes the students amuse themselves by dressing up and mimicking the passers-by. They have developed it to such an art that the victim seldom if ever realises what is sending everyone else into fits of laughter.

The town on either side of the Cours differs as much as the two pavements themselves. Behind the banks is the Mazarin quarter, built in the 17th century by the Archbishop of Aix whose brother was the famous statesman. It was laid out on the grid system, provided homes for his aristocratic friends and has hardly changed at all in the past 300 years.

On the opposite side the streets of the older town twist and wriggle about, some of them lined with little shops and restaurants, others stony-faced and rather severe. A taxi ride through the few which are open to traffic is quite an experience. The car races along between shuttered houses towards a blank wall, makes a 90-degree turn at speed and repeats the same process until it eventually arrives at a main road. Nine times out of ten this is one-way in the wrong direction, so off you go again, realising that the driver was quite right when he said that it would be easier, quicker and cheaper to walk.

The thermal baths are built on the site of the original Roman ones but the

116

Fontaine des Quatre Dauphins

only remaining evidence of these is one small piece of stone displayed inside. They are highly organised and rather clinical and you cannot just pop in for a swim if you feel like it. First it is necessary to find a doctor—and there are many of them about—who will decide if the treatment would help your particular complaint. Then you register and put yourself in the hands of the white-coated staff, hoping that eventually you will be allowed a dip in the pool. A very boring and functional drinking fountain in the entrance supplies a constant trickle of water which is warm, full of highly concentrated chemicals and cannot hold a candle to the local wine, although they say it does you much more good.

It is necessary to have a car, catch a bus or hire a taxi to visit the **Vasarély Foundation** on the western outskirts of the town. It is a long, modern building on the Jas de Bouffan designed by the artist a decade ago to house his works and tributes from his contemporaries. His experiments with light and movement are demonstrated and explained, which is just as well for anyone whose appreciation and knowledge lie in quite a different direction. It is open from 10am to 5pm and is closed on Tuesdays, 1 May and Christmas Day. The entrance fee is 12 F.

117

WHERE TO STAY

Although Aix has plenty of hotels, some of them fairly large but not extremely expensive, it can be very difficult to find a room.

Le Pigonnet, 5 Avenue Pigonnet ·(tel. 42–59.02.90), is outside the old town, has a most beautiful garden and a lovely view. It costs 485 F per night. The restaurant, which closes on Sunday evenings and from November to March, has a set menu for 130 F and a number of specialities that taste even better on the terrace under the chestnut trees.

The **Hôtel du Globe,** 74 Cours Sextius (tel. 42–26.03.58), is both modern and comfortable behind its old façade and it would be hard to find anyone more delightful or more considerate than the directrice, Madame Bottoni. She spends most of the day looking after her guests, many of whom have come to 'take the waters' opposite, and brushes aside their thanks with the assurance, 'It is nothing. We do the same for everyone.' The rooms are priced up to 190 F but there is no restaurant, although the hotel does have a garage. The hotel closes from Christmas to the beginning of March.

You will find one or two camping sites in the countryside round Aix, most of them with swimming pools and shops. The majority of these sites are open all the year.

EATING OUT

There are a considerable number of restaurants, from little places where the students sometimes bring their own food, order a cold drink, borrow a knife and fork and settle down at a table on the pavement, to large open-plan establishments that can be rather formal.

Les Caves Henri IV, 32 Rue Espariat (tel. 42–27.86.39), occupies a 16th-century cellar in the old town and is so popular that it is wise to book in advance. The memorable set menus run from 200 to 280 F. The restaurant is closed on Sundays and Mondays, for most of August and from the last few days in February to the middle of March.

La Rotonde, 2A Place Jeanne-d'Arc, just off the Place Général-de-Gaulle (tel. 42–26.01.95), is airy and very pleasant. It specialises in fish which they cook to perfection and lamb that has fed on lavender and melts in your mouth. You get a good dinner including wine and coffee for about 170 F.

The **Vendôme,** 2 bis Avenue Napoléon-Bonaparte (tel. 42–26.01.00), is next to the casino and holds dinner-dances on Saturday nights when one is expected to dress accordingly. There is a set menu for 250 F and the res-

118

taurant is closed on Tuesday evenings and on Wednesdays except during July and August.

Apart from these you will find a lot of other places to eat on the Cours Mirabeau and the Place Général-de-Gaulle, a Vietnamese restaurant in the Rue des Cordeliers and, in the Cours Sextius, **Le Clams**, which has an unusual way with fish.

FESTIVAL

The Summer Music Festival, in July and August, is famous throughout Europe. It is held at the Archbishop's Palace.

TOURIST INFORMATION

Details of the Festival and the excursions below are obtainable from the tourist office in the Place Général-de-Gaulle (tel. 42-26.02.93).

EXCURSIONS

There are good bus services to several places round about, including Marseille, and excursions are available throughout the year. They run to places of interest as far apart as the Gorges du Verdon for 87 F and the Pont du Gard which costs 120 F. You can also take a coach to local festivals like the January Mimosa Fête at Mandelieu or the Flower Carnival at Hyères at the end of March. A local bus will also take you to **Entremont**, to the north of Aix, is an ancient Celtic settlement which pre-dates the town by a few hundred years. The inhabitants came into conflict with the Romans, were defeated and their capital was sacked by Sextius in 123 BC. Recent excavations have uncovered enough to show where the ramparts were, the foundations of a few houses and the remains of an entrance gate. You have to walk a short way up to the plateau where you can see everything for yourself between 9am and noon and from 2pm to 6pm any day except Tuesday and 1 May.

Mont Ste-Victoire

Less than half a century after the Celts had been put to flight, the Romans had an even more serious problem with hordes of barbarians who had decided to emigrate from eastern Europe and settle themselves near the Mediterranean. They were soundly defeated by General Marius who is credited with killing 100 000 invaders and taking about the same number prisoner. Some people believe this is how Mont Ste-Victoire got its name. It is a long limestone ridge, towering more than 915 metres (3000ft) above the plain and made even more famous by Cézanne who painted it in all its changing moods and colours. Looking at the incredibly pure light on the white stone cliff, the vivid colours of the fields below and the strangely dappled trunks of the plane trees, it is easy to realise that if the Impressionists had not emerged on their own someone would undoubtedly have invented them. On the summit of Mont Ste-Victoire is the enormous iron **Cross of Provence** which can be seen for miles around. To get up there you have to walk from **Les Cabassols,** at the far end of a string of man-made lakes to the north. It is a good two-hour climb up a mule track with an occasional excuse to draw breath at the chapel of Ste-Victoire or the ruins of an old priory, but the view from the top is worth all the effort.

Vauvenargues, near Les Cabassols, is known only for its 17th-century château which was bought by Picasso in his later years and where he is buried in the grounds. It is not open to the public, so you have the option of carrying on to **Pourrières** and then to **Puyloubier** where the Foreign Legion has its Pensioners' Hospital, spending an afternoon by the lakes or joining the autoroute for a quick run down to Marseilles.

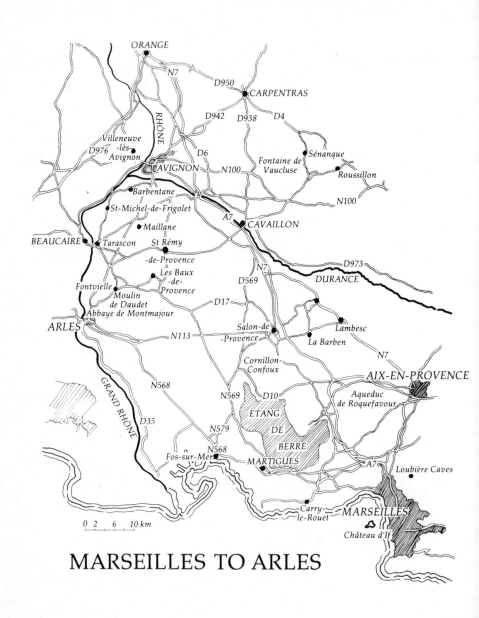

MARSEILLES TO ARLES

Chapter VI

MARSEILLES TO ARLES

Château d'If, Marseilles

Marseilles

Marseilles is one of those places that you either like or you loathe—I have never met anyone who was completely indifferent to it. It is a tough uncompromising city, far more interested in the present and the future than it is in the past which, broadly speaking, it leaves to take care of itself. Writing at the turn of the century, Augustus Hare said it possessed few items of interest and that no one would linger there for pleasure. Today that is not strictly true. It has plenty of atmosphere, some of which is rather unendearing, several attractions to keep its visitors happy and enormous commercial interests which are gobbling up the countryside. Few people would describe it as a holiday resort, but it is a popular venue for conferences and many professional and business people prefer to meet there than anywhere else on the coast.

HISTORY
In order to trace the history of Marseilles, the oldest city in France, it is

123

necessary to go back to 600 BC when Greek traders from Asia Minor sailed in to the bay, ingratiated themselves with the local tribes and converted one small inlet into a port. This expanded as trading posts were set up as far afield as Arles and Nice, contacts were made with countries 1000 miles or more away and the coast was opened up to agriculture, mainly fruit and olive trees. Explorers from Massilia, as it was called, pushed back the boundaries of the world as they knew it, sailing to Cornwall for cargoes of tin, up to Scandinavia, across to Iceland and down the west coast of Africa. The more successful the port became, the more its warlike but less adventurous neighbours resented it and at last Massilia had to ask the Romans for help. This settled all the immediate problems but created many more to take their place.

Playing politics, which has always been a popular local sport, the new republic joined Rome against Hannibal and won, but later threw in its lot with Pompey against Caesar and lost. It was besieged, its fleets were captured and everything of value was removed. After a setback like that it was not until the time of the crusades that things began to improve. Trade picked up, particularly when it came to transporting armies to the Holy Land and returning with merchandise from the Middle East, and soon the port was rivalling Genoa and Venice in the commercial stakes. After the fighting stopped, Marseilles was faced with another batch of problems, including the plague of 1721 which reduced the population by some 50 000. The discovery of America and the opening up of the sea route round the Cape of Good Hope to India and the Far East did not help either because they diverted trade from the Mediterranean to more accessible French ports on the Atlantic coast. However, when Ferdinand de Lesseps obligingly built the Suez Canal in the mid-19th century, the port staged another dramatic recovery only to be knocked sideways again when the Germans blew a good deal of it up in 1943. The inhabitants, and especially those who lived in the rough areas along the water front, had always made a practice of defying anyone in authority. The Germans found them so impossible to handle that they decided to raze the whole area and gave the householders an ultimatum to get out or be blown up along with everything else. After the war Marseilles re-established itself as a major port but, at the same time, turned more and more towards industry. As a result the whole western side of the city has expanded into a vast conglomeration of oil storage tanks, factory chimneys, petro-chemical plants and other such adjuncts to progress in the 20th century.

WHAT TO SEE

With all these changes of fortune nobody worried very much about relatively unimportant matters like preserving churches or accumulating art treasures. If a building fell down, the logical thing to do was to use the stones to replace it with something useful as soon as possible. It was, therefore, only fairly recently that the remains of the original Greek quays and fortifications were uncovered and incorporated into gardens in the vicinity of the old port.

The **Roman Docks** were discovered only when the dock area was demolished and are now happily preserved in the basement of a block of flats in the Place Vivaux. The museum attached to them has an interesting collection of maps and models but the main fascination is in seeing the docks as they were, complete with the quay and storage jars for grain standing about as they did 2000 years ago. The ancient Greeks would no doubt be taken aback if they could see all the pleasure boats tied up in their original port hardly a galley's length away. Although it was constantly dredged and enlarged, the demand for space outstripped its capacity and new commercial docks were built just round the corner, leaving the historic inlet free for fishermen and smaller vessels that never ventured out of the Mediterranean. The Roman Docks and the museum are open from 9am to noon and from 2pm until 6pm but are closed on Tuesdays, Wednesday mornings and on some holidays. The entrance fee is 3 F.

The **Museum of Old Marseilles,** more or less opposite, also looks back over the years but with rather more emphasis on things like furniture and articles that were used around the home, frequently made of either copper or pottery. There are hundreds of little *santons*, none of which is particularly old, providing a fascinating picture of life as it used to be. For card players the Camoin Gift is a 'must' because it shows the equipment and technique involved in making playing cards from the 18th century onwards. The museum is open from 10am to noon and from 2pm until 6.30pm. It is closed on Tuesdays, Wednesday mornings and on public holidays and costs 3 F to get in, except on Sunday mornings when you can look round for nothing.

The **Maritime Museum,** in the former stock exchange on the Place Général-de-Gaulle, is only a short walk away, especially if you wander along the quay, which is a good 300 years old. It is lined with cafes and restaurants and can be extremely lively, but that is nothing compared to the row which broke out when the Mamelukes celebrated Napoleon's escape from Elba, just as the city was deciding to support the Royalists after all. They regretted it later because, when he was defeated and packed off to St

125

Helena, the townspeople threw them into the port, just to show them the wisdom of changing sides like everyone else. The museum concerns itself mainly with the last 300 years, is open from 10am to noon and from 2.30pm to 7pm, restricts afternoon visiting to 2pm to 6.30pm between October and April and closes on Tuesdays and public holidays.

If you continue on round the old port and turn left when you reach the entrance to the tunnel, you will come upon the **Basilique St-Victor** which was a sanctuary before it was turned into a fortified church. The large crypt dates back to the 5th century and services are still held among the catacombs where the graves of two early Christian martyrs were examined about 20 years ago and found to contain bones and other relics from AD 250. Some people maintain that St Mary Magdalene and St Lazarus once hid in the cave which forms the crypt but, as with so many similar legends, nothing has ever been found to substantiate it. You can look round for 3 F from 10am until noon and from 2.30pm to 5.30pm every day except Sunday when it is only open from 3pm to 6pm; and it keeps the same hours on public holidays.

Other places of interest in the vicinity include the **Parc du Pharo,** a large and attractive garden that was laid out originally for the wife of Napoleon III, and **Notre-Dame-de-la-Garde,** a newish church on an ancient site near the Rue du Fort-du-Sanctuaire, where you get a particularly good view over the city and along the coast.

The **Palais Longchamp,** built in the 1860s at the end of the boulevard of the same name, houses the **Fine Arts Museum** and the **Natural History Museum** in two classical pavilions linked by a colonnade with an impressive fountain in front and a small zoo in the gardens behind. The former has startling pictures of the city during the plague and a considerable amount of space devoted to Pierre Puget, the famous sculptor who had great plans for redesigning Marseilles that never got further than the ideas stage. The latter is exceedingly full of stuffed animals, skeletons and fossils with a small aquarium to bring things up to date. The Arts Museum is open from 10am to noon and from 2pm until 6.30pm. It is closed on Tuesdays, Wednesday mornings and some holidays, is free on Sunday mornings but charges 3 F at all other times. The Natural History Museum keeps the same hours apart from closing half an hour early in the evenings and opening on holidays, and makes the same charge. The zoo costs 5 F and is open from 9am to 7pm in the summer but closes at 5.30pm from the beginning of November to the end of March.

La Canebière, which runs straight up from the old port, was once one of the great streets of the world but it is now a little shoddy and second-rate for such a famous thoroughfare. If you pull up at a traffic light the chances are that a very small Arab boy with a very large sponge will leap out and cover your windscreen with water, holding out his other hand at the same time in the hope of being paid the going rate for a car-wash. Marseilles, like so many other large ports, is a place where visitors should be reasonably careful. It would be stupid to go into some areas wearing a lot of jewellery or with a wallet temptingly obvious to casual passers-by. The seamy side of Marseilles with its long history of violence and gang warfare puts it outside the usual run of popular holiday resorts but it is an interesting city to visit if you exercise the same care as you would at home.

The **Château Borély,** on the Promenade de la Plage, is a mansion built in the late 18th century which contains three excellent museums mainly concerned with antiquities. It is especially proud of a pre-Roman sanctuary that has been reconstructed from remains discovered at Roquepertuse. Incidentally, the Egyptian collection is considered to be one of the finest in Europe. The château stands in its own park close to the sea and is open from 9.30am until noon and from 1.00pm to 5.30pm but is closed on Tuesdays, Wednesday mornings and on some holidays. It costs 3 F but is free on Sunday mornings.

The **Unité d'Habitation,** quite close by, was designed in 1952 by Le Corbusier and at that time it was unique. It consists of several hundred apartments with all the services you would expect to find in a miniature town encased in one giant concrete block. It may not be a novel idea today but in the 1950s it opened up a fresh chapter in the history of modern architecture.

WHERE TO STAY
One thing Marseilles does not do is pander to tourists but, as you might expect, it has several large hotels which meet all the needs of visiting businessmen. They are moderately expensive and the best one to choose would probably be close to the old port.

The **Sofitel Vieux Port,** 36 Boulevard Charles-Livon (tel. 91–52.90.19), is ideally placed near the Parc du Pharo. It has an excellent view, a swimming pool and ample parking, is open all the year and charges up to 810 F for a double room. Its more expensive restaurant, where a set menu can cost up to 250 F, closes in August; but **Le Jardin,** which closes at weekends in the winter, provides meals at 180 F with similarly priced wine.

The **Européen,** 115 Rue Paradis (tel. 91–37.77.20), is a little closer to the city centre, has no restaurant or special parking facilities and charges up to 167 F.

127

If you are travelling with a tent or a caravan, there are a couple of small sites within reach of the city which are open all the year round.

EATING OUT

Marseilles has literally hundreds of restaurants, some of which are very good and fairly expensive, particularly if they specialise in local delicacies like *bouillabaisse*, *bourride* and the medieval *brandade de morue* which is all done up with truffles and garlic.

The **Michel** (tel. 91–52.64.22) and the **Calypso** (tel. 91–52.64.00) are almost opposite each other in the Rue des Catalans. Both have delicious specialities and good local wines, offer set menus starting at 200 F and are open at different times, which is useful. Michel closes during July and on Tuesdays and Wednesdays, while Calypso shuts up shop in August and on Sundays and Mondays.

FESTIVALS

Marseilles does not make a big thing of festivals but if you happen to be there in the winter the Santons Fair, which runs from the end of November to the beginning of January, overlapping a few days in each direction, is worth a visit.

ACTIVITIES AND EXCURSIONS

The shops are more or less what you would expect to find in a large city and, generally speaking, are in and around la Canebière. The open-air markets are more fun, like the Marché de la Gard de l'Est near the old port and the fish market on the quay where you can pick up your own lunch any morning from Monday to Saturday.

The nightlife is not particularly exciting, although there are a few discos and bars where you can listen to the local music. With this thought in mind it is interesting to reflect that one of Marseilles' most lasting contributions to the history of France appears to be the *Marseillaise*—but, in fact, the anthem did not originate from the city. The townspeople, acting in character, threw themselves wholeheartedly behind the Revolution and their soldiers left hot-foot for Paris singing the *Battle Hymn of the Army of the Rhine*, composed in Strasbourg, at the top of their voices. It soon became associated with them, was christened accordingly and before long there were few Republicans who either knew or cared that it had nothing whatever to do with the famous port on the Mediterranean.

128

Before you leave in search of a quiet beach or a secluded family hotel, make a point of taking a boat trip round the bay. This usually starts with a visit to the **Château d'If,** the grim island fortress that features so prominently in Dumas' novel *The Count of Monte Cristo.* It dates from the early 16th century and was intended as part of the city's fortifications until it proved to be much more valuable as a state prison. You will be shown the miserable little cells where thousands of prisoners were herded together, waiting to be sent to the galleys, and a particularly dreadful one, without either light or air, which was reserved for anyone who was not meant to leave the fortress alive. Thankfully very few survived for more than a month or two, although it is said that one man existed there for over 20 years. Slightly better accommodation was provided for special prisoners like the Man in the Iron Mask and Mirabeau who ran up large debts and had to pay the price before marrying money and going on to become a pillar of the Revolution.

Other places of interest include the **Frioul Islands** which have been turned into a sports centre, where you can sail, windsurf, skin-dive and generally work off any surplus energy, and the modern docks that stretch from the old port along the coast to the mouth of the Canal du Rove. This 6½-kilometre (4-mile) tunnel under the mountains was built as a link between the sea and the Berre Lagoon and was used extensively by barges until a landslide put it out of action in 1963. The lagoon, which shares its name with the mountain chain behind, is filled with fishing boats and privately owned craft but has nothing to recommend it to the ordinary tourist.

Carry-le-Rouet

Just beyond this point the road leaves the coast—although there is a path for anyone who wants to continue westwards on foot—and after a fairly straight run through featureless country branches off to Carry-le-Rouet. The woods around this little seaside resort are filled with holiday villas and, although it is not over-blessed with hotels, you should be able to find somewhere to stay, except in the high season. A camping site is available for people who take their homes with them. **L'Escale** (tel. 42–45.00.47) is an excellent restaurant overlooking the bay which specialises in local dishes and charges high prices for them, though you can get a set menu on most days except Sundays for around 230 F. It is open from March to October but closes on Sunday nights and Mondays depending on the season. Apart from swimming and riding, there is very little in the way of entertainment; however, it is the best of all the small villages along this part of the coast.

Martigues

A short drive by way of main or secondary roads takes you to Martigues on the Berre Lagoon, which has been described as the Venice of Provence. To my mind this flatters it considerably, although there are some attractive places tucked away behind the encroaching industry. The town is made up of three fishing villages grouped round the Canal St-Sebastien, a pictur-esque waterway with typical, box-like houses lining the roads on either bank and little boats tied up alongside. Although it makes quite a fuss about the past with a parade of water-borne floats in July, a festival in August and numerous folklore events throughout the year, the whole place has a slightly impersonal atmosphere about it. There are a number of hotels and restau-rants, most of them easily forgettable, space for more than 3000 tents and caravans and a fairly large beach flanked by rocks on either side. At one time it numbered several artists among its regular visitors but now the crowds are more likely to come from the industrial areas round Fos and the Berre Lagoon.

Loubière Caves, Roquefavour, Lambesc and La Barben

There are roads up either side of the lagoon but those to the east have rather more in the way of places to explore. You might start off at the Loubière Caves, just north of Marseilles, which are very colourful and seem to go on for miles. Then thread your way up to the Roquefavour Aqueduct, built a little over 100 years ago, which is higher and longer than the Roman Pont du Gard and quite impressive in its own way. The next stop could be at Lam-besc, an enchanting old town in the shadow of the Chaine des Côtes. It has an ancient gateway and a converted mill called the **Moulin de Tante Yvonne** (tel. 42–28.02.46) where the food is delicious but very rich. It closes, most independently, during February and August and on Tuesdays, Wednesdays and Thursdays.

A somewhat larger road cuts across to the **Château de Barben**, a medieval castle surrounded by trees which once belonged to Pauline Borghese, Napoleon's somewhat extravagant sister. Her apartments are still decorated in the style to which she became accustomed but the annexes have been converted into homes for fish, reptiles and birds. There is also a zoo and an attractive formal garden, seen to the best advantage from a terrace outside the château reached by a stairway that was added when the castle was enlarged in the 16th century. It is open from 10am to noon and from 2pm to 6pm, and closes on Tuesdays out of season. The entrance fee is 10 F. The little town of La Barben is a good place to stop if you are hungry. The **Touloubre** (tel. 9055.16.85) has set menus from 85 F to 200 F although the cheaper ones are not served on Sundays or holidays. Rooms are also available from around 200 F.

Salon-de-Provence

The nearest large town is Salon-de-Provence, a short drive away, which has been the centre of the olive oil industry for the past 500 years. It is busy, but not aggravatingly so, perhaps because the old city that climbs up the hillside to the castle is separated from the more modern town by wide avenues lined with trees. One of its most famous citizens was Nostradamus, the doctor turned astrologer whose predictions were an immediate success in 1555 and still cause a good deal of argument today. The house where he lived has been turned into a museum but it is closed at the time of writing. He is buried in the Church of St-Laurent nearby where there is also a portrait of him painted by his son.

The **Empéri Castle,** which seems to be an integral part of the rock, is undoubtedly the most impressive building in Salon. It was started in the 10th century, rebuilt 300 years later and modernised before Nostradamus was born. Apart from the state apartments used by the Archbishops of Arles and their small private chapel, most of the heavy stone fortress had been turned into a splendid military museum. The exhibits, and there are said to be 10 000 of them, trace the history of the French army from the reign of Louis XIV to the end of the First World War. A portrait of the Sun King shows him to be much fatter and less attractive than novels set in France at that time would have us believe. Naturally special attention is given to Napoleon, covering everything from his exploits in the field to personal possessions like his unmistakeable hat, but it is the enormous range of swords and firearms that draw and hold the largest crowds. The uniforms—which

131

must run into hundreds—are surrounded by the various items that were worn or used with them, and in the case of cavalry regiments the horses are dressed overall as well. The colonial troops, not forgetting the Mamelukes, are well represented in a colourful array that must have provided an ideal target for the enemy. The whole display contrasts sharply with the uniforms of young Air Force officers from the training school which was established in the town about 50 years ago. The museum is based on a private collection that belonged to two brothers, Raoul and Jean Brunon, and probably for that reason includes a wonderful miniature army that must send lovers of tin soldiers into transports of delight. It is open from 10am to noon and from 2.30pm to 6.30pm in the summer, but from 2pm to 6pm on winter afternoons, and is closed on Tuesdays, 1 January and 1 May as well as Christmas Day. The entrance fee is 6 F.

There is a small selection of hotels and restaurants in the town—two of each to be found in the Allées Craponne, and a very pleasant combination of the two at Cornillon, 4 kilometres (2½ miles) to the south, called **Devem de Mirapier** (tel. 90–55.99.22), a ranch-type establishment built round a swimming pool. The information office at 56 Cours Gimon (tel. 90–56.27.60) will help you with hotels as well as all other questions relating to your holiday.

About 3 kilometres (2 miles) to the north of Salon there is a **monument to Jean Moulin**, the operational name given to the greatest of all the French Resistance heroes who is buried in the Panthéon in Paris.

Château Bas, Vernègues and Cavaillon

After so much concentration on war it is almost a relief to head for the country again, ignoring both the main road and the autoroute in favour of the smaller roads that zig-zag their way northwards. Depending on time and inclination you can pause at Château Bas where there are some Roman ruins in the castle grounds, or take a short walk up from Vernègues to all that remains of the original village which was destroyed in the earthquake of 1909. From here onwards agriculture begins to take over in a big way and the last part of the drive to Cavaillon is through interminable market gardens that are famous for such delicacies as early asparagus and those smooth-skinned melons which are pink inside and absolutely delicious. The small town is another relic from Roman times with an arch and a museum that glories in its collection of coins and other articles discovered

132

in the locality. Also included are a few exhibits from the days when the building was part of an old hospital where the books of ancient remedies were referred to with varying degrees of success. The 18th-century synagogue, built on the site of an earlier one, has its own museum exhibiting items such as an oven for baking unleavened bread.

Carpentras

Both Cavaillon and Carpentras have a number of sites for tents and caravans which are usually rather full because they make ideal centres from which to explore Provence. The majority are shaded, a fair selection have swimming pools, you will occasionaly find tennis courts as well, and the shops are seldom more than a few minutes' drive away. One example is **Camping Les Verguettes** at Villes-sur-Auzon (tel. 90–61.88.18) at the foot of Mont Ventoux.

Carpentras itself is slightly larger than Cavaillon but without much more left of its ancient past. The former Cathedral of St-Siffrien, an ornate building, has a door called the Porte Juive, dating from 1404 through which any Jew converted to Christianity had to pass on the way to be baptised. The synagogue, about two blocks away, is the oldest in France and is also highly decorated as befitted a community whose financial wizards were largely engaged in running the money side of things for the Popes at Avignon. It dates from the 15th century but was restored as recently as 1958. Opening hours are 10am to noon and 3pm to 5pm from Monday to Friday, and from 10am to noon on Sundays.

The town is fairly open-plan with large gardens outside the boulevards that trace the line of the old ramparts, and several small museums and places of interest inside. The only visible reminder of Roman occupation is a small triumphal arch, built at the same time as the much grander one at Orange. The **tourist office** on the Avenue Jean-Jaurès (tel. 90–63.00.78) has a fund of information about places in the area.

Probably the most outstanding tourist attraction is the **Fontaine-de-Vaucluse** which is reported to have more than one million visitors every year. There is nothing particularly spectacular about it in the dry season, but after a period of heavy rain or when the snows are melting it is a different story. Then literally thousands of gallons of water a second are hurled through the mouth of a cavern and thunder down the hillside in a foaming torrent. The little village, overlooked by the ruins of an ancient castle, is only a few minutes' walk away. Its museum is dedicated to the Italian poet Petrarch who lived there from 1337 to 1353, and there is a small church containing the tomb of a 6th-century bishop who is said to have dispatched a local monster known as the Coulobre. The whole area is peppered with small villages, each with something of interest to offer if you are prepared to spend enough time looking for them.

Roussillon

Exploring is hungry work, so if you find yourself in the vicinity of Roussillon with its colourful houses and memorable views you might call in at the **Val des Fées** (tel. 90–75.64.99). It is a most attractive restaurant with set menus ranging from 95 to 145 F and a large selection of local wines for less than 100 F. However, I would be inclined to chose something *à la carte* such as *rognons de veau* cooked with wine and herbs, followed by one of the mouth-watering deserts. If you want to spend a night in the mountains, the **Mas de Garrigon** on the road to Apt (tel. 90–75.63.22) is a delightfully secluded hotel that charges 440 F.

Orange

There is no doubt that it is well worth while making time to visit Orange if only to see the Arc de Triomphe and the theatre which are two of Europe's greatest monuments to the power and achievements of Rome.

HISTORY
Modern Orange stands where the Romans founded their city of Arausio on the site of an old Celtic town in 102 BC after the local tribes had wiped out about 100 000 legionaires. By the time Augustus arrived it was a hive of activity with all the obligatory aids to gracious living such as baths, a gymnasium, temples, a circus and, of course, a theatre capable of holding 8000–9000 people. With the departure of the Romans the city fell prey to the Saracens and other invaders, but by the 13th century had recovered sufficiently to become the capital of a small principality. This, in turn, was inherited by William, Prince of Nassau, 300 years later and he was so pleased with it that he decided to retitle his dynasty the House of Orange. He was also the founder of the Dutch Republic whose ruling family were allowed to

keep the title after the town was handed back to France in 1713. In this way the Netherlands still has its House of Orange, we had William III in Britain, Ulster has its Men of Orange, Dutchmen in South Africa preserved the title by naming a river and their new Free State accordingly and there are any number of little Oranges scattered about America. The town returned the compliment by naming a square after Queen Juliana when she was there on an official visit in the 1950s.

WHAT TO SEE

Partly because of the troubles it had to cope with during the Dark Ages and partly due to the habit of vandalising ancient ruins to provide building materials in the 17th century, there is not much left of Arausio apart from a few excavations, the theatre and the arch.

The **theatre,** which stands right in the middle of the old town, is a fantastic sight. The great sandstone façade is over 30 metres (100ft) high and more than 90 metres (300ft) long, is rather severe and is sometimes embellished with the scaffolding necessary to keep it in a good state of repair. The only reason it survived is that it was incorporated into the city defences, to be described by Louis XIV on one occasion as the finest wall in his kingdom. Backing on to the façade is the stage with its entrances and exits, but unfortunately the ceiling as well as most of the columns and all the statues disappeared a long time ago. However, the larger-than-life statue of Augustus was discovered in pieces, stuck together and returned to its alcove high above the centre of the stage. Standing immediately below him one is faced with tier upon tier of stone seats, forming roughly three-quarters of a circle and cut into the slopes of the Capitol Hill. There are also quite a few modern seats which increase the size of the audience for the music festival held there in July. The acoustics are said to be perfect and if you are energetic enough to climb up to the 'gods' it is possible to judge the claim for yourself.

Next to the theatre are the foundations of an exceptionally large temple and the remains of a sports arena but precious little else. The theatre is open from 8.30am to 7pm on weekdays between April and September but closes from 12.30pm to 2pm on Sundays and holidays. During the rest of the year the hours are 9am to noon and 2pm to 5pm. The price of entry is 5 F.

The **Arc de Triomphe** dominates the main road from the north which, thanks to the new autoroute, has lost its 2000-year-old position as the most important road in France. At one stage it looks as though you are going to drive right through the archway, but in fact it stands on an island and, provided there are not too many cars about, it is just possible to pause under the trees for a closer look at this impressive piece of local history. The arch is one of the largest and best-preserved to be found anywhere. It commemorates Julius Caesar's victory over the Greek fleet at Massilia and the exploits of the Roman legion that colonised the town in 36 BC.

Any time you have to spare could be usefully employed in visiting the **Municipal Museum** where, apart from anything else, there is a collection of works by Sir Frank Brangwyn including such unexpected sights as London Bridge. It is open between April and September from 9am to noon and from 2pm to 6.30pm, closes at 5pm during the rest of the year and on 1 January, 1 May and Christmas Day, and charges 5 F. Another interesting museum is to be found at Serignan a few miles away. It was the home of the famous entomologist, J. H. Fabre, and contains his collections of insects in the rooms where he carried out the greater part of his research. To find out more about Orange and its surroundings, call in at the tourist office on the Cours Aristide-Briand (tel. 90–51.80.06).

The 14th-century fortified palace built by the Popes of Avignon, Avignon

Avignon

Avignon is a city which gears itself to tourists and handles its publicity so well that there is nothing new to discover when you get there. The

Pont St-Bénézet, commemorated in song as the Pont d'Avignon, is exactly as most people visualise it, stopping abruptly in mid-stream at one end and disappearing into the city ramparts at the other.

The **Palace of the Popes,** which you could hardly miss no matter how hard you tried, is medieval, enormous and claims to be the most impressive building of its kind in Europe. From the early 14th century the Popes ruled their Christian world from Avignon in preference to Rome where the intrigues were becoming too hot to handle, but by the time the palace was completed in 1352 there was very little to choose between the cities. The earlier of the two castles which make up the palace is rather austere, in keeping with the Cistercian training of Benedict XII, but when Clement VI was pontiff the pendulum swung right the other way. The court then wallowed in luxury to such an extent that the Italian poet Petrarch described it as a sewer where all the filth of the universe had gathered. When Gregory XI was persuaded to return to Rome in 1377, a number of cardinals stayed behind and elected their own Antipope. After this the venerated gentlemen spent their time squabbling over their possessions and handing out excommunications like parking tickets. In 1403 the Antipope of the time was driven out of Avignon and Rome governed from a distance until the city was united with France during the Revolution. When that happened, the palace was looted and then turned into a prison before eventually becoming an army barracks. Under the circumstances it is hardly surprising that, apart from some tapestries and wall paintings, all the great echoing rooms and corridors are completely empty. The only way to look round is to join a conducted tour, costing 15 F. The tours are given in different languages, so check carefully beforehand the time of the one you want.

There are so many little chapels and churches, imposing mansions and museums in Avignon that the best thing to do is to collect a map from the **tourist office,** 41 Cours Jean-Jaurès (tel. 90–82.65.11), order a coffee or a cold drink at one of the cafes in the Place de l'Horloge and figure out exactly where you want to go.

The **Petit Palais Museum,** built in 1317 and remodelled about 100 years later, is devoted to medieval paintings and sculptures. It is in the Place du Palais, is open from 9am to noon and 2pm to 6.15pm but closes on Tuesdays and public holidays. It is free from October to March but costs 5 F at other times of the year.

The **Aubanel Museum,** a block away from the main palace, would be of particular interest to people from the literary world because the family of the same name have been printers and publishers for nearly 250 years and have gathered together quite a collection of old books and documents as well as the machinery that was used to produce them. There are guided tours from 9am to 11am but the museum is closed at weekends, on holidays and throughout August.

If you are heading for the Pont St-Bénézet, walk down the Rue de Limas quite close to the ramparts where you can see glassblowers at work and spend some time in the **Rocher des Doms** wandering through the rose gardens, feeding the birds on the lake or simply enjoying the view. On the other side of the old town it is pleasant to stroll down the Rue des Teinturiers beside the River Sorgue where the old paddle wheels supplied power for the textile mills. Shopping is easy but quite expensive in the masses of little establishments which tempt the passer-by with antiques, clothes, accessories and souvenirs as well as food. Parking can be something of a problem, so if you find a spot in one of the designated areas it would be shortsighted not to drive straight into it and do the rest of your exploring on foot.

Avignon tends to stay up late at night, especially during the Festival Season from mid-July to mid-August when many of the productions are staged in the courtyard of the Palace of the Popes. There are jousting tournaments on the Rhône using boats instead of horses, orchestral concerts at the weekends and at least one striptease which would have delighted the Papal Courts of old, though the thoroughly modern discos might have produced a different reaction altogether.

Whatever you are looking for in the way of hotels and restaurants, you are quite certain to find it. For the most part they are functional with an eye on groups of tourists, the bigger the better, but now and again you come across one that is full of atmosphere.

The **Europe,** in the Place Crillon (tel. 90–82.66.92), was going strong when Napoleon stayed there in 1799 and is highly decorative. It costs up to 590 F for a room and has a restaurant which closes for odd weeks here and there and charges from 150 F for a set menu.

Villeneuve-lès-Avignon

Villeneuve-lès-Avignon, just across the river, is a much quieter town, although it had its moments when the Popes agreed to expand into foreign parts. At that time the Rhône was the border between France and Provence and the **Tour de Philippe-le-Bel** had been built in the 13th century to keep a sharp eye on what was happening at the other end of the bridge.

Apart from just being there, it is singularly devoid of interest unless you think the view from the top is worth a clamber up the spiral staircase, passing the time by counting the 176 steps.

A century later the French decided that more was needed in the way of fortifications so they put up the great **St-André Fort**. It has only one gateway which is exceptionally deep and protected by towers on either side. Within the walls there used to be a monastery, a couple of churches and houses for the villagers, but all those have disappeared. Nothing in this warlike attitude upset a group of cardinals who made up their minds to evacuate the overcrowded papal city and build themselves bigger and better mansions on the opposite bank. Presumably everyone else thought it was a good idea too because 15 luxurious establishments were set up in record time and continued to flourish long after the Popes had gone back to Rome.

Thanks to the destructive zeal of the revolutionaries, only two or three of these mansions still exist. The **Chartreuse du Val de Bénédiction** came through mainly because the monks were thrown out and the property, covering about 2½ hectares (6 acres), was sold off piecemeal to the highest bidders. A certain proportion of it has already been restored, in particular the three main cloisters lined with cells, the little church and the chapter house. It is open from 9am to noon and 2pm to 6.30pm from April to September, from 10am to noon and 2pm to 5pm during the rest of the year. It stays open all day in July but closes on 1 January, 1 May and Christmas Day. A ticket costs 9 F but if you buy one for 12 F you get into the St-André Fort as well.

Villeneuve is also justly proud of two religious works of art. One is the Coronation of the Virgin, painted in the 15th century and housed in the **Municipal Museum.** It is described by experts as one of the great pictures of the world. You can see it and all the other contents of the museum from 10am to 12.30pm and 3pm to 7.30pm between April and September, but only between 2pm and 5pm on winter afternoons. It is closed on Tuesdays, during February, at Easter, on 1 May and on Christmas and New Year's Day. The entrance fee is 7 F. The other masterpiece is an ivory carving of the Virgin and Child set at an unusual angle in order to follow the line of the elephant's tusk, a fact which both figures seem to find faintly amusing. It is one of several good reasons for visiting the **Church of Notre-Dame.**

WHERE TO STAY AND EATING OUT

Another good reason is that you can slip round the back afterwards to an ancient priory which has been converted into a hotel. **Le Prieuré** stands in beautiful gardens with its own swimming pool and tennis courts, but you might have to take out a mortgage to stay there as the price is 800 F a night. This did not put off the Duke and Duchess of Windsor who are remembered by the management with considerable pleasure. The restaurant has a set menu for 220 F. The whole place closes from early November to roughly the first week in March.

La Magnaneraie, 37 Rue Camp-de-Bataille (tel. 90–25.11.11), has the same advantages, apart from royal patronage, at more realistic prices. The building dates from the 15th century and is delightfully quiet and comfortable with rooms for 380 F. You can eat in a charming dining room or outside under the trees for 125 F upwards, but gourmets will go for one of the many specialities recommended by Monsieur Prayal, who is both the chef and the proprietor.

Barbentane, St-Michel-de-Frigolet and Maillane

From Villeneuve-lès-Avignon you can join a major road that follows the river down to the fortress towns of Beaucaire and Tarascon, perhaps deviating to include Barbentane on the far side of the Rhône. It is a medieval village overlooking the plain with an occasional reminder of its origins and a very superior château belonging to the local duke. The rooms are decorated and furnished in the grand manner but it should not take more than an hour to see everything.

While you are in the area it is an idea to carry on to the St-Michel-de-Frigolet Abbey, tucked away in a valley, which started out as a recuperation centre for monks in the 11th century, was turned into a boarding school for a time and then reverted to being a monastery some 100 years ago. The poet Frédéric Mistral was a pupil there for a while. He was born in Maillane, a short distance away, lived a good deal of his life in a house that is now a museum and is buried in the village cemetery. The **museum** is open from 10am to noon and 2pm to 5pm in the summer, closes an hour early in the winter and on Tuesdays and holidays, and costs 4 F.

Beaucaire

It is almost impossible to separate Beaucaire and Tarascon, although they were at loggerheads for the best part of 700 years. The castle at Beaucaire was built in the early 13th century to guard the interests of Languedoc, but Cardinal Richelieu virtually demolished it in the 1600s. All that is left is a most impressive shell with a staircase in the wall of the keep leading to a triangular platform where you get an excellent view over the valley of the Rhône.

A midsummer fête is held in the town every year to commemorate one of the greatest trade fairs ever staged in Europe. During the Middle Ages nearly half a million people would converge on Beaucaire each July bringing boatloads of goods to sell and exchange. Entertainers of every description were to be found on the flat lands between the castle and the river bank, and the improvised city of tents would burst at the seams with local merchandise and exotic offerings like furs and amber, silks from the Far East, Turkish carpets, swords from Toledo and dates grown and packed in Africa. The **Museum of Old Beaucaire** gives you a pretty good idea of what it must have been like before the railway arrived and put an end to the whole thing. Nowadays a bull-ring below the castle provides most of the excitement instead.

Tarascon

Tarascon, across the river in Provence, is older and got off more lightly than its sister town on the whole. It was a trading post before the Romans added their fortifications which, in turn, provided the basis for the present castle that dates partly from the 12th century. It was added to by Good King René, completed in the 15th century and was released from prison service only in 1926. The interior, which was largely undamaged, has been completely restored and many people insist that it is head and shoulders above any other French medieval castle. One woman said she could smell meat roasting over an open fire in the great banqueting hall but no one admits to seeing the ghosts of Robespierre's cronies who were thrown over the battlements into the Rhône when he was no longer around to protect them. From the writing on the walls it appears that quite a few British subjects were held in the castle during the 18th century, many of them presumably after being captured at sea.

Tarascon also has its annual festival which, unlike the fête at Beaucaire, has changed very little over the years. It is based on a legend involving St Martha of Bethany and a large monster, the Tarasque, that used to live in the Rhône. The creature had a taste for children, cattle and any odd traveller who attempted to cross the river, to say nothing of anyone foolish enough to copy the example of St George. Eventually the townspeople appealed to St Martha who released them from its tyranny by making the sign of the cross, putting a rope round its neck and leading it back to the water. She is reputed to have stayed on in the town and to be buried in a little church which is named after her.

Both towns have pleasant old quarters with an occasional church or museum but not a great deal in the way of small parks and gardens. Tours of both castles are arranged between April and September and you can get details from the tourist offices, 59 Rue Halles (tel. 90–91.03.52) in Tarascon or 6 Rue Hôtel de Ville in Beaucaire (tel. 66–59.26.57).

One thing that all these towns down the valley of the Rhône have in common is the mistral, an aggravating wind that lashes at everything with considerable force. In pagan times people built altars to it without any marked success. Later the inhabitants decided that the icy blasts from the north purified the air and got rid of diseases that bred in the dirty streets, and organised their lives accordingly. Farmhouses were built with all their windows facing south and heavy stones were hauled up on to the roofs in the hope—occasionally, no doubt, a vain one—that this would prevent them from being blown away. The practice continues today, as does the habit of protecting fields and buildings with thick cypress hedges, although some of these are bent almost double by the force of the wind. It is said that the mistral blows for three, six or nine days at a time, but visitors who are unfortunate enough to encounter it feel as though it has been raging for months.

St-Rémy-de-Provence

Logically, the next place to visit after Tarascon is St-Rémy-de-Provence, a rather nice little town which earns its living as a market garden centre and entertains its visitors to the best of its ability. There are only two museums and they face each other across the Rue de Parège which runs off the Place Favier. The larger of the two, the **Pierre de Brun Alpilles Museum,** occupies a splendid 16th-century mansion and is filled with costumes, *santons* and examples of local art. It also has reminders of the poet Mistral and of Nostradamus who was born in St-Rémy but moved later to Salon. It is open from 10am to noon and 2pm to 6pm in the summer, stays open an hour later in July and August but closes at 4pm in the winter. It is shut on Tuesdays and from December to February. Entrance costs 5 F.

The **Lapidary Museum** is in the Hôtel de Sade, a house which also dates from the 16th century and was once the home of relatives of the infamous Marquis. It concentrates on items discovered at Glanum, a pre-Christian trading post outside the town. Guided tours are available at 10am, 11am, 3pm, 4pm and 5pm from July to September costing 5 F, but the museum is closed on Tuesdays.

The countryside round St-Rémy is rather flat for walking unless you happen to like it that way and a tour of the older streets turns out to be nothing more than a gentle stroll. There are quite a few hotels and restaurants and some comfortable camping sites. The swimming pools get fairly crowded in hot weather, but if you want to go off on your own there is no difficulty in finding a horse or a bicycle. As usual you can get all the details from the **tourist office** in the Place Jean-Jaurès (tel. 90–92.05.22).

Glanum

On the way to Glanum you pass the old **St-Paul-de-Mausole monastery** which was turned into a mental home in 1605. The small church and the cloisters are open to the public but visitors are not usually allowed into the cell where Van Gogh spent the last year of his life. He was admitted after cutting off his ear and presenting it to an incredulous lady in Arles. He did at least one of his most famous paintings in the quiet little garden but failed to respond to treatment and committed suicide within a few weeks of leaving the hospital. Another famous inmate, for quite a different reason, was Albert Schweitzer who, as a German from Alsace, was interned there during the First World War. The cloisters are open from 8am to 7pm but close at 5pm in winter.

You will not see much of Glanum if you persist in looking up instead of down because not much of it stands more than about 1 metre (2–3ft) above the ground. However, excavations have shown that the Gauls were there in 500 BC with a small village built next to a sacred spring. Two hundred years later the Greeks, probably from Marseilles, contributed several houses and fortifications which were enlarged and embellished by the Romans when they took over quite peacefully later on. It is very simple to follow the town plan and pick out the old forum, the covered canal that ran under the main road, the baths, half a dozen temples and the spring which supplies water to an ancient swimming pool. Some of the mosaics are said to be the oldest ever found in Gaul.

The town was totally destroyed in the 3rd century AD but for some unknown reason the two Roman monuments opposite were left intact. One is an arch that was built in about 20 BC, making it among the oldest in the South of France. Although the top has disappeared, it is still an impressive sight with the weatherbeaten remains of sculptured prisoners chained to a tree, some garlands of leaves and, inside the vaulted roof, a mass of geometrical shapes that look rather like Tudor roses.

The cenotaph is in a much better state of repair. The large square base is carved with hunting and battle scenes and, above the arches, two statues are visible through the columns which support the roof. According to the inscription they are Caius and Lucius Caesar, the grandsons Augustus appointed to succeed him but who both died young. The monuments can be seen at any time as they are open to the road but the excavations are enclosed. You can wander round the latter from 9am to noon and from 2pm to 6pm between April and September but they open an hour later and close an hour earlier during the rest of the year and are closed on Tuesdays and Wednesdays out of season. The entrance fee is 8F but you will get in for half-price on Sundays and holidays.

Les Baux-de-Provence

The famous and so-called 'deserted' village of Les Baux-de-Provence looks quite incredible from a distance but once again commercialisation and the feet of millions of visitors are slowly overwhelming it. As recently as 1952 James Pope-Hennessy described it as 'terrifyingly lonely', but then he must have timed his visit fairly carefully. To get the best out of Les Baux it would be necessary to avoid the tourist season when the occupied part of the village reverberates to the cries of souvenir hunters and the ruined section can hardly be seen for the milling crowds. There is even an early checkpoint for cars where a handful of francs allows you to drive further up the hill in the hope of finding a parking space. Notices are posted, as they are at the Pont du Gard, warning you to lock your car and take anything of value with you.

From this point you walk up the road to the Magi Gate and then follow a clearly defined route that passes every building of note in the village. You can afford to ignore the old town hall and the post office but spare a glance for the Eyguières Gate which used to be the main entrance. The 12th-century Church of St-Vincent, facing a small shady square, is interesting in itself and also because a midnight mass is held there every Christmas Eve when a newborn lamb is presented to the Christ Child just as it has been for the last 400 years. There are two or three museums to distract you before you tackle the ruins themselves where, fortunately, very little has been done apart from the necessary job of cleaning them up. You obtain a ticket for 5.50 F which covers the museums and the old village—just queue up at the Lapidary Museum on your way through.

If it were possible to wander round alone, the atmosphere could easily be quite oppressive because a good deal happened in the hilltop fortress, much of it unpleasant. The Lords of Les Baux were among the most important and the most feared rulers in Provence during medieval times, and although they claimed to be descended from Balthazar of Three Kings fame, the nearest they got to proving it was by including the Star of Bethlehem in their coat-of-arms. One way and another they extended their domains to take in Sicily and Albania as well as large chunks of Provence and for a while were famous for their Courts of Love. In the 14th century love was about the last thing anyone would have associated with them: the ruler of the period amused himself by kidnapping people and, if no ransom were forthcoming, took pleasure in pushing them over the castle walls on to the rocks far below. Eventually the King of France, the Pope and the Count of Provence decided to put an end to his crimes and when he tried to escape from their combined armies at Tarascon he was providentially drowned in the Rhône.

For a while Les Baux became the property of Good King René who in turn presented it to his wife, Jeanne de Laval. When she had no further use for it the Manvilles ruled in the name of the French King, but they became power-crazed and turned it into a Protestant stronghold from which they backed any revolt that took their fancy. In 1632 Richelieu decided that enough was enough and ordered the castle and its fortifications to be destroyed and the inhabitants fined so heavily that recovery was out of the question. Even the title was disposed of to Prince Hercules of Monaco, which is how the son of an American film star is now the Marquis des Baux.

WHERE TO STAY AND EATING OUT

The valley below the fortress boasts a small pavilion built in memory of Queen Jeanne and three luxurious hotels. The restaurant **Oustau de Baumanière** is considered to be one of the best in France and was chosen to provide dinner for the Queen and Prince Philip during their state visit in 1972. Both the hotel and its dining room are definitely out of the ordinary, but you can see for yourself at 660 F for a room, 925 F for an apartment and as little as 260 F for the cheapest set menu.

The Hostellerie de la Reine Jeanne (tel. 90–97.32.06) is much more modest but it does have the advantage of being in the village itself. It closes from mid-November to the beginning of February and on Tuesdays from mid-October to mid-March. You can book a room for 185 F and choose a set menu for between 65 and 100 F.

Fontvieille

The town of Fontvieille, to the south-west, cannot hold a candle to Les Baux as far as medieval history is concerned, but it has a parish church where the ancient ceremony of the shepherds and their Christmas offering also takes place every year. However, it is better known for the windmill immortalised by Alphonse Daudet in his bestselling *Letters from my Wind-mill*. The **mill**, which he used to visit but never owned, is in full working order and has incorporated a small museum in appreciation of all he did to make it famous. It is open from 9am until noon and from 1pm to 7pm, reducing the afternoon hours in winter to 2pm to 6pm. A fee of 4 F is charged to visitors.

Abbey of Montmajour

A little way down the road you come to the ancient **Abbey of Montmajour**, founded by Benedictine monks in the 10th century on what used to be an island surrounded by marshes. After rising to very respectable heights of power and prosperity, during which it was visited by 100 000 pilgrims a year, it went into a decline. This was not helped by the abbot getting involved in the scandal of Marie Antoinette's necklace, and the building was closed before eventually being sold off cheaply after the Revolution. Sections were pulled down to provide building materials, but when the State took it back every effort was made to restore the parts that were left. These included a 14th-century keep, an earlier church with a crypt which is partly carved out of the rock, and one of the finest cloisters in Provence. There is also an ancient burial chapel of Ste-Croix which has been standing for 800 years without a window on the world in what was once a cemetery but is now an open field. In its heyday the abbey was involved in draining the marshes that covered the surrounding plain and, with some help from a Dutch engineer, had converted them to cornfields by the middle of the 17th century. Although much of the area has now been flooded over again and turned into paddy fields, we still have something to thank the monks for— instead of taking a raft or a flat-bottomed boat you simply get into your car and drive to Arles.

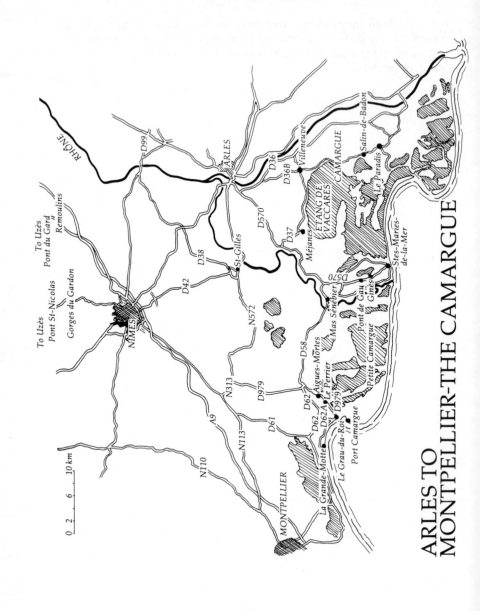

ARLES TO
MONTPELLIER-THE CAMARGUE

Chapter VII

ARLES TO MONTPELLIER

St Trophime, Arles

Arles

Arles, like Aix-en-Provence, becomes more and more attractive as you get to know it better. It fascinated Constantine the Great, captivated the Roman Emperor Honorius and entranced Van Gogh. One of its most appealing characteristics is that everything is done in moderation. The buildings are neither the biggest nor the best in the country, its museums are well-stocked and particularly informative without being too overcrowded and the town gives you room to breathe as you wander round. One visitor was heard to remark that it was the most satisfying place he had seen during his tour through France and that, to my mind, just about sums it up.

HISTORY
Historically Arles came into being around 600 BC when the Greeks from Marseilles decided to establish a trading post on the banks of the Rhône. Some 400 years later the Roman Consul Marius edged it towards prosperity

149

by building an important ship canal to link the port directly with the Mediterranean, slicing straight through the southern marshlands to emerge in the Golfe de Fos. It was quite an accomplishment as you will see if you drive down the D35 towards Port-St-Louis. For the first few miles the Grand Rhône flows steadily along on one side with the Canal de Marseille au Rhône more or less parallel on the other. Julius Caesar completed the good work after he defeated Marseilles in 49 BC. To impress on the little republic that it had been most unwise to side with Pompey against him, he took away nearly everything it possessed and distributed the booty among other towns along the coast. Arles got its fair share, enhanced by the decision to set up a colony for the Sixth Legion there. Strategically the town was also important as it stood guard over the Aurelian Way, connecting Italy with Spain, as well as commanding a fairly accessible route to the northern and western parts of Europe.

Following their usual practice of making themselves very much at home, the Romans built temples, a theatre and an arena as well as providing all the essential services. Water was piped in for public baths, marble lavatories and fountains, with a certain amount diverted to private homes, before being flushed away through an efficient drainage system. The whole place was a going concern by the time Constantine the Great arrived in the 4th century. One look at the prosperous trading and industrial centre was enough to convince him that it would make an ideal spot for a sumptuous riverside palace which, by the way, has completely disappeared apart from a section of the royal baths. When the Emperor Honorius took a fancy to Arles in AD 400, he made it the capital of the three Gauls, one of which was Britain, but as the empire was by then on the wane the town's influence was never really felt on the far side of the Channel.

With the arrival of Christianity, Arles had also become an important religious centre on the way to acquiring a kingdom of its own. In AD 597 St Augustine was consecrated the first Bishop of England on the site of what is now the Church of St-Trophime. But when the present building was completed, and Frédéric Barbarossa was crowned King of Arles there in 1178, the good times were running out and at the close of the 15th century the town became a part of France.

WHAT TO SEE

Arles in this day and age is a drowsy, contented sort of town with a great deal to offer anyone who cares to stroll about in search of small squares, attractive gardens and houses that retain much of their original character. At the same time it fully appreciates the value of its tourist trade and there are all the usual cafes setting up their plastic chairs and commercially printed umbrellas on the pavements, vying for custom with stands full of postcards and rather unimaginative souvenirs. There are no longer many craftsmen about, although the little traditional figures known as *santons* are still made locally, some of them destined for the winter trade fair.

The majority of the ancient sites are grouped together in a small area and a ticket costing 12 F will get you into all the ones that are listed here apart from the Museon Arlaten. They are open from 8.30am until 7pm from June to September with a break for lunch from 12.30pm until 2pm. The opening and closing hours vary a little during the winter and everything is closed on Christmas Day, New Year's Day and 1 May.

The **arena**, from the point of view of size, is probably the first place to see and you will find it with no difficulty at all in a slight depression near the centre of the old town. It was built in 46 BC to hold approximately 25 000 people and, although it has been damaged and has lost its top section altogether, a few of the covered galleries and stairways are still in good working order. The main reason why the arena escaped the indignity of becoming nothing more than a glorified stone quarry was that it was turned into a fortification during the Middle Ages. Three towers were added to keep a lookout for the enemy and something approaching 200 houses and a church were crammed inside. They mouldered away until the debris was finally removed in 1828 when, for some reason or other, the towers were left standing. They make the silhouette look a trifle odd but are really no more incongruous than the posters announcing the next bull-fight plastered over the ancient walls.

The bull-fights which are held regularly in the arena fall into two categories. In the first instance both the matadors and the bulls come from Spain and it is a fight to the death, almost invariably the bull's. When the fights are conducted Provençal-style, both the men and the bulls are local. The amateur *razeteurs* are expected only to snatch a rosette (*cocarde*) that has been suspended on a cord between the animal's horns. The razeteurs derive their name from *razet*, the half circle into which they have to run to remove the rosette. The prize goes to the first young man to grab it successfully, even if he has to make a rapid getaway over the barrier, followed on rare occasions by the bull. It is an exciting and dangerous sport but the advantage is that no blood is spilled intentionally and when it is all over the bulls return to their grazing grounds in the Camargue.

151

The **theatre** next door to the arena did not escape so lightly when the demolition squads moved in during the Middle Ages. All that remains are the foundations of the stage, a couple of columns which are almost intact, the stumps of a handful of others and 20 or so rows of seats. Everything else was appropriated by the local builders to supply stone for the ramparts and the town that was growing up inside them. Even a convent which occupied the site when nobody could think of any further use for it has vanished into thin air. Now the interior has been repaired to the height of a few feet and surrounded by walled gardens, making an ideal setting for the festival of music, drama and dancing which is held there during July.

The **Church of St-Trophime,** only a minute's walk away on the Place de la République, has a splendid west door guarded by statues of the apostles under a frieze that shows in no uncertain manner what lies ahead for the saints and sinners of this world. It was a cathedral when the Emperor Frédéric Barbarossa was crowned, but since then it has lost its status. Early Christian sarcophagi enriched with biblical scenes take the place of the font and a conventional altar and are much easier to see than the details of tapestries hanging high up on the dark walls of the nave.

The way in to the cloisters is through a porch next to the old Bishop's Palace. They are justly famous for their intricately carved pillars and are worth inspecting quite closely. You should not have much difficulty in identifying the scenes from the New Testament, but when it comes to Provençal legends it may be necessary to brush up on St Martha and the efficient way she dealt with the monster at Tarascon.

The **Museum of Pagan Art,** housed in what was once the Church of Ste-Anne, built in the 17th century on the opposite side of the Place de la Republique, is full of ancient statues and other items that were discovered in the vicinity. Augustus, for example, once kept an eagle eye on the original theatre productions but the same cannot be said for the Venus of Arles. When she was dug up in the 17th century, some local dignitary had the bright idea of presenting her to the King who in turn put her in the Louvre. Arles was left to make do with copies of the original which somehow do not seem to have quite the same appeal.

The **Museum of Christian Art,** which is usually bracketed with its Pagan counterpart, has been set up in a 16th-century Jesuit chapel practically next door. In fact you can relax for a few minutes in the medieval Plan de la Cour before passing from one set of antiquities to the other. Simply take a few steps down the Rue Balze and you will find yourself among what has been described as the best collection of early Christian sarcophagi outside Rome. If the prospect strikes you as being rather dull and funereal, I would suggest you go along anyway if only to visit the cryptoporticus underneath. This vast gallery was built by the Romans in the 1st century BC and was used by them as a grain store. After 2000 years it came into its own once again when it did sterling duty as an air-raid shelter during the last war. At one end are the foundations of a temple, but if you want to see the columns you will have to go into the Place du Forum about a block away. Without being in quite the right place to justify its name, it is a pleasant square with several cafes where you can sit out under the trees.

The **Museon Arlaten** should perhaps be the next place to visit before you set off for distant parts, mainly because it is all of a piece with the Museum of Christian Art in the Rue de la République. An even better reason is that it has the most fascinating collection of items depicting life in Provence that you are likely to come across anywhere. It was founded in a 16th-century mansion by the poet Frédéric Mistral who was so keen on getting all the details right that he did a lot of the arranging and writing of labels himself. When he won the Nobel Prize for Literature in 1904, he used the money to add to the collection until it spilled over into more than two dozen different rooms.

There are tableaux showing various aspects of everyday living ranging from an affluent Christmas party to a dressmaker's workroom, a section devoted to the fisherfolk of the Rhône and another that concentrates entirely on the Camargue. In fact it would be difficult to think of anything that has been left out, whether it is the type of loaves baked for different festivals, the use of herbs both magical and medicinal or the work of artists and craftsmen who lived in the area. There are even reproductions of a few of the 300 or so works painted by Van Gogh during the short time he spent in Arles. You would probably need two visits to do justice to all the exhibits. The museum is open from 9am until noon and from 2pm until 6pm in the summer. It closes an hour earlier from November until Easter, every Monday from October to June and on New Year's Day, Christmas Day and 1 May. The price of a ticket is 3 F.

The **Baths of Constantine,** just off the Quai Marx Dormoy on the banks of the Rhône, are a bit further away but it is a pleasant walk through the old town where the streets wind a little, but not too much, and the atmosphere is surprisingly unspoiled. As you might expect, they were the largest and most impressive baths in Provence—in fact there would not be a lot of grass left over if some modern eccentric decided to re-create them in the middle of the Wembley Stadium. Unfortunately only a small part has survived but it is enough to give you an idea of how they were built and the scale on which emperors lived in those days.

The **Réattu Museum** next door is an old priory which once belonged to the Knights of St John of Jerusalem 500 years ago. It contains a good many reminders of the days when they were a force to be reckoned with along the Mediterranean. There are some outstanding tapestries, a few pieces of furniture, some sculptures and ceramics, but otherwise the museum concentrates on pictures, including literally dozens of drawings by Picasso. In winter the key to the Baths of Constantine is kept there.

The **Alyscamps** on the opposite side of the town at the end of the Boulevard des Lices has its full quota of visitors in spite of the fact that there is not really much of it left. Until about the 12th century it was an enormous burial ground, a mile or so long and nearly half as wide, with literally thousands of tombs going back as far as the Roman occupation. All sorts of legends grew up round it and people in the Middle Ages are said to have gone to extraordinary lengths to make sure that they ended up there. According to one story they would even order that their bodies should be floated down the river with the necessary fees attached, rather like being buried with coins over their eyes to pay for the boat ride across the River Styx.

Perhaps these ancients might not have gone to quite so much trouble if they had been able to see far enough into the future. When it became the custom to present sarcophagi to important visitors and anyone else who needed to be placated or impressed, they were shipped off in their hundreds to foreign parts. All that remains is the ruined Church of St-Honorat, an avenue edged with trees and empty tombs, a forlorn atmosphere and the noise from nearby factories and a railway line. Anything worth seeing that has been overlooked found its way into the local museums, but I suppose it is something to be able to say that you have walked in the Elysian Fields.

WHERE TO STAY

You should not have much difficulty in finding a hotel in Arles except at the height of the season. The majority are quiet and comfortable without being too expensive, but generally speaking you will have to look outside the old town if you are hoping for things like a swimming pool and unlimited parking space. There are *logis* on the outskirts where you get value for money and good home cooking, and camping sites are available within a radius of a mile or so.

The **Hôtel Jules César**, in the Boulevard des Lices (tel. 90–93.43.20), is probably the best-known and correspondingly the most expensive in

Arles. The building is an old monastery within easy walking distance of the main sites which has been modernised to the degree expected by well-heeled American visitors. You should expect to pay up to 650 F a night for a double room and breakfast in bed is extra. The restaurant is excellent and the food imaginative, but check the menu for prices if you are economising as they tend to be rather high with the cheapest set meal costing 140 F.

The **Hôtel d'Arlatan,** 26 Rue du Sauvage, near the Place du Forum (tel. 90–93.56.66), was once an ancestral mansion dating in part from the 15th century, and it has more than a touch of the same elegant atmosphere today. It is wholly delightful with a secluded garden and a patio where you can have breakfast and sit out for drinks in the evening, but there is no restaurant. It is in the middle-income bracket with double rooms up to 358 F a night.

The **Hôtel Le Cloître,** 18 Rue du Cloître, near the church of St-Trophime (tel. 90–96.29.50), is a delightfully quiet if rather basic hotel among the Roman remains with all creature comforts but very few frills. It has no restaurant or private parking and no dogs are allowed. It is, however, very good value with a top price of 180 F.

The **Camping Municipal des Pins** (tel. 90–97.78.69), 8 kilometres (5 miles) along the road to Avignon, is a good base for touring the area. It is quiet and well-shaded, with all the basic requirements, and is open from April to October.

Les Roses (tel. 66–59.22.38), across both the Rhône and the Petit Rhône on the D15 to Beaucaire, has the advantages of both a swimming pool and fishing in the river but the shops are 8 kilometres (5 miles) away. It is open all the year but can be crowded, so it is as well to book in advance.

EATING OUT

The **Restaurant Vaccarès,** in the Place du Forum (tel. 90–96.06.17), is a fairly expensive choice but the local dishes are well worth the money and the wines are reasonably priced. It is on the first floor above what was once the rendezvous made famous by Van Gogh in his *Cafe du Soir.* The set menu without wine costs 145 F.

The **Hostellerie des Arènes,** 62 Rue du Refuge, near the arena (tel. 90–96.13.05), is cheerful, frequently over-crowded and outstanding value for money. You can get a plain meal for less than 55 F with wine at a comparable price, but unless you are having trouble with your bank manager splash out on one of the specialities like Provençal lamb.

FESTIVALS

Festivals play a large part in the life of Arles and the majority have some-thing to do with bulls.

The Easter Festival starts things off with religious services and bull-fights, many of them along Spanish lines. There is a cowboy festival on the last Sunday in April and bull-fights roughly once a fortnight right through to October.

The Music Festival, held in the Roman theatre from the last part of June until late in July, gives you a chance to see some of the national costumes which spend the rest of the year in private wardrobes if they are not already in the museums.

The Festival of the Santons starts before Christmas and goes on until after New Year. It is mainly a show by the trade for the trade but is none the less interesting for that.

TOURIST INFORMATION

The information office in the Esplanade des Lices (tel. 90–96.29.35) will tell you all you want to know about local bus and train services, coach tours and where to hire a car or a bicycle, as well as providing details about places of interest in and around the area.

The Camargue

Anyone who prefers to see the bulls in their natural environment rather than beribboned in the arena has only to drive down to the Camargue. It is a large and extremely flat plain with very few hamlets and no towns apart from Stes-Maries-de-la-Mer. The roads are either filled with tourists dashing along so fast that they would probably not see a dinosaur if one happened to be about, or else the whole place is silent and somewhat desolate. For bird watchers and anyone whose inclination is to get as far away from other people as possible, there are two important things to remember. First, most of the **Vaccarès Lagoon** is inside the national reserve and no one is allowed on to it without a permit which is almost impossible for the ordinary tourist to obtain. Second, a large proportion of the area is marshland and if you were unfortunate enough to fall into a bog or a patch of quicksand it is unlikely that there would be anyone to pull you out.

The northern part of the Camargue has been largely reclaimed for agri-culture and is given over to vineyards, wheat and other crops and planted with trees. Some of these stand in long lines to break the force of the mistral, others provide shelter for the farmhouses, and there are quite a few orchards where fruit is grown on a large scale. Further south the main harvest is rice and on all sides small dykes separate the oblong paddy fields which look decidedly muddy and unattractive until the plants are tall enough to give them a greenish tinge.

WILDLIFE

The plain is cobwebbed with little roads, some of which have not even been tarred, and the amount and variety of wildlife you see depends to a certain extent on the route you decide to take. One option is to follow the D36 down the side of the Grand Rhône towards the sea, branching off whenever you feel like it in the direction of the lagoon. **Salin-de-Badon**, about two-thirds of the way down, is a good place to start looking for flamingoes and other species, although keen observers may already have seen hoopoes, partridges and an occasional purple heron busy fishing. From **Le Paradis** causeways have been built to link some of the larger pools, passing small islands where the flamingoes build their nests. Once you get as far south as **Salin-de-Giraud** the outlook is mostly salt pans and a smattering of industry, so the time has come to retrace your steps. However, there is no need to double back further than **Villeneuve** to join the D37 which skirts the top of the lagoon. Among the birds to look for here are bee eaters and black-winged stilts, but it is necessary to get much closer to the sea to find marsh harriers, avocets and even a small egret or two. It is said that more than 300 different species have been reported in the Camargue, from vultures to skylarks and falcons to owls. Something like 100 000 ducks migrate there every year to spend the winter on the small islands that poke their backs up above the salty waters of the lakes. From mid-July the mud flats are invaded by lapwings, sandpipers and other visitors from the north, and when the winter is over the flamingoes desert North Africa to raise their young in nests along the water's edge.

Not all the local inhabitants are feathered. Some of the last beavers to be found in Europe have set up home there and stories are told of a particular type of hog that makes itself a little mat of chewed grass and hides underneath when it does not like the look of the world outside. By far the most famous animals of the Camargue are the black fighting bulls and the white horses, but if you expect to see the stallions pounding through the surf with manes and tails flying you will be sadly disappointed. They graze quite peacefully a few hundred yards from the roadside and by no means all of them are white. The foals are brown when they are born and only change colour when they are about three years old. The black bulls are just as docile as the cattle you see anywhere else, although the odd one can get a bit stroppy if it is separated from the herd. They are looked after by *gardians* who literally live on the job. Their homes are the tiny thatched cottages dotted about over the marshlands with a blank white wall facing northwards to beat the mistral.

Méjanes, just off the D37, is one of dozens of farms that make tourists part of their everyday business and it is a good deal more commercialised than most of the others. The attractions of the so-called amusement centre include a bull-ring, a small electric railway that charges 6 F for a short trip along the shores of the Vaccarès Lagoon and horses for pony trekking at 35 F an hour.

All along the main road you will see horses tied up in little roofed enclosures, saddled and ready for hire. Parties are made up and go out in the care of a *gardian* but you don't have to be a cowboy yourself to join in. The ponies are intelligent, generally quite amiable and wonderfully surefooted, and they seem to know by instinct how to avoid all the dangerous spots.

To get a complete rundown on all there is to see and do in the Camargue call in at **Ginès** where the information centre is open every weekday from 9am until 6pm with the customary two-hour break for lunch. During the summer it is also manned on Sundays and public holidays but the doors do not open until 10am. If you have to hang about, the best place to pass the time would be the **Pont de Gau bird sanctuary** which is open between 8am and sunset and costs 8 F. It will also cost you 8 F to get into the **Boumian Museum** any day from the beginning of April to 1 October from 10am to 12.30 pm and 2pm to 7pm. It specialises in tableaux representing various aspects of life in the Camargue with the sort of things that you might not see in the flesh like a gypsy camp or a typical *ferrade* where the young steers are branded.

Stes-Maries-de-la-Mer

Feelings about Stes-Maries-de-la-Mer vary considerably because its past as a fortified outpost and a place of pilgrimage is very much at variance with its present role as a rapidly expanding holiday restort.

HISTORY
According to popular belief a boat without any sails or oars drifted in from the Holy Land on some unspecified date around AD 40. On board were St

158

Mary Magdalene accompanied by St Lazarus and his sister St Martha; St Mary Jacobe, the sister of the Virgin Mary; St Mary Salome, the mother of James and John; St Maximin and St Sidonius, as well as an African servant called Sara who had insisted on going along with them. When the bulk of the party set out to convert the heathen the Sts Maries Jacobe and Salome remained behind with Sara. They appear to have led supremely uneventful lives and were eventually buried in a small oratory on the site of the present church.

By AD 869 a new church had been built, the town was being fortified and the Archbishop of Arles travelled down to inspect the defences. Unfortunately his visit coincided with a Saracen raid and he was kidnapped and held to ransom. By the time the full quota of gold and silver, swords and slaves had been collected, the poor old gentleman had died. Nothing daunted, his captors dressed him up in ceremonial robes, tied him to a throne and were sailing off with the payout before the townspeople realised what had happened. In the 12th century it was decided to build the present more impregnable church on the lines of a fortified castle complete with thick stone walls and battlements topped by a sturdy watch tower. In 1448 Good King René had the two Sts Maries exhumed and their relics placed in an upper chapel which has been their shrine ever since. Sara stayed down in the crypt with an altar and a reliquary all to herself.

WHAT TO SEE

Apart from the old houses still grouped round the church, Stes-Maries is very much like any other popular seaside resort. It has magnificent sandy beaches that stretch for miles, but the sea front is lined with very ordinary buildings, a few unremarkable hotels and the ubiquitous cafes that seem to have no ambition whatever to get into anybody's good food guide. Most of the streets are fairly wide; however, that does not prevent them from being very overcrowded during the season when you would be lucky to find a convenient parking space or even somewhere to cool off in the shade.

The church, in the Place de l'Église, has always been a place of pilgrimage and acts as a beacon for the thousands of gypsies who arrive once a year for a ceremony that has remained unchanged since the Middle Ages. It is a rather gloomy building with very little in the way of decoration apart from a carved boat with the Maries standing side by side, apparently not at all sure that what they are looking at is really land at last. A practical note is introduced by a covered well in the nave where the defenders could be sure of finding fresh water in times of siege. The shrine of the Maries can be seen through a window high up above the steps leading to the crypt.

Sara, who was appointed long ago as the patron of the gypsies in spite of not being a saint, is a rather mottled figure wearing far too many clothes. During the gypsies' pilgrimage they keep an all-night vigil in front of her altar when the crypt is so crowded and the atmosphere so personal that a tourist would have to be exceptionally brash to squeeze in. Officially the crypt is open from 7.30am until 7.30pm from April to September but closes half an hour early during the rest of the year. It is always closed from noon until 2pm and whenever there is a service in the church. There is no entrance fee, but if you want to turn on any of the lights, the time switches only respond when they are given 1 F apiece. However, it will cost you 5 F and a bit of shoe leather to climb up to the sentinel's walk round the ramparts where the view is exceptional.

The **Baroncelli Museum,** off the Avenue Victor-Hugo, concerns itself only with the Camargue through items ranging from literature to landscapes and furniture to clothes. It is open from 9am to 6pm in the season apart from the usual two hours for lunch, closes an hour early from October to the end of March, every Wednesday and right through December. The entrance fee is 5 F.

WHERE TO STAY

There are several hotels in Stes-Maries-de-la-Mer, none of which are opulent or even expensive. If you decide to look outside the town, you could not do better than choose one of the many ranch-type establishments which have large grounds, often put up their guests in bungalows and provide facilities like tennis courts, swimming pools and horses, plus the occasional disco.

The **Mas de la Fouque,** on the shores of a lake about 5 kilometres (3 miles) away up the D38 (tel. 90–47.81.02), is probably the most luxurious. It is modern with a good restaurant, adds fishing to its other attractions, is open from the end of March to the beginning of November and charges up to 1020 F a night. The most expensive set menu for dinner is 220 F, but you have to eat out on Tuesdays when the dining room is closed.

The **Hôtel Galoubet,** in the Route de Cacharel (tel. 90–97.82.17), is comfortable without being in any way out of the ordinary. It has a swimming pool and a car park but, in common with nearly all the hotels in the town itself, there is no garden, no restaurant and no dogs are allowed. It closes over Christmas and from early in January to the beginning of March and charges up to 225 F a night.

EATING OUT

The **Brûleur de Loups,** in the Avenue Gilbert-Leroy (tel. 90–97.83.31), is a very pleasant restaurant overlooking the sea with a terrace that catches any breeze that is going. The food is appetising, the service attentive and the set menus range from 101 to 112 F. It is closed for four months from the middle of November and also on Tuesday nights and Wednesdays except during August and September.

The oddly-named **Hippocampe,** in the Rue Pelletan (tel. 90–97.80.91), is one of those places that make you turn your ideas upside down and choose a restaurant where you can live in rather than a hotel where you have to eat out. The food is good and not expensive with the cheapest set menu costing 80 F all in. The handful of rooms are reasonably priced at 176 F. It is open from mid-March to about the middle of November and the restaurant is normally closed on Tuesdays but stays open all the week from July to September.

FESTIVALS

Where festivals are concerned the most important is undoubtedly the gypsy pilgrimage which takes place every year on 24 and 25 May. The caravans start arriving the day before and although the sheer weight of numbers is impressive they are less colourful now that all the horsepower is under the bonnets. They settle like locusts on every available piece of ground and then the gypsies go off to pay their respects to Sara, thanking her for past favours and putting in a few requests for the year ahead. The next day there is a service in the church during which the relics of the two Maries are lowered from their chapel on to the altar where they remain for a little over 24 hours. The small boat is removed from the nave, Sara is brought up from the crypt and they are both carried in procession to the beach attended by the clergy, mounted cowboys, gypsies decked out in all their finery, townspeople in national dress and tourists weighed down with cameras. After the sea has been blessed, the whole lot turn round and stream back again. When eventually the relics and the statues have been returned to their normal places, everyone gets on with the less serious business of dancing and singing, fighting bulls and racing horses, after which all the caravans disappear as suddenly as they arrived.

There are similar festivals at the end of October and in early December but they are not nearly so well attended or so colourful. They are held on the penultimate Sunday in October and the first Sunday in December.

EXCURSIONS

For anyone who would like to combine nature study with a boat trip there are regular services up the Petit Rhône between Easter and the beginning of November. They last for something over an hour and cost 32 F with half-price tickets for children. There are four trips a day during the high season, at 10am, 2.30pm, 4.15pm and 6pm, but these are reduced to one a day as the demand slackens.

Groups of about 30 to 40 people are made up regularly for trips into the Camargue which cost between 135 and 160 F. You can get all the details you need from Les Grandes Cabannes du Vaccarès (tel. 90–97.10.14) and Méjanes en Camargue (tel. 90–97.00.51).

Aigues-Mortes

When you feel the time has come to delve back into antiquity, take any of the minor roads to Mas Sénébier, turn left on to the D58 just before it crosses the Petit Rhône and head westwards where you will find a perfect example of a small, unspoiled medieval town that has remained almost intact behind its fortress walls. Until quite recently this city of Dead Waters, which is the literal translation of the name, was out on a limb as far as tourists, industrialists and second-home owners were concerned. As a result it is not an old quarter wrapped up in glass and concrete but an ancient walled town, still invisible behind the ramparts which have protected it for upwards of 700 years.

HISTORY

Aigues-Mortes was built by St Louis in the 13th century on the site of a small fishing village owned by Benedictine monks. The King needed a port of his own because he was planning to liberate Jerusalem; the abbey did not want its marshy little piece of coastline; so they had no difficulty in coming to an amicable arrangement. People were attracted to the area with a series of promises like tax incentives, the Tower of Constance was built to protect them, some houses were added and the King sailed away on the 7th Crusade. It was a singularly unfortunate venture as far as he was concerned because he was captured, held to ransom and when he finally got back he had to land at Hyères instead of Aigues-Mortes as planned. When he tried again in 1270, the port gave him an enthusiastic send-off but unluckily he made for Tunis where he caught the plague and died. His son, Philip the Bold, decided that the town would be much safer if it had ramparts surrounded by a moat, an idea which proved so effective that the security of the town has never since been seriously threatened.

WHAT TO SEE

The best way to see Aigues-Mortes is to walk round it because, although cars are allowed inside, there are very few places to park. It is so small that you can stand at one gate and look straight down the road and out through its companion on the opposite side. The town has been maintained rather than restored and any of the inhabitants returning after 400 or 500 years should feel very much at home. They would obviously miss the moat, which has been filled in, and the odd hotel and restaurant might give them food for thought, but otherwise the 20th century has hardly encroached at all.

The **Tour de Constance**, the only place to visit apart from the ramparts themselves, consists of two enormous circular rooms, one on top of the other, with all the stairways and dungeons built into the walls which are $5\frac{1}{2}$ metres (18ft) thick. It could hardly be called a museum, although there are some manuscripts preserved from the days of St Louis and several reminders of the 400 years when it was used as a state prison. Among the last people incarcerated there in the 18th century were the Huguenots, probably the best-known being Marie Durand who went in as a child of eight and was only released on compassionate grounds 30 years later.

Right on top is the watch tower which doubled as a lighthouse before the canals silted up and put an end to the town's activities as a port. From this vantage point it is possible to see for miles around and also to get a comprehensive view of the ramparts if you do not feel like spending the better part of an hour examining them more closely. This solitary two-for-the-price-of-one attraction is open all the year round, from 9am until 6.30pm in the summer and from 10am to 5pm from October to March with the regulation two hours off for lunch. The price of a ticket is 6 F on weekdays but only 3 F on Sundays and holidays.

WHERE TO STAY

For obvious reasons there are very few hotels in Aigues-Mortes and those that do exist behind their old stone walls are quiet and reasonably priced.

The **Hôtel St-Louis**, in the Rue Amiral-Courbet (tel. 66–53.72.68), is probably the best value for money with the most expensive room costing 195 F. It has a restaurant, closed on Wednesdays, with set menus from 80 to

180 F and the whole place is shut from New Year to the end of February.

EATING OUT
The **Camargue**, 19 Rue de la Republic (tel. 66–53.86.88), is more tourist-conscious than most. In the evenings it sets itself out to attract visitors with extensive menus and gypsy music and takes an obvious pleasure in the number of well-known people who have dined there. It is closed from early January until mid-February and on Mondays except during the season, and you can order the set menu for 80 F.

The restaurant **La Grange**, 15 Boulevard Diderot (tel. 66–53.69.31), just outside the ramparts, is quite easy to miss unless you are looking for it. There is plenty of parking opposite where the moat used to be and the décor is definitely rural with cart wheels, pitch forks and the like. The *soupe de poisson,* served by Marc and André, was the best I tasted anywhere and if not too many people are waiting you may be given a lesson in the ritual of rubbing the rusk-like bread with garlic before adding all the other ingredients. The restaurant is closed on Mondays except during the high season, and a good dinner with wine will set you back about 200 F.

TOURIST INFORMATION
The information office in the Place St-Louis (tel. 66–51.95.00), which is closed for only one month a year from the third week in October, will give you details of excursions into the Camargue including a special Photo Safari which leaves three times a day from the Porte de la Gardette.

Le Grau-du-Roi and Port Camargue

If you feel the need for a sandy beach or a dip in the Mediterranean, Le Grau-du-Roi is less than 15 minutes' drive away. At heart it is an attractive little fishing village, somewhat spoiled by holiday villas and sprawling urban development, with rather basic hotels, typical cafes and the odd restaurant or two. Although the village is not strictly in the Camargue, that area's tourist office will put you in touch with people who organise trips into the surrounding countryside and arrange visits to a local rodeo or a display of gypsy dancing. It is a popular centre for anyone on the lookout for somewhere to camp or park a caravan as there are a number of sites within a radius of a few miles.

The Campexel **Les Jardins-de-Tivoli** (tel. 66–51.82.96), off the D979, is open all the year round and provides its guests with a whole range of facilities including a restaurant, a shop and a swimming pool. The only drawback is that there are no trees. However, the beach is not far away and you can fish, play tennis and ride.

La Petite Camargue, further north off the D62 (tel. 66–88.32.36), has roughly the same facilities including take-away meals and the same variety of sports laid on. Although it is a fair way to the beach, trees provide a certain amount of shade and there is a games room and a disco which can be rather noisy when the place is crowded.

A beach sweeps round from the mouth of the canal to link Le Grau-du-Roi with Port Camargue, a relatively modern development designed entirely for the convenience of yachtsmen. There is a large marina and a series of small islands linked together in groups and edged with moorings, most of which have a house attached. Behind the protecting walls of the outer harbour, the planners have included everything anyone could possibly want. On the business side there is a crane and three travelling hoists, maintenance and repair services, a slipway, fuel and all the usual chandlers. Entertainment is provided by a nightclub and casino, boats can be hired, short trips are available and the Club Nautique will help with anything like deep-sea fishing, water-skiing and learning to sail. You can even leave your boat there safely for the winter, either in the water or under cover ashore.

La Grande-Motte

The City of Pyramids, as it likes to be called, started from a mosquito-ridden swamp 15 years ago and is now a thriving town in every sense of the word. It is wonderfully green with forest areas and acres of grass where you can walk or sit under the trees. Like its famous pyramid-shaped buildings, most of which face on to the harbour, the sculptures are ultra-modern. It has a town hall and a library, an open-air theatre and conference halls, a casino and half a dozen discos, as well as a number of specialist clubs. You can learn to use a computer, play bridge or scrabble, go to the cinema or book an indoor tennis court.

Outdoor activities cover the whole spectrum of sport from archery to soccer and basketball to golf. A little gaily painted train runs about on rubber wheels taking visitors on a 25-minute tour beginning at the casino and costing 16 F. Yachtsmen are just as well catered for and so are children who can be left at their own club, Point Zero, to play on the beach, go for picnics or even try their skill at local handicrafts.

165

WHERE TO STAY

Whatever your inclination La Grande-Motte does its best to meet your requirements. There are hotels of all shapes and sizes, mostly in the middle-income bracket, you can hire a villa or an apartment, stay in a village or holiday camp or bring your own caravan. Many places are open throughout the year and the Office Municipal de Tourisme (tel. 67–56.62.62) in the Place de la Mairie will send or give you all the details you need.

The **Hôtel Azur** (tel. 67–56.56.00) is a delightfully small establishment with rooms overlooking the swimming pool. It stands alone, almost at the entrance to the harbour, looking across to the familiar skyline of La Grande-Motte, is open from the beginning of April to the end of November and charges up to 300 F for a double room.

EATING OUT

The restaurant **Alexander** (tel. 67–56.63.63) could almost be described as part of the Hôtel Azur and has all the same advantages because there is nothing anywhere near to hem it in. It is fairly expensive, charging 160 F for a basic menu, but both the food and the service are excellent. It closes in November and from early January to the middle of February, which is probably not a bad idea when you think of the mistral whistling all around.

Other and less expensive restaurants are scattered about everywhere especially along the Quai Général-de-Gaulle, in the Place de l'Épi near the casino and the Rue Frédéric Mistral which runs off it. The best way to choose is to study the menus and prices and pick the one that suits you best.

St-Gilles

One pleasant excursion from La Grande-Motte, or for that matter from any other town round the Camargue, is to St-Gilles which was positively inundated with pilgrims during the Middle Ages.

HISTORY

According to legend St Giles the Hermit, after giving away all his money, arrived in Provence from Greece on a raft in the 8th century and when he died was buried in the local church. The town took his name—and so, incidentally, did Edinburgh Cathedral—and by the 13th century it was a hive of activity exporting crusaders and handling the rich cargoes that were brought back in their stead. The abbey that was built in the 12th century was partly knocked down 400 years later by the Protestants who murdered the resident monks by throwing them down the well. The Revolution also took its toll on the abbey, but enough has been restored to make it worth a visit.

WHAT TO SEE

By some fortunate chance—there are those who call it a miracle—the great west front of the church, a magnificent example of medieval sculpture, escaped almost intact. There is very little to see inside apart from the crypt where a tomb which was discovered in the middle of the last century is believed to be the place where St Giles was buried. Between March and November the tourist centre in the Place de l'Église will arrange for you to see the spiral staircase known as the Vis de St-Gilles which once led to the ancient chapels to the east of the choir. It is slightly claustrophobic because it is roofed over with stone.

From St-Gilles it is an easy run to Nîmes.

The Roman arena in Nîmes

Nîmes

From a distance Nîmes looks anything but an ancient town with whitish highrise buildings punctuating the skyline and suburbs fanning out in all directions. This impression is not entirely misleading because it is predomi-

167

nantly a commercial centre with the emphasis on industries like the manu-
facture of textiles. In the last century it produced a tough material for
working clothes called *serge de Nîmes* which we know today as denim. However, it has retained enough of the past to hold its own in the constant battle
for tourism.

HISTORY

After the Roman Emperor Augustus defeated Antony at Actium, he needed
a place where a large number of soldiers who had fought in Egypt could
settle. He chose an old Celtic settlement which had grown up round a natural spring and had already attracted the attention of the Romans. He gave it
the symbol of a crocodile chained to a palm tree to commemorate the Nile
victory.

By AD 50 Nemausus, as the town was called, had everything it needed in
the way of houses and temples, baths and sanitation and the final touches
were being put to the arena. However, this state of affairs lasted for only
another hundred years or so, after which everyone from the invading Saracens to the destructive forces of the Revolution played a part in knocking it
down again. Fortunately each group in turn found some use for the arena
and the temple nearby, as a result of which they are among the best-
preserved buildings of their kind to be found anywhere.

WHAT TO SEE

Not even its most ardent admirer would claim that Nîmes had much in the
way of tourist attractions apart from its few ancient buildings, the 18th-
century Jardin de la Fontaine, a small section of the old town and a devotion
to music and bull-fighting. The buildings are rather spread out compared
with places like Arles, but the area is so beautifully preserved and includes
so many delightful little shops that walking about is a pleasure rather than a
chore.

The **arena** at the southern end of the Avenue Victor-Hugo may not be
the largest in existence but it certainly is more intact than most. Once the
Romans stopped using it for chariot races and feats of arms, not to mention
flooding it occasionally for water sports, it was turned into a fortress which
prevented anyone from making off with the stones. In the Middle Ages a
group of knights used it as their headquarters and in the early 13th century it
became a slum with more than 2000 people living inside the walls. Around
1809 the whole area was cleared out and has now reverted to its original
function with bulls taking the place of lions and several thousand spectators
crowding into every available inch of space. Except when the bull-fights are

168

going on, the arena is open from 9am to noon and again from 2pm until 5pm with the times extended to 8.30am and 7.30pm between June and September. It is closed on Tuesdays during the winter as well as on 1 and 2 January, 1 and 11 November, Christmas Day and Boxing Day. It costs 10 F for a ticket but this also takes you into the Maison Carrée, Diana's Temple and the Tour Magne.

The **Maison Carrée,** at the opposite end of the Avenue Victor-Hugo, is in fact a Roman temple built by Agrippa in about 20 BC and dedicated to his sons Caius and Lucius. It is a magnificent oblong building reached by a flight of steps with columns supporting the roof in the style of ancient Greece. It has survived down the ages because someone has always had a special use for it, either as a public building, a private house, a church or a stable. Its present function, apart from just being there, is to house the Museum of Antiquities where you can see such things as a large statue of Apollo and the marble head of the Venus of Nîmes. It is open at the same time as the arena (although the extended hours apply only during July and August), it is closed on the same days and you use the same ticket to get in.

The **Tour Magne,** standing on the top of the hill behind the Jardin de la Fontaine, is said to be one of the towers built at intervals in the original city walls. It dates from about 16 BC and has lost its top storey but in spite of this there is an excellent view of the country all round provided you have the energy to climb up the seemingly endless steps to the top. Its opening times are the same as those of the arena and the same ticket applies.

The **Jardin de la Fontaine,** which includes the ruined Temple of Diana, is at the end of the Avenue Jean-Jaurès. The fountain referred to is the spring around which the town grew up, though its setting has changed considerably since then. The water still gushes out, but instead of being directed into Roman baths it finds its way through pools flanked by balustrades, past a conventional layout of terraces, shallow steps, urns and statues to a water garden and finally disappears into the canal. The garden is open during the day and floodlit on summer evenings but the Temple of Diana keeps the same hours as the arena and the Tour Magne.

Scattered about the old town you will find a handful of churches and museums including the **Cathedral of Notre-Dame and St-Castor** on the Place aux Herbes which was almost entirely restored in the last century, and the **Museum of Old Nîmes** practically next door. It was once a palace but is now devoted to furniture, clothes, textiles and bulls. Like the **Museum of Archaeology** and the **Museum of Natural History** on the Grand Rue, where you will find glass, pottery, coins and more bulls, it is open from 9am

169

to noon and from 2pm until 5pm. They all close on Tuesdays and occasionally on public holidays.

WHERE TO STAY

There are quite a number of hotels in Nîmes ranging from the fairly expensive to the cheap and cheerful with a good many commercial ones in between. Holidaymakers usually choose one in or near to the old town, although you have to look further afield if you want things like a swimming pool.

The **Imperator,** just off the Quai de la Fontaine (tel. 66–21.90.30), is no distance at all from the Jardin, added to which it has a splendid garden of its own and a good restaurant where you can eat in or out of doors. The rooms cost up to 440F and the hotel is closed from the middle of January to the middle of March. The restaurant closes for only a month from mid-January and offers set menus from 110 to 190F but the specialities work out at a good deal more.

EATING OUT

Nîmes is not over-blessed with good restaurants but there are quite a few bistros, especially in the streets round the arena, that serve local dishes at prices local people are willing to afford.

Au Chapon Fin, 3 Rue Château-Fadaise (tel. 66–67.34.73), is within easy reach of both the arena and the Maison Carrée, closes on Tuesdays and has a most acceptable set menu for 190F.

FESTIVALS AND SPECTACLES

Like Arles, Nîmes makes quite a feature of bull-fights which are held two or three times a month in the arena. They are mostly Spanish-style from June to September and usually take place on Sunday afternoons.

The Whitsun Festival, which lasts for five days—from Thursday to Monday—is an extremely popular event. Apart from the inevitable bull-fights there are concerts, folk dancing and a certain amount of jubilation all over the town.

For music lovers there are operas in the arena and the theatre, a jazz festival in July and a folklore festival that spills over into August as well as open-air concerts in the Jardin de la Fontaine.

TOURIST INFORMATION

All the relevant details of the above spectacles are available from the tourist office in the Rue Auguste, less than a block from the Maison Carrée (tel. 66–67.29.11), which will also help you to find a hotel.

Pont du Gard

In 19 BC the Romans discovered that the natural spring, delightful as it was, could not produce nearly enough water for their everyday needs, so Agrippa arranged for an aqueduct to augment it from the river about 50 kilometres (30 miles) away. To do this he had to build a bridge which is still regarded as one of the most outstanding sights in France.

Roman aqueduct, the Pont du Gard

The Pont du Gard is about 275 metres (900ft) long and 49 metres (160ft) high, built of enormous blocks of stone without a trowelful of mortar to be seen anywhere. When you come in off the main road there is a car park that charges 8 F, a motorway type of restaurant and not a sign of the bridge, which is rather disconcerting because one would think that it is far too big to be hidden by the trees. However, if you approach it from the D19A to the north, you not only get in for nothing but the road runs along the lower tier of arches before coming out in the car park on the other side.

The best view of the Pont du Gard is from outside the St-Privat Château a little further upstream although, provided you are not afraid of heights, there is nothing to beat a head-spinning walk along the stone roof of the

171

canal that runs across the top. Far below you can see people swimming and boating—it is a favourite spot for picnics and excursions from Nîmes and Avignon.

Gorges du Gardon, Pont St-Nicolas Remoulins and Uzès

For anyone with a whole day to spend in the area there are plenty of places to visit. Nature lovers would probably opt for the Gorges du Gardon, the Pont St-Nicolas built in the 13th century or the bamboo forest near Remoulins. Others with an unquenched thirst for old buildings would be better advised to make for Uzès. It has a **ducal palace** with a resident duke, a perfectly restored square called the **Place aux Herbes** that takes its name from the herb market held there in the Middle Ages and is all set about with the houses of ancient noblemen. Any member of the party who is fed up with the Renaissance can pass the time in the **Museon di Rodo** which specialises in model railways and vintage cars.

WHERE TO STAY
There are any number of camping and caravan sites in this part of the world but if you are heading south a good choice would be at Bezouce on the N86 just north of Nîmes. **Les Cypres,** Rue de la Bastide (tel. 66–26.24.30), is open from March to September; here you can get something to eat or replenish your own supplies from the shops next door, plug into the electricity and have a shower.

Perrier

The country to the south of Nîmes is undulating, largely covered with vineyards and there are not a great many places of interest along the way. For visitors who just like to wander there are minor roads leading southwards into the Camargue and about the same number heading north towards the mountains. Perrier, some 16 kilometres (10 miles) to the south off the main N113, is famous for its bottled water which was brought to public attention by St-John Harmsworth, a member of the English newspaper family. It is possible to see over the factory, learn how the whole enterprise works and even have one for the road before driving on to Montpellier.

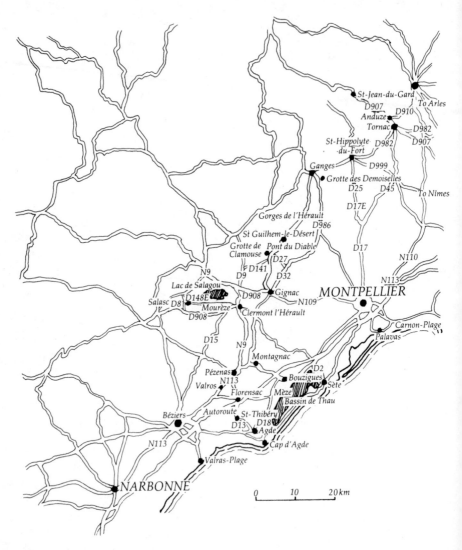

St-Jean-du-Gard
To Arles
D907
Anduze D910
Tornac
D982
St-Hippolyte D982 D907
du-Fort
Ganges D999
Grotte des Demoiselles
D25 D45
To Nîmes
D17E
Gorges de l'Hérault
D986
St Guilhem-le-Désert
Grotte de Pont du Diable
Clamouse D27
D17
N9 D141
D9 D32
N110
N113
Lac de Salagou
MONTPELLIER
D148E D908 Gignac
Salasc D8 N109
Mourèze
D908 Clermont l'Hérault
Carnon-Plage
Palavas
D15
N9
Montagnac
Pézenas D2
Valros N113 Bouzigues
Florensac Mèze Sète
Béziers Autoroute Bassin de Thau
St-Thibéry
D13 D18
N113 Agde
Cap d'Agde
Valras-Plage
NARBONNE
0 10 20 km

MONTPELLIER TO NARBONNE

Chapter VIII

MONTPELLIER TO NARBONNE

Cathedral of Maguelone, Languedoc

Montpellier

Montpellier is first and foremost a university town in spite of the fact that it is the capital of Bas-Languedoc and, in common with other centres along the coast, is paying increasing attention to the importance of light industry. It is neither self-consciously ancient nor aggressively modern and although it welcomes visitors they are accepted as part of the community rather than being treated as if the whole place depended on them.

HISTORY

Little or nothing remains of the days when Montpellier was a staging post for Romans on the Via Domitia which ran down through Narbonne and on to Spain. There are no ruins to be seen, no pilgrim shrines, not even a

175

plaque announcing proudly that Hannibal slept here. For all practical purposes its history begins in the 10th century when it was famous for the herbs and spices rich merchants imported from the Middle East. Naturally a certain amount of attention was paid to their medicinal properties and gradually young men started to arrive from other parts of the country to learn what they could from the experts. This led, in the early 13th century, to the formation of a medical school; other faculties were added and in 1289 it was given the status of a university.

At this time Montpellier belonged to the kingdom of Majorca but 50 years later Jayme III ran into financial problems and sold the whole place lock, stock and barrel to the King of France. Both the university and the town continued to thrive under their new management until the Protestant community joined in the Wars of Religion, indulged in an orgy of self-destruction and were finally defeated in 1622. Louis XIII immediately ordered his forces to destroy the ramparts and build a citadel to keep the population in order. Today, as the Lycée, it confines itself to the younger generation. It was Richelieu, acting for the king, who made Montpellier the administrative capital of the area and as soon as the forces of government moved in new houses were built, the cathedral was restored, roads and gardens were added and all the while the university went from strength to strength.

WHAT TO SEE
Apart from the specific places of interest Montpellier is not a town which tempts you to wander round. There are no brooding alleys or mysterious little covered stairways, and when you do find a square with a fountain it is liable to be filled with students swapping notes or having an al fresco lunch. Most of the impressive old houses rise straight up from the pavement Spanish-style and you have to be inside to appreciate the attractive courtyards, decorated columns and wide staircases that recall the wealth and influence of the 17th and 18th centuries. Fortunately many of them have been turned into museums or are used by government departments which are open to the public and tolerate visitors during office hours. On the other hand, the city's gardens are large and beautiful and parking, although difficult, is not impossible to find.

The **Promenade du Peyrou** at the end of the Rue Foch is guarded by an Arc de Triomphe built in 1691 to recall the victories of Louis XIV. A statue of the Sun King, riding a splendid charger with one arm raised as though he is about to let off a rocket, overlooks the town below. A small building at the end of the promenade has all the attributes of a temple with sweeping steps, an ornamental basin and decorative archways flanked by columns, but it flatters to deceive. The Château d'Eau, as it is called, is in fact an integral part of the aqueduct that supplies the town with water, although in the summer it doubles as a concert platform in the evenings.

The **Jardin des Plantes,** roughly a block away on the Boulevard Henri IV, is considerably older. It is actually the oldest of its kind in France, having been created on the orders of the said Henri in 1593. You do not have to be very knowledgeable to enjoy walking round looking at all the trees and flowers yet it does help to be able to identify a few of the more exotic ones. The garden is open from 8am to noon and from 2pm until 6pm but is closed at weekends and on public holidays. Guided tours, which cost 5 F, have to be arranged about a fortnight in advance.

The famous 14th-century **Faculté de Médecine** is on the opposite side of the Boulevard Henri IV, close to the only part of the ramparts that were not demolished. It was originally the Abbey of St Benedict, then became an Archbishop's Palace and ended up as a state prison during the Revolution. It has a fantastic library of books and manuscripts, some going back more than 1000 years, and also includes the **Atger Museum** with drawings presented to the medical school early in the last century. The museum is closed at weekends, on holidays and throughout August, but otherwise is open for inspection from 10am until noon and from 1.30pm to 7.30pm.

The **Cathedral of St-Pierre,** which adjoins the medical school, is the only medieval church in Montpellier. It is disappointing because it was almost totally restored in the 17th and 19th centuries. There is really nothing to show that it was once the abbey chapel and the whole atmosphere is rather dark and gloomy.

The **Fabre Museum,** on the other hand, which you will find on the Rue Montpelliéret, just off the Boulevard Sarrail opposite the Esplanade, is the most outstanding art gallery in the South of France. Its contents are extremely varied and are based on a collection presented to the city by Fabre in 1825. It appears that he was remarkably friendly with the Countess of Albany, the widow of Charles Stuart who failed in his ambition to become King of England. When she died she left him everything and he in turn decided to found a museum. A good many other people have added to it since and there are rooms devoted to sculptures, to French and Italian artists, to modern painters and even a few corners set aside for other nationalities. The best-known British contribution is *The Infant Samuel in Prayer* by Sir Joshua Reynolds which must have fathered as many reproductions as *The*

177

Monarch of the Glen. The museum is open from 9am to noon and from 2pm until 5.30pm but closes half an hour early on Sundays, all day on Mondays and on 1 January, 1 May, 14 July, 15 August, 1 and 11 November and on Christmas Day.

The **Hôtel du Lunaret**, 5 Rue des Trésoriers-de-France, one of the most impressive of the 17th-century mansions, is now the Archaeological Museum with exhibits from prehistoric times to the 18th century. It is open only on Saturdays between 2pm and 5pm and closes completely during August.

The **Place de la Comédie**, a bare two minutes' stroll away, is a favourite meeting place for the townspeople, visitors and students alike. Apart from the Opera and the Fountain of the Three Graces, it is largely given over to cafes but opens out at one end on to the Esplanade. This runs for 1 kilometre (more than half a mile) along the site of the old ramparts with a delightful park containing a lake and plenty of trees on what was once the parade ground.

WHERE TO STAY

There are any number of hotels in Montpellier, quite a few within easy walking distance of the Esplanade.

The **Hôtel Metropole**, 3 Rue Clos-René (tel. 67–58.11.22), is, like so many others in the top bracket, completely self-contained apart from lacking a swimming pool. All the buses run nearby, the tourist office is conveniently near and the station is at the bottom of the road. It is open all the year round and charges up to 580 F a night.

The **Novotel**, 125 bis Avenue de Palavas (tel. 67–64.04.04), is the only one with a swimming pool and is outside the town centre. It is modern and rather impersonal in the manner of commercial hotels, but the service is quick and friendly, they will serve a snack lunch if you want one and the price of a comfortable room is 352 F. It is open all the year.

The **Hôtel Nice**, 14 Rue Boussairolles (tel. 67–58.42.54), is only a stone's throw from the Place de la Comédie. It is rather basic but pleasant and good value at 100 F and is open 12 months of the year.

EATING OUT

With something like 100 different restaurants to choose from in Montpellier, many of them side by side and frequently specialising in a particular kind of cooking, it is difficult to pick out one or two. It is better by far to decide what you want to eat and then find out where to get it.

Le Rolin, 11 Boulevard Ledru-Rollin (tel. 67–60.47.50), does a nice line in *foie de veau aux framboises* with set menus for between 90 and 200 F. It is open all the year but closes every Monday.

Le Chandelier, 3 Rue Leenhardt (tel. 67–92.61.62), has a wonderful way with lobster and herbs and a set menu for 95 F, although this is not available on holidays when the cheapest one costs 190 F. It is closed on Sundays, for lunch on Mondays and all through August.

If you are looking for something really inexpensive, there is no need to go further than the Place de la Comédie. Order a grill at **Le Bison,** or try the couscous at **Le Yam's.** By dint of a little exploration you can start thinking in terms of Greek or Russian dishes, something exotic from Mexico, Japan, North Africa or the South Seas, an American steak or an Italian pizza.

ENTERTAINMENTS
Montpellier does not go in for annual festivals to any great extent, although the grape harvest is celebrated in October, but there is something going on most of the time, especially in the fields of music and drama.

ACTIVITIES
Anyone who feels particularly energetic might be interested in fishing in the River Lez, playing tennis at the Complexe Sportif de Grammont, swimming in any of the four public baths or keeping the children happy by taking them to the local zoo.

TOURIST INFORMATION
The tourist office at 6 Rue Maguelone (tel. 67–58.26.04) will provide details of all current events and advise on the variety of conducted tours both in and out of town.

Carnon-Plage and Palavas

All the way down the coast, stretching approximately from La Grande-Motte to le Cap d'Agde, there are a series of lagoons protected from the sea by a narrow belt of sand. Wherever it widens out enough you will find a coast road linking the various holiday resorts and connected to the mainland at more or less regular intervals. Montpellier has two of these seaside towns practically to itself—Carnon-Plage, which is quite new but growing fast, and Palavas, a well-established fishing port. They have quite a few things in common such as long sandy beaches and sizable marinas that have been designed to meet all the needs of both local and visiting yachtsmen. Each has an individual sea-orientated club which will point you in the right direction if you want to learn to sail, water-ski or skin-dive, go deep-sea fishing or simply take a mini-cruise along the coast. However, Carnon has no boats for hire at the time of writing and has fewer hotels and restaurants from which to choose.

Palavas scores on both these points as well as being more picturesque. The waterway linking it with the lagoon behind is usually lined with fishing boats whose owners draw the crowds by just sitting on board mending their nets or spreading them out on the quay to dry. Shops and cafes line the streets on either side, the former tempting you to buy with boxes of colourful fruit and vegetables or fish that were alive and swimming a few hours before, while the latter are kept busy providing light snacks at very reasonable prices.

There are at least a dozen hotels in the resort, none of which is particularly expensive, and half of them stay open all the year. The local restaurants cater for every taste and pocket while upwards of six camping sites can accommodate about 2500 tents and caravans between them. They open at various times between the beginning of April and the middle of June, but they all close quite firmly in September.

Apart from the advantages of a large, sweeping beach and the promise of 300 sunny days a year, Palavas attracts its visitors with a Festival de Marionnettes in the spring, jousting tournaments using boats instead of horses, nightclubs, discos, a casino and, quite literally, all the fun of the fair.

Maguelone

A short drive or a brisk walk along the sandspit leads to the isolated **Cathedral of Maguelone**. It was a religious centre as long ago as the 3rd century but it fell among thieves and had to be restored and fortified 800 years later. In the 12th century it gave the Pope much-needed sanctuary and in return was elevated to the status of a major religious entity with an enviable reputation for wisdom and generosity. However, sitting out all alone on its little patch of sand, Maguelone was neither very safe nor very lively and gradually the population packed its bags and moved inland. The crunch came during the Wars of Religion and in 1622 Richelieu, who was nothing if not thorough in demolishing errant churches, had all the houses knocked down and the protecting walls removed. The cathedral itself was so strongly built that it managed to survive into the 19th century when the family who owned it had both the sense and the money to do all the work that was needed without spoiling its essential character.

Today the dignified old church stands almost alone, surrounded by trees and vineyards, empty apart from an ancient sarcophagus, some remarkably well-preserved tombs and a great deal of atmosphere. The thick stone walls have all the stubborn appearance of a fortress and by climbing up to the gallery, built half-way up the nave and supported by arches, you can get a pretty good idea of how it looked when the Pope celebrated mass there in the Middle Ages.

Anduze and St-Jean-du-Gard

If you prefer exploring the countryside to lounging on the beach, particularly if you are a railway enthusiast with a day to spare, a trip to Anduze could be right up your street. The town lies due north of Montpellier and is something over an hour's drive away if you take the quickest route up the N110. However, it is more fun to pick any of a dozen small roads that meander past vineyards and tree-covered hills towards the Cévennes. With an occasional pause to admire the view or look round one of the many little villages along the way, you could easily be feeling quite hungry by lunchtime, in which case a good place to eat would be **Le Ranquet.**

The restaurant is on the outskirts of Tornac on the D982, in the direction of St-Hippolyte-du-Fort, and has attractions like a swimming pool to complement the excellent food. Admittedly it is a trifle on the expensive side for a midday break, but you can have a light lunch for 75 F plus service or toy with any number of dishes from the *à la carte* menu at about the same price. Alternatively you can go the whole hog with the Menu Plaisir at 180 F and economise on dinner if necessary.

The **Train à Vapeur des Cévennes** operates from May to September between Anduze and St-Jean-du-Gard, where Robert Louis Stevenson parted from his donkey. The fare is 26 F one way or 38 F return with half-price tickets for children. The fascinating little steam engine puffs its way over rivers and streams, through tunnels and forests and over impressive aqueducts for approximately three-quarters of an hour. It takes a lunch break in St-Jean, or a much shorter rest at each end to turn round at other times, and then trundles back the way it came. The departure times vary according to the day and the season but you can get full details by ringing 66–85.13.17.

Should you decide to stop the night in St-Jean-du-Gard where there are two modest *auberges* and a restaurant with rooms to let, all three specialising in regional dishes, you would have time to visit the **Grotte des Demoiselles** the next day. These fantastic caves are open all the year round but the times vary between winter and summer and there are some evening trips in the season. The best way to ensure that you do not have to wait about is to telephone 67–58.44.12. A funicular carries visitors to the heart of the mountain with hardly a dull moment on the way. The stalactites and stalagmites conjure up endless pictures, provided you give a certain amount of reign to your imagination, the most famous being a likeness of the Virgin and Child in a grotto known as the Cathedral.

Clermont l'Hérault and St-Guilhem-le-Désert

Still on the subject of grottos and the like, the area round Clermont l'Hérault is well worth a visit. It is a pleasant enough little town that is rather short on hotels and restaurants but makes up for it with an attractive old quarter and a 13th-century church. It has a swimming pool, tennis courts and a riding centre, you can walk or cycle to your heart's content, and whichever direction you take there is bound to be something of interest quite close by.

The **Gorges de l'Hérault** makes an ideal starting point with an excellent road that runs along above the river past the famous **Grotte de Clamouse**. The caves plunge for a good half-mile into the mountainside and are full of crystalline deposits and strange formations in a surprising variety of colours. They are open 12 months of the year, 9am to 5 or 6pm during the summer but only on winter afternoons. To find out any other details you have only to ring 67–57.71.05.

Further up the road is St-Guilhem-le-Désert, an old mountain village that goes back to the days of Charlemagne. It is a picturesque jumble of antiquated stone houses clustered round an abbey that was founded by Guilhem in AD 804. Its history is just as chequered as that of other monasteries thereabouts, but it also has a legend that sustained it through the lean and hungry years. The story goes that Guilhem, a childhood friend of Charlemagne's, went to Rome with the Emperor where they met Zacharius. For some reason, apparently unrecorded, he presented Charlemagne with a

Les Gorges de l'Hérault, St-Guilhem-le-Désert

sliver of the Cross which Ste Hélène had left for safekeeping at a church in Jerusalem. The friends decided that it should be kept in the abbey from where it is still paraded through the streets of the village on 3 May every year. The splendid old building has been completely restored and is open to the hundreds of visitors who converge on the village during the summer.

Close to the **Pont du Diable** which jumps the gorge near to the Grotte de Clamouse, just before the river widens out and becomes a great deal more placid, there is a restaurant called **La Bergerie**. It used to have a resident sheep but now each new arrival is greeted by an alsatian that barks furiously but does not mean a word of it. The owner welcomes English visitors with a friendly 'Hallo', a habit he picked up in London where he was training to be a dentist before he decided that he preferred to run a restaurant. If you do not want to eat inside there is a veranda overlooking the gorge with a large open fireplace for grilling the meat and baking potatoes in their jackets. You help yourself from a cold table, drink the local wine and pay only for what you select. There is quite a large parking space, which is more than can be said for the grotto where finding somewhere to leave the car presents quite a problem.

A mile or two outside Clermont l'Hérault in an easterly direction is the **Lac du Salagou**, a man-made expanse of water which is both useful and decorative. Its main purpose. is as a source for irrigation but it is also

183

extremely popular with holidaymakers. The water is on the chilly side, so if you don't feel like swimming you can sail instead. There are no hotels in the immediate vicinity, but if you bring your own tent or caravan, the Camping des Vailhes is clearly visible on the way in. It has a bar and a restaurant as well as facilities for takeaway meals but otherwise is fairly basic. The main drawback is the total lack of trees which comes as a shock to all the dogs that are allowed in provided they are on a leash. Most people who go to Lake Salagou come away with vivid memories of sunbathing on the shore and delightful picnics under large umbrellas but we were not so lucky. It was pouring with rain, the water everyone describes as blue was extremely murky and the red soil all round had dissolved into a series of vermilion puddles. It was so depressing that, if the weather turns sour on you, I would strongly recommend going somewhere else instead.

Mourèze and Salasc

You also need good weather for Mourèze, which is no distance from the lake although you have to get back on to the D908 and watch for the turning, thereby putting a few miles on the clock. Immediately on the right-hand side is the **Bir-Hakeim memorial** commemorating the members of the local Maquis who died in the closing years of the war. It is a faceless statue with folded wings holding a sword and among the 100 or so names listed is the inscription: *'Inconnu tué à la parade État Major Anglais.* Captain Fowler. Alsace 44/45.'

Mourèze is an enchanting village with narrow streets and old stone houses topped by a ruined château and is all but invisible behind a perpendicular rock face. It is totally unspoiled by the new houses which have been built further along the road and in fact gives the impression of disowning them completely. Some of them are very attractive with well-kept colourful gardens set slightly back from a small hotel which has no restaurant and does not allow dogs inside. Charming though the village is, its main attraction is a vast natural amphitheatre known as the **Cirque de Mourèze**. This consists of countless rocks scattered over a considerable area and eroded down the ages into weird and wonderful shapes like the Head of the Devil, the Serpent and the Sphinx. It is interesting—and time-consuming—to clamber about the scrubland for a closer look, although the local people maintain that it shows to the best advantage at sunrise or in the late afternoon.

The road through Mourèze carries on to Salasc where you can pause for refreshments, buy some pottery and wander round under the trees. From there it is simply a matter of rejoining the D908, heading for the D15 which zig-zags across the country and selecting any of the minor roads which will take you eventually to Pézenas. If you stop at all, possibly to look at the rows of young vines pushing their way up through long strips of black plastic, the chances are that you will see and hear dozens of birds which seem to put in hours of choral practice every day.

Pézenas

Pézenas is famous mainly because it is a place where time stands still and has done so for the last three centuries. Nobody invites you to inspect the ruins for the simple reason that there are none to be seen anywhere. The Romans, who originally fortified the town, have disappeared without trace and so have the generations who lived and died there during the next 1400 years. A few 15th-century houses have survived, largely because they were considered grand enough to be included in Le Prince de Conti's 'Versailles-du-Languedoc'. While he was Governor of the region, Pézenas underwent a dramatic change with the mansions of noblemen springing up like mushrooms and Molière staying at the home of Gély, the barber, in order to get material for his plays. Everything was in apple-pie order when the Prince died in 1666 and the town, like Rip van Winkle, immediately fell into a deep and dreamless sleep.

WHAT TO SEE
The extraordinary charm of Pézenas lies in the fact that the old quarter is exactly as the Prince left it with the same heavy doors and wrought-iron balconies gazing at each other across one street after another. There is no need for a town plan to pinpoint an ancient cathedral or a fabulous palace, both of which are non-existent, but the route map supplied free of charge by the Syndicat d'Initiative comes in very useful. It leads by numbers from mansion to mansion, pointing out their various claims to fame, whether architectural or historic.

Numbering the sights is a particularly happy idea because you cannot make any mistakes as you move off from the Place du 14-Juillet where, incidentally, there is room to park the car with a statue of Molière to keep an eye on it. Along the way you will see the house where he lived, opposite the

185

16th-century Tribunal de Commerce, and also the Hôtel d'Alfonce where his plays were staged during the winter of 1655–6. If, having admired the fountain with its four little cherubs riding dolphins, you are pulled up short by the sight of a yellow postbox, try to ignore it. Apart from cars and people in modern dress it is one of the few things that bring you back to the present with a jolt. This is borne out by the fact that French film makers have used Pézenas for several years and it is still liable to appear on the cinema screen if any of them need an authentic setting instead of going to the trouble of building one.

When you lose count of all the different courtyards, splendid staircases and decorative stonework, which is extremely likely because there are more than 70 classified buildings in a very small area, you can take a breather in the **Musée de Vulliod-St-Germain**. Among the items on show are banners, tapestries and sculptures, to say nothing of the archives that go back about 1000 years. It is the only place of historic interest in Pézenas where you have to pay to get in and it costs 3 F. The museum is open from 10am until noon and from 2pm to 7pm in the summer but closes at 5pm between October and May, on Mondays in the winter and on Tuesdays throughout the year as well as on public holidays.

Pézenas has more local craftsmen than you will find anywhere else in the area with the possible exception of Cordes. They turn out everything from pottery and glasswear to jewellery and wrought iron, they work with leather and pewter and have pictures, sculptures and some beautifully embroidered clothes for sale. The tiny shops that look out from under old stone archways are a treasure trove of souvenirs which very few tourists can resist.

WHERE TO STAY AND EATING OUT

Strangely enough there is a dearth of hotels and restaurants in Pézenas, but if you care to drive a short distance down the N113 you will come to **Valros** and the **Auberge de la Tour.** There is nothing memorable about the outside but the hotel is becoming so popular that you may well have to book in advance. The rooms all look out over vineyards at the back of the building so you have no problems with traffic noise from the main raod. The dining room is spacious with an open fire for cool evenings and the food is excellent whether you go for a set menu costing up to 160 F or something more expensive *à la carte* accompanied by Coteaux du Languedoc, the recommended house wine. Monsieur Grasset, his family and staff are kindness itself and nothing is too much trouble, even if they are being run off their feet. The price of a double room is 160 F and pension terms are available up

186

to 286 F. The *auberge* is closed in November and the restaurant on Wednesdays except during July and August. If you want to telephone ahead, the number is 67–98.52.01.

Failing Valros you could stop at **Montagnac,** to the north of Pézenas, which is also on the N113 after it branches off towards the coast. There is a church spire which, for some reason, brings to mind a witch's hat and a similarly priced *auberge* called **Les Rocailles.** It would then be a pity not to visit Sète. The road carries on straight to **Mèze,** where you will find 15th-century church but not much else of interest, and turns sharply to run along the side of the Bassin du Thau. Not only does this give you an uninterrupted view of the oyster beds stretching far out into the lagoon, but you can also stop at any of the little stalls beside the road at **Bouzigues** to buy oysters and mussels for lunch.

Sète

Sète is both a busy port and a popular holiday town, especially where British visitors are concerned. It was built in the 17th century to handle traffic using the recently completed Canal du Midi that still links the Atlantic with the Mediterranean. Obviously the town has expanded considerably since then and now covers a number of small islands separated by canals that are usually crammed with pleasure boats and commercial craft. One seems to spend a lot of time driving backwards and forwards across the various bridges, although there is no need to do more than head straight down the Quai de Bosc, beside the main canal, to reach the old port. In addition to its deep involvement in the export of wine and petro-chemicals, Sète is the largest fishing port on the Mediterranean coast and the ancient harbour is mainly reserved for boats unloading quantities of sardines, tunny and the like, maintaining their equipment and preparing for the next trip.

During the summer the roads on either side of the Canal du Midi are thronged with people shopping for run-of-the-mill articles, sitting outside the cafes or taking a gentle constitutional. This quite often includes the Môle St-Louis, where there is a good view back towards the town and across to Mont St-Clair, and the **Paul-Valéry Museum** which overlooks the cemetery where the poet is buried. It is a modern building that divides the focus of attention between Valéry, who was born in Sète, and artists of the calibre of Cézanne, Manet and Renoir. It is open from 10am to noon and from 2pm to 6pm but closes an hour early between October and March as well as on Tuesdays and public holidays.

For about a month during the summer the port entertains visitors and residents alike with its annual Festival of the Sea. Covered stands appear along the quay without really spoiling the view from the lines of straight-fronted houses behind, and two boats, painted red and blue respectively and manned by ten oarsmen apiece, are manoeuvred into position for the jousting tournaments. Armed with shields and lances and perched on platforms over the stern, two warriors attempt to unbalance each other and although each team has its supporters the sight of either body plunging into the canal sends the entire audience into paroxysms of delight. Other entertainments are also laid on, including an open-air theatre festival at the **Fort St-Pierre** on the Route de la Corniche.

There are several hotels and restaurants in Sète, both in the town itself and out along the Corniche, ranging in price from 180 to 400F for a double room and 55 to 200F for a set menu. Many of them close for at least a month during the winter but you will always be able to find a bed for the night and somewhere to eat unless the resort is crowded to capacity.

Cap d'Agde

The coast road continues on its leisurely way down the sandspit to Cap d'Agde which really prides itself on being a modern holiday centre. The marina, divided into sections, can accommodate nearly 2000 boats and supply most of them with their own water and electricity. Everything like repairs, fuel and chandlers can be had for the asking and so can boat trips, sea fishing, diving and water-skiing. The marine club (tel. 67–94.76.21), will give advice on all these and supply details of the local sailing school. Boats can be hired, you can ride and play tennis and spend the evening at a night club or a disco. When you have exhausted all these possibilities, visited Aqualand and decided for or against hiring a bicycle or a pedalo, you might give a thought to the beaches. On the northern side you will find an unbroken stretch of sand nearly the whole way to Sète, deserted apart from Marseillan Plage, backed by the road, the railway line and the lagoon, but sadly devoid of any shade so it is necessary to provide your own. In the opposite direction the beach is just as sandy with no coast road and only an occasional pin-point of civilisation before it reaches the Hérault River with the pleasant little resort of Tamarissière on the far side.

Cap d'Agde is typical of all the new *ports de plaisance* springing up along the coast, leaving you with the impression of colour which, at the moment, does not include a lot of green. The buildings are very new, so much so that notices offering flats and villas for sale are everywhere. The walls are flat and painted in shades of cream, pink, dull yellow, old gold and dusky rose and look for all the world like a cardboard cut-out designed for a puppet version of *Beau Geste* or *The Desert Song*. There is a tendency to compare these new and often unfinished towns with places like La Grande-Motte, deploring their lack of vegetation and absence of character, but when all the building is finished and the parks have taken root they should be equally attractive in their own individual ways.

WHERE TO STAY AND EATING OUT

As far as hotels go, Cap d'Agde has a round dozen or thereabouts including some fairly large ones like the **Golf** on the Ile des Loisirs (tel. 67–26.72.40) where you can arrive just as easily by boat as by car and tie up in the marina alongside. It is open from mid-March to mid-November, charges 399 F and has a restaurant on the premises where the cheapest menu is 140 F. As a change from eating in sea-front cafes you would undoubtedly appreciate dinner at the restaurant **Les Trois Sergents** at the Hôtel St-Clair, another of the larger establishments. It is closed on Sunday evenings and on Mondays from October to June and puts up the shutters completely during December and January. To book a table, which would probably be necessary in the summer, ring 67–26.73.13. However, if you want to contact the hotel itself the number is 67–26.36.44. The set menus range from 65 to 130 F.

Agde

The town of Agde, a short drive away, is one of the most ancient in France, having been founded by the Greeks from Marseilles who called it Agathe, meaning 'Good Place'. The 12th-century **Cathedral of St-Étienne**, with its massive stone tower, is more than usually sombre, mainly because it was built with black lava from Mont St-Loup, an extinct volcano overlooking the town. A solid, heavily fortified building on the banks of the river, the cathedral gives the impression of being a prison rather than a church. This is hardly to be wondered at since one of its original functions was to provide a refuge for the villagers and, if necessary, withstand a siege. There was even a hole in the roof of the nave through which the defenders could be supplied with food, water and ammunition.

You can spend a very enjoyable hour or so exploring the town, particularly the old quarter where several houses are also built of lava, making the narrow streets darker than they would otherwise be. As an alternative, there is a lot to be said for an idle saunter along the river banks. In some places they are lined with trees, in others with typical weather-worn houses, and all the way along fishing boats by the dozen are tied up to heavy bollards set in to the old stone quays. You might also spare a moment, if you have one, to visit the **Musée d'Agathois,** in the Rue de la Fraternité, which is closed on Tuesdays and will cost you 5 F. It was founded just before the last war and includes an interesting collection of local costumes as well as several reminders of the early days of the town.

If you are hoping to find a reasonably large hotel with all that implies, you will have to go back to Cap d'Agde, but if you are quite happy with something smaller and perfectly comfortable there are at least half a dozen scattered around the town. However, most people prefer a room by the sea and you would probably be happier if you followed their example.

The countryside round Agde is peppered with camping sites, some quite up-market, others rather basic with little to offer apart from a convenient beach. Several people have reported favourably on La Carabasse south of Vias, where you can not only take your own equipment but also hire a tent complete with beds, a gas stove and a small fridge. There is a restaurant and a shop carrying all the usual items where you will also find everything you need in the way of fresh produce and local wines at realistic prices. Facilities for recreation include tennis courts, horses and a swimming pool, and there are organised entertainments referred to by some campers as a blessing but described by others in less complimentary terms.

Florensac and St-Thibéry

Any of the minor roads, especially those within nodding distance of the river, make a pleasant afternoon's drive or give you a good excuse for a picnic. The small towns like Florensac and St-Thibéry are full of character and there is usually something going on in the way of a market or a display of local craftsmanship. You are bound to find a cafe round the corner where the atmosphere is cheerful and food is available, even if there is nothing outstanding on the menu. Should this idea not appeal to you, the answer is to time your arrival in Florensac to coincide with lunch. The **Hôtel Léonce** (tel. 67–77.03.05) in the Place République puts on a good table for anything from 100 to 180 F.

None of these little villages offers anything in the historic monument line: for that you will have to go on to Béziers. As it is one of those places that should really be seen for the first time from a special vantage point, you would be well advised to make a detour through the vineyards and approach it by way of the N113 from Narbonne.

Béziers

The main reason for creeping up on Béziers from the south is that you get such an unforgettable view of the Cathedral of St-Nazaire. Its fortified walls appear to grow straight up out of the rock with a necklace of red-roofed houses separating it from the River Orb. One way in is over a heavy 13th-century stone bridge which complements the whole scene to perfection. It would be logical to assume that the cathedral is the focal point from every direction, but anyone approaching from the north could be forgiven for overlooking it altogether, or a any rate until it was too late to appreciate it fully.

HISTORY

Béziers is definitely not inundated with ancient churches, museums and monuments and, to the casual observer, has apparently forgotten that it existed before the Romans arrived. They established a small colony but, as far as one can see, did not think it worth putting up much in the way of buildings, baths and trophies. They must have had a forum and at least a couple of temples to placate the gods, but no one is very sure where they were, although a likely place is thought to be the site of the 18th-century town hall. Nor is anyone profoundly interested in the comings and goings of the next 1200 years, preferring instead to concentrate on a wholesale massacre that swept the town into history at the beginning of the 13th century.

As usual the trouble was firmly based in religion. A particular sect which called itself Christian but disagreed violently with everything held sacred by the Church of Rome had moved into Béziers in large numbers from Albi, on the River Tarn. The Albigenses, as they were called, did not accept a single word of the New Testament and had little time for the Old Testament either, believing that the world had been created by the devil and the only hope of redemption lay in renouncing the pleasures of the flesh

191

altogether. The Popes tolerated this for close on 200 years and then decided that something drastic would have to be done. In 209 Simon de Montfort the Elder led a crusade against the sect and started with a flourish by capturing Béziers. The entire population of 20 000 men, women and children, Catholic and disbelievers alike, were slaughtered. The cleaning-up operation in Languedoc lasted for another 20 years, but it was not until their stronghold at Mont Ségur was eventually captured in 1245 that the Albigenses were totally eliminated.

After the massacre Béziers was accepted back into the fold. Life there went on rather more quietly until the 17th century when Paul Riquet, who was born there in 1604, had the bright idea of building the Canal du Midi. This nudged the town into the age of commerce which it accepts in a half-hearted sort of way without making a great thing of industrial development.

WHAT TO SEE
The old part of the town does not stand out as a masterpiece of urban planning, but if you are prepared to walk about, or drive from one place to another in the hope of finding a parking place when you want one, you should not be disappointed. The most important church is without a doubt, the **Cathedral of St-Nazaire** which suffered considerably at the time of the massacre but was quickly rebuilt and has been well maintained ever since. It has a number of beautiful stained-glass windows and the usual collection of tombs, workmanlike cloisters and a magnificent view from the terrace across miles of vineyards to a line of distant hills.

The **Musée du Vieux Biterrois** in the Rue Massol has an archaeological section, goes very deeply into the history of wine and instructs visitors in the folklore of the region. If it is pictures you are after, have a look round the **Fine Arts Museum** in the Place de la Revolution which also has an extensive collection of Greek vases. Both of them are open from 9am to noon and from 2pm to 6pm. The former closes at 5pm in the winter, on Mondays and on public holidays, while the latter is closed on Sunday mornings, Mondays and on 1 and 2 January, 14 July, 1 and 2 and 11 November and on Christmas Day.

Life in the town centres round the Allées Paul-Riquet, a tree-lined promenade starting from the Plateau des Poètes, a garden that takes its name from the statues which are dotted about, and ending at the theatre 460 metres (500 yards) away. Somewhere approximately in the middle is a statue of Paul Riquet, booted if not spurred, clutching what looks like a roll of drawings and patently deep in thought. There is nothing special about the shops and at least one bank may throw you out at closing time, even if you have been waiting for some while in the queue. Of course, a successful raid on their branch in Perpignan shortly before this happened could have made them unusually jumpy, so perhaps one should give them the benefit of the doubt.

WHERE TO STAY

You should not have too much trouble finding a hotel in Béziers because there are many to chose from with a proportion, ranging from the expensive to the modest, either on or near to the Allées Paul-Riquet. Many of them do not bother about a restaurant but one exception to the rule is the **Hôtel du Midi,** 13 Rue de la Coquille (tel. 67–49.13.43), which is across the street from the theatre. It charges up to 300 F a night and closes for about three weeks from the middle of November.

EATING OUT

Apart from the restaurant **La Rascasse,** at the Hôtel du Midi, which is open throughout August but closes on Sundays during the rest of the year and charges up to 120 F for a set menu, you might try the **Brasserie Ragueneau** (tel. 67–28.35.17), a little further down the Allées Paul-Riquet on the same side. You can eat there for as little as 82 F and watch the world go by at the same time.

SPECTACLES AND ENTERTAINMENTS

The first half of August is the time for bull-fighting in Béziers when a whole programme of events is staged in the arena. It is built on Roman lines with tiers of seats looking down on to the ring but, unlike the ones at Nîmes and Arles, it has no pretensions as a tourist attraction in the historical sense.

If you happen to be in town on the third Sunday in October, you will find crowds celebrating the wine harvest and trying to deplete existing stocks as far as possible. To absorb local colour at other times of the year you might drop in at the Sunday-morning market at which the shopping is done under cover or at any of the open-air stalls round about.

TOURIST INFORMATION

The information office is at 27 rue 4 septembre (tel. 67–49.24.19).

Valras-Plage

The nearest coastal resort to Béziers is Valras-Plage, another up-and-coming seaside town that is bound to improve with age. At the moment it is a carbon copy of all the rest with superb beaches, a comparatively small but efficient marina and as many holiday attractions as the authorities have been able to get together in the time. The countryside around is extremely flat and not of any great interest unless you happen to be a glutton for agriculture but, because Valras is at the mouth of the Orb, anyone who dislikes the idea of putting to sea can hire a boat and have a splendid time messing about on the river. The hotels and restaurants are of the typical seaside variety and if you look round carefully it is possible to enjoy a good meal for less than 55 F.

Oppidium d'Ensérune

In complete contrast, any visitor who feels like wallowing in antiquity should put aside enough time to see Oppidium d'Ensérune, off the main Béziers–Narbonne road. It is all that remains of a settlement that existed in approximately 800 BC and was a place of some importance more than 100 years before the Romans started to clean up the population with swords and public baths. Excavations have uncovered enough to show how the inhabitants lived and a museum, built on the site, has an interesting collection of finds, the most modern of which are bits and pieces left lying about by the Greeks.

On a clear day it is possible to look across from Ensérune to Mont Canigou, far away to the south near the Spanish border. It is a magnificent sight, particularly if you see it covered with snow in the late spring as we did. However, nothing is ever quite perfect in this world and under these conditions a bitter wind plays havoc with the young vines and causes serious trouble to people towing caravans. We saw three blown over in the space of a mile; if you find yourself having to cope with these conditions, it really would be wise to follow the example of the heavy transport drivers and pull into the lee of a house or a sturdy row of trees until the worst is over.

It does not seem to matter when you go or where you go: people always trot out the observation that the weather is exceptional, by which they usually mean exceptionally awful. In this case the oldest inhabitant, undoubtedly somebody's great-grandmother with bad eyesight and an even worse memory, insisted that she had never seen anything like it in her life. Snow was unheard of except in the mountains and not even at those altitudes in the spring. The local paper could not have consulted her on the subject because it had pictures of a young man busy clearing inches of snow off the cafe tables where it had settled during the night. Our well-informed hotel owner said the conditions were unusual but far from unique and that, at certain times, strong winds rushing down from the mountains take an annual toll of caravans that are driven too fast or in circumstances that are obviously dangerous. However, you should not let any of this put you off travelling out of season. Provided you take your time and are prepared for the occasional strong gust, you will arrive in Narbonne quite safely, as literally thousands of other motorists have been doing for years.

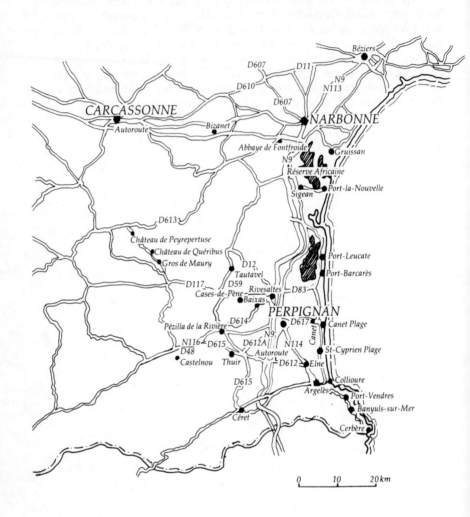

NARBONNE TO CERBÈRE

Chapter IX

NARBONNE TO CERBÈRE

La Cité at Carcassonne

Narbonne

Although Narbonne is no larger than Béziers, its history is considerably more impressive. This is possibly because the Romans got it off to a good start and succeeding generations took the trouble to preserve as much as they could and add a few touches of their own for good measure. The town is quite open-plan compared with its contemporaries, and the Canal de la Robine running through the middle is a tranquil place to pause and take stock of your surroundings.

HISTORY
After making a modest start in about 100 BC Narbonne soon became a flourishing port, providing the Romans with all the supplies they needed from wood and oil to butter, meat and cheese. in return it received buildings

197

by the score until the town was sufficiently important to have a whole province attached to it and to compete for the title of first city of Roman Gaul. Naturally the Saracens were envious and when the legions moved out they moved in, totally destroying everything in their path.

In the years that followed Narbonne continued to be a rich prize in any war that happened to be raging at the time, but on each occasion it picked itself up and continued more or less where it left off. In the 12th century the troubadour Bertrand de Bar sang of great ships with rich cargoes keeping it in a constant state of prosperity. Human nature being what it is, wealth created power and power fostered ambition, so it was not surprising that the local nobility got ideas above even their elevated station. The young Cinq-Mars, not content with an important position at court and the friendship of Louis XIII, decided to pit his wits against Richelieu. When the French laid siege to Perpignan, which was a Spanish possession at the time, he opened up secret negotiations with Spain, Richelieu got his hands on the paperwork and Cinq-Mars was beheaded in 1642.

By that time nature had started to take a hand and the gulf on which Narbonne's value as a port depended was silting up at an alarming rate. It is now a series of lagoons enclosed by sandspits with the Canal de la Robine running through them to meet the sea at Port-la-Nouvelle.

WHAT TO SEE
The only evidence of Roman occupation to be seen in Narbonne nowadays is part of the canal bridge leading to the Place de l'Hôtel de Ville and a large number of old pieces of stone preserved in the appropriate museum. They are no doubt fascinating if you can tell one from the other, but to the uninitiated it is easy to see how builders in the Middle Ages carried them off thankfully to complete a new palace or a contemporary church.

If you overlook a mere handful of exceptions, the main places of interest are all of a piece with the Hôtel de Ville and include the anything-but-self-effacing palaces of the Archbishops, said to have inspired the Palace of the Popes at Avignon. The **Cathedral of St-Just**, which is also included, was planned on a monumental scale to take the place of a 4th-century church. It had the blessing of Pope Clement IV, a previous Archbishop of Narbonne, who sent over a foundation stone by way of encouragement. For one reason or another it was never completed, which is unfortunate because it would have ranked among the most splendid buildings of its kind in France. As it is one has to settle for the choir, the cloisters and very little else, but these alone are worth a visit. Because they never got round to building the nave, the vaulted roof seems much too high, but there is nothing wrong with the beautiful stained-glass windows, the rich tapestries or the intricately carved marble tombs. Other treasures are kept under lock and key and you can see them during the season between 9am and noon or from 2pm to 6pm for the price of 1 F. During the winter you have to rush round looking for someone to open the door. The way out is through the cloisters and down some steps into the Passage de l'Ancre, which separates the old 12th-century palace on the left and the new 14th-century palace opposite.

To reach the **Museum of Art and History** it is necessary to climb up a broad stairway to the State Apartments, trying not to envy the Archbishops who did it with much less effort on a mule. The **Archaeological Museum** is in the same palace and there are all sorts of rooms and courtyards to be visited and admired. A fact-finding tour will lead you from prehistoric times through the Stone, Bronze and Iron Ages to the days of the Romans. There are a great many items recalling the splendour of the Middle Ages, an outstanding collection of pottery and a considerable number of pictures and statues. The whole place, including the crypt of the cathedral, is open from 15 May to the end of September from 10am to noon and from 2pm to 6pm. It is closed on Mondays for the rest of the year and also on 1 January, 1 May, 14 July, 1 November and Christmas Day. The ticket, costing 3 F, also takes you into the Musée Lapidaire and the Horreum which share the same opening hours.

On the opposite side of the canal, about a block from the Place des Pyrénées, you will find the ancient church of St Paul which can trace its history back to the 4th century. As well as many conventional treasures it has a marble frog sitting happily in a basin of holy water. There are some rather far-fetched versions of how it got there but I liked the attitude of a young priest who, when asked 'Why the frog?', replied simply, 'Why not?'

A little further along the Rue de l'Hôtel Dieu is the 16th-century Maison des Trois Nourrices where Cinq-Mars is said to have been arrested.

WHERE TO STAY
If you want to spend the night in Narbonne, you could do a lot worse than put up at the **Hôtel Midi** which is very conveniently placed at 4 Avenue Toulouse (tel. 68–41.04.62). There is somewhere to park, the top price for a double room is 165 F and the restaurant has a set menu for as little as 43 F. However, the hotel is closed from the middle of December for a month and on Sundays between mid-October and the end of April, and the restaurant

is shut at midday and on Sundays from the beginning of October to the end of May.

There are plenty of camping sites in the vicinity but for a long stay the best are probably at Narbonne Plage. You might try the **Camping Municipal La Falaise** (tel. 68–49.80.77), which is on the D168. It has a restaurant, shop and bar with individual sites and most of the usual facilities including a swimming pool, although the beach is not all that far away.

EATING OUT

If you are looking for something a little out of the ordinary try the lobster or the duck at **Réverbère** (tel. 68–32.29.18) in the Place Jacobines, just off the canal. It is closed in February and on Sunday nights and Mondays. Set menus are available here for 145 to 220F.

It is only a short drive from Narbonne to the coast, whether you head for Narbonne Plage, which is quite an ordinary sort of place, or for Gruissan, which is not. To reach either of them you have to skirt the Montagne de la Clape, a limestone ridge that is arid and uninviting but commands an excellent view if you can be bothered to climb the 213 metres (700ft) or so to the top.

Gruissan

At Gruissan you have a wide choice of atmosphere and it would be possible to meet two families who had stayed there and decide that one or other had got all the facts wrong. In the first place the whole town is surrounded by water but only a very small part of its gets to within sight or sound of the Mediterranean. The old section consists of an island that is, to all intents and purposes, a perfect circle jutting out into the lagoon. The ruined castle, perched on a rock at the top, is surrounded by trees with paths threading their way up to the summit. Below this are concentric rings of old houses, all with the usual terracotta roofs and flat, bland faces, surrounded in turn by stone quays with boats tied up alongside. It is fun to wander about, but if that sort of thing does not amuse you there is no reason why you should go anywhere near it.

A long straight road cuts across a sandspit to the sea where there is a wide expanse of beach and a good deal of evidence that development is under way, but one could be forgiven for thinking that it is a dreary, inhospitable sort of place with nothing much to recommend it. It is only when you explore a little further that you find the town with all its promised holiday attractions. There are modern buildings grouped together on small square-shaped islands with plenty of open spaces everywhere, not many hotels at the moment but an assortment of cafes and a handful of camping sites. For yachtsmen there are marinas with room for about 700 boats and all facilities to keep both the craft and the crews in prime condition. The Yacht Club (tel. 68–49.01.30) is the place to go for advice on everything from water-skiing to windsurfing and you can hire a boat, play tennis, fish and ride before living it up in the evening at a casino, disco, nightclub or cinema.

There is no coast road from Gruissan to the south so you have to retrace your steps towards Narbonne, a most convenient state of affairs if you have a mind to visit the **Abbey of Fontfroide**, a truly splendid building encased in trees and guarding the entrance to a gorge. It was founded in the 11th century and became a Cistercian monastery about 100 years later. For the next 600 years it behaved exactly like any other religious centre, dabbling in power games and politics and reaping the attendant penalties and rewards until it finally came to grief in 1791. The work of restoration began early in this century and it is now on a par with other famous monasteries like the Abbaye du Thoronet in Provence. A conducted tour leads visitors through the Grande Salle into an open courtyard named after Louis XIV, on to the cloisters which are some of the loveliest in southern France, and ends in the ancient church. The price is 9 F and the building is open from 9am to noon and from 2.30pm to 6pm between April and September. For the rest of the year the times are 9.30am to noon and 2pm to 5pm any day except Tuesday.

Bizanet

When you have had your money's worth, or if you arrive just before lunch and have a longish time to wait, you could picnic in the forest and then climb up to see the ruins of the **Château of St Martin-de-Toques** a mile or two away. Being a bit short on energy we gave them a miss and followed a series of tiny roads to Bizanet, to be given a lesson on the stupidity of judging a restaurant from the outside. A few steps and a glass door separate the local *auberge* from the Rue de Paris. Inside a fruit machine was causing much hilarity around the place. The owner rustled up some wine and sandwiches from a bar-counter inside the entrance and removed a pile of papers from a solitary table near the door. During the course of conversation it turned out that he was a local hunter and the *spécialités de la maison* included wild boar and *canard à l'orange flambé au Grand-Marnier*, to mention only two. A door led through into a rustic dining room where the walls were decorated with guns and a boar's head gazed out above an open fireplace over which he and his kind were roasted. In the corner was an extremely modern disco that was demonstrated loudly and enthusiastically for our benefit. The sole occupant of the room was an elderly American who had obviously escaped from his usual round of conducted tours to mop up a little local colour and he clearly objected to the intrusion. As the rhythms of a very lively pop group reverberated round the old stone walls he looked up and observed to no one in particular, 'I never did believe in all that crap about the walls of Jericho but I sure do now!' The restaurant **Chez Jumbo** in the **Auberge de Bizanet** is open all the year and its telephone number is 68–45.16.13.

People whose idea of a perfect holiday is exploring out-of-the-way places on their own will find any number of little towns and villages to interest them, some with an ancient building or two, others hardly large enough to support the small cafe where refreshments do not go much beyond coffee, beer and the local wine. On the whole the roads are good but there are some very minor ones indeed that wander about aimlessly, come on an isolated farm or vineyard and give up the unequal struggle altogether. This is particularly true up in the mountains where the interminable streams and rivers have etched deep grooves for themselves, creating grottos and outstanding views at the same time. It is not hard to believe the odd story of strange goings-on in the backwoods or an occasional hint of sorcery as long as it comes from someone not patiently drawing on his imagination to keep the tourists happy.

Minerve

When historical facts exert a stronger appeal than local superstitions, a good place to visit is Minerve, an ancient fortress in the Gorges de la Cesse. It was built on a rocky outcrop beside the river towards the end of the 9th century but got involved in the crusade against the Albigensians, provided refuge for the heretics and was sacked by Simon de Montfort in 1210. A small section of the ramparts still exists alongside a tiny church with an altar dated 456 that is said to be the oldest in the country. A little museum, open every day from 9am to noon and 2pm until 7pm and costing 2F a head has got together quite a reasonable collection of fossils and antique remains discovered in the area. A road circles the town and provides a short cut to Lézignan-Corbières on the main road to Carcassonne.

Carcassonne

If you feel inclined to visit this famous city, the drive will only take another half an hour but do not go along thinking that you are about to discover a genuine medieval masterpiece because you are not. The truth is that the town was reconstructed in the 1840s, shortly after the powers that be had inspected the ruins and decided that the best plan would be to get rid of them altogether. However, the decision was overruled and work started on re-creating the city built by St Louis in 1240 and partly burned down by the Black Prince in 1355. Seekers after the unvarnished truth tend to dismiss it as little more than a copy, but that is totally unfair.

The original city was important enough to be attacked by Charlemagne who kept up a siege that lasted for five years. Legend has it that Lady Carcas, the widow of the last Saracen governor, fed the sole remaining pig with the last of the grain and pushed it over the battlements. The unfortunate animal burst on impact, scattering its lunch all round and thus giving the impression that nobody inside was starving. Discussions were called for to the triumphant cries of 'Carcas sonne!'. However, the fortress did not escape as lightly in the crusade of 1209 and gave so much trouble to St Louis that he arranged things to his own satisfaction 30 years later.

Time and the introduction of the cannon proved to be its eventual downfall but enough of the ruins remained to enable the architect, Viollet-le-Duc, to recreate it as it was in the 12th century. Perhaps it is just a little too perfect and too commercialised but, as a close friend observed recently, it is better to see it like that than not at all. The main sights are the **Château Comtal** and the **Basilique St-Nazaire,** for most people, though, the attraction of Carcassonne is that it is all there.

Sigean and Port-la-Nouvelle

From Carcassonne you can go on to Perpignan, by autoroute if necessary, or double back to the coast. Either way, when you skirt the Étangs de Bages et de Sigean keep a look out for the **Réserve Africaine** a few miles north of Sigean. It is a most enjoyable place to pass an idle hour, starting off with a slow ride round the first enclosure where white rhinoceros and Tibetan bears live side by side in apparent harmony. The speed limit is 11 kilometres

(7 miles) an hour and you are warned to keep the windows closed and not to leave your car. The same applies next door where lions roam about freely in the vicinity of a small lagoon. You can spend as much time as you like watching them, which is entertaining if they are awake and playful but can get monotonous if they are all asleep in the long grass. An equally large area of parkland is set aside for the more conventional type of zoo where you can see dozens of different animals gathered from far and wide. Elephants trumpet at the camels next door, giraffes look down on ugly little Vietnamese pigs and alligators gaze longingly at the thousands of birds which have a lake all to themselves. You will find plenty of parking space, a cafeteria and two bars as well as a souvenir shop that will replace your film when it runs out. Nor is there any objection to your using the special picnic spot, always provided you do not feed the animals or leave your rubbish lying about. The reserve is open from 9am to 6.30pm in the summer and from 10am to 4.30pm between October and March. It costs 27 F per adult and 16 F for each child.

WHERE TO STAY AND EATING OUT

Rather than stop in Sigean, where none of the hotels looks at all inviting, I would be inclined to go on to the **Méditerranée** (tel. 68–48.03.08) on the front at Port-la-Nouvelle. Although the town is too new and too industrialised to rate as a leading holiday resort, the beach is magnificent and the hotel rooms looking out over the sea are quiet and comfortable. A bright and breezy young man takes your car round to a secure parking place, probably remarking with the confidence of an expert, 'Very nice, but you come with a Rolls-Royce next time.' The restaurant, also looking out on the sea, specialises in local dishes as well as providing set menus for 55 F and upwards. It pays to take the advice of the staff when ordering because if you do not everybody else's dinner looks so much more exciting than your own. The hotel is closed from the third week in November until Christmas and charges up to 225 F a night.

Port-Leucate

If you want something more than just good food, a comfortable room and a sandy beach, follow the N9 down to the point where there is a sign off to Port-Leucate and Port-Barcarès. The former is yet another of the new resorts, poised on the sandspit between the lagoon and the sea, which is doing its best to catch up but still has quite a way to go. The buildings follow the usual pattern and there is a choice of marinas that collectively provide all the necessary goods and services for more than 1000 boats. Three hotels are all the town can muster apart from one reserved for nudists who have a special area all to themselves with holiday flats, seaside cafes and a swimming pool. Some clothing is required for playing tennis, riding horses or bicycles and travelling in the little rubber-tyred train. Entertainments are laid on for children during the day and there is an open-air cinema and two nightclubs for their parents when the sun goes down.

Port-Barcarès

Port-Barcarès is making even greater strides towards becoming a sandspit metropolis but at the moment it is more like a series of tiny villages scattered about on islands between the sea and the lagoon. It has spread itself out deliberately, leaving plenty of open space for trees that are coming along nicely, tennis courts both covered and uncovered, swimming pools and parking spaces. Whatever you want to do, whether you are young or not so young, energetic or lazy, a beginner or an expert, you will find exactly what you are looking for. You can learn to sail anything from a dinghy to an authentic Catalan barque, to say nothing of water-skiing, for which all the necessary equipment is supplied for beginners and the only stipulation is that you can swim.

Anyone who prefers wheels to water can learn the art of driving a four-wheel-drive vehicle over rugged country at prices ranging from 450 F for half a day to 1600 F that cover two days, one night, breakfast and three other meals. If you simply want to try your hand for half an hour, it will set you back 100 F. Horses can be hired for 50 F an hour, up to 300 F for an all-day pony trek. Should you simply want to look round the town, the Barcarès Express with its open carriages is more amusing than driving yourself. Organised entertainments include a marine zoo, sardine barbecues where all the work is done by local fishermen, and traditional evenings when the accent is on folklore and colourful firework displays.

One thing that distinguishes Port-Barcarès from all the other seaside resorts is a large white liner rejoicing in the name of *Lydia*. Thirty years ago she operated between Marseilles and Beirut but eventually she was retired, given a sand berth on the beach and became part-night club, part-casino and part-exhibition hall. Someone has added artificial waves to balance the authentic lifeboats on the upper deck and when the occasion warrants it she is dressed overall. There are marinas dotted about with facilities for several hundred boats in additional to individual moorings attached to some of the holiday flats which have their own waterfronts.

WHERE TO STAY
There is a choice of half a dozen hotels, only one of which is open throughout the year.

The **Lydia Playa** (tel. 68–86.25.25) is large and comfortable, looks out over the sea and provides both indoor and outdoor swimming and its own tennis courts. You will pay up to 390 F a night and anything from 65 to 130 F for a set menu. The hotel is closed from the beginning of October until the end of April. Most people, however, prefer to rent a house or an apartment, while others bring their own tents and caravans. The sites for the latter range from two- to four-star, a couple staying open all the year, with attractions that can be anything from a football pitch to equipment for hire or a bungalow to let. For information about excursions and any other details you need simply contact the **tourist office** on the sea front (tel. 68–86.16.56).

EXPLORING THE AREA
One place that figures on nearly every list of important sights is the great **Fort de Salses** on the other side of the lagoon. Standing all by itself, well below ground level, it marks the site of a Roman camp on the Via Domitia. Legend has it that Hercules passed close by but history, dealing in fact rather than fantasy, will not go further back than Hannibal who was there in 218 BC. Nothing remains from Roman times but traces have been found of a 12th-century castle that pre-dates the existing fort by some 300 years. Intended as a garrison for 1500 men, the fort consists of a giant parade ground surrounded by barrack-type buildings and watched over by circular towers. It takes about an hour to walk round accompanied by a guide and costs 7 F. The fort is open from 9am to 11am and from 2pm until 5pm from the beginning of April to the end of September. It opens and closes an hour earlier out of season and you will not get in on 1 January, 1 May, 1 or 11 November or on Christmas day.

There is no direct route from the fort to a clutch of ruined castles crowning the mountaintops north of Maury but they are so impressive that it is worth driving down to **Rivesaltes** and cutting through from there. The **Château de Quéribus,** near the Grau de Maury, and the **Château de Peyrepertuse** are perfect examples of feudal strongholds that recall the days of Simon de Montfort and the equally unpleasant Counts of Toulouse. It requires a lot of energy to climb about inside the ramparts, some of which are only a continuation of the sheer rock face, but there are enough paths and steps to make it unnecessary to mountaineer unless you feel that way inclined. If you have time on your hands, follow the road round the valley and back through the limestone **Gorges de Galamus** to **St-Paul-de-Fenouillet**, the tourist centre of the area.

The countryside between the mountains and the sea gives the impression of being an enormous semi-circular vineyard criss-crossed by small roads and tiny rivers and spangled with hamlets that seem to have at least one historic building or ancient ruin apiece. It is a great pity that so many people rush through as though the devil was at their heels because it is a land made for leisure. Most of the châteaux you see hidden in the trees produce their own wines and are delighted when passers-by drop in to sample a little for themselves. It would be quite impossible to make a definitive study of the subject and still be capable of driving afterwards, but taken slowly and interspersed with sightseeing, picnics and walks it is an ideal way of getting to know the area.

Tautavel, Cases-de-Pène, Baixas, Pézilla de la Rivière and Thuir

You might, for example, start exploring at Tautavel where the cellars are well-stocked and the **museum** is crammed with prehistoric discoveries including the skull of the Caune Arago man, said to be 320 000 years old. It is open every day from 10am until noon and from 2pm to 6pm, but it is closed on Tuesdays.

From there a winding road leads through the mountains to Cases-de-Pène with offers including such attractions as the 17th-century **Notre-Dame-de-Pène hermitage**, complete with an excellent view, and summer exhibitions of paintings and sculpture at the **Château de Jau**. There is a restaurant that opens at 12.30pm but you have to book a table in advance (tel. 68–64.11.38).

The next stop might well be Baixas, one of the most attractive villages on the plain and only a short drive away. It has a 17th-century Gothic church, the remains of some ramparts and exhibitions of local handicrafts at the **Cellier Dom Brial**.

Pézilla de la Rivière, to the south on the much larger D614, formerly a fortified city, still has a handful of small churches and oratories that appear to be open most of the time. The **wine cellars** belong to a co-operative and you can visit them between 9am and 7pm. Yet another small road leads to Thuir, the wine capital, after which I would suggest that you head for the mountains.

Les environs de Thuir, Castelnou

Castelnou

You would go a long way to find a more captivating hill village than Castelnou, a mere handful of houses reached through an ancient gateway in the ramparts which climb up the hillside to the castle as they have done for nearly 1000 years. There is a shop just inside the entrance filled with dried flowers, herbs and corn-on-the-cob that looks as though it started life at about the same time as the village. A little further on, along a narrow street, is a restaurant called **L'Hostal** where you can have a good lunch for between 70 and 130F, wine included. It is closed on Mondays and also during January and February. Before leaving, have a look at the delightful little church outside the walls, almost opposite the gateway. The tiny cemetery in front is a mass of flowers, visited regularly by hundreds of bees that drone lazily round the clock tower, and almost as many butterflies. It must be rather a waste of time as far as they are concerned because all the flowers are artificial, made of china and other materials that withstand both time and weather but contribute nothing to the job of making honey or of providing a meal of nectar.

Following the usual pattern there are three ways out of Castelnou and you have to decide whether to wind your way up into the mountains in search of spectacular views and isolated hermitages or to return to Thuir and join the comparatively straight but reasonably scenic route to Ceret.

Céret

The best time to visit Céret is in the spring because it is the cherry capital of France and is famous for producing bumper crops long before anywhere else. However, there are plenty of other things to see, namely the 14th-century **Pont-du-Diable**, the gates of the old town and the medieval **Church of St-Pierre**. It also has two other attractions which are much more up-to-date. One is a monument by Maillol in the Place de la Liberté which shows a woman mourning the dead of the First World War and the second is the **Museum of Modern Art**, started by Pierre Brune in 1950 and including works by such artists as Matisse, Dali, Picasso and Chagall. From June to September it is open from 10am to noon and from 3pm to 7pm but closes on Tuesdays. For the rest of the year the morning hours are the same, but it is open from 2pm to 4pm and closes on Monday mornings, on Tuesdays, Thursdays and Fridays. The museum also closes throughout November and on public holidays. The entrance fee is 5 F.

Elne

Another First World War memorial by Maillol can be found in the main square at Elne, which is old enough to boast that Hannibal slept there although admittedly it was in a camp outside the walls. From early Roman beginnings it became the capital of Roussillon but started to fade in the 17th century and now has little to show for its past glories apart from the 800-year-old **Cathedral of Ste-Eulalie**. Try to arrange your visit so that you can see the **cloisters** which are really splendid. These are open from 9am to noon and from 2pm to 6pm, but close an hour early on winter evenings; they are also closed on Tuesdays and on Sundays in the winter. Entrance costs 4 F but this also includes the museum, housed in an ancient chapel on the premises.

Perpignan

After all this stopping and starting, walking and sampling the wine, you may well feel like a short rest, in which case you will be glad to know that Perpignan is only 14 kilometres (about 9 miles) away along a good, straight road.

HISTORY
Perpignan is believed to have started not as a Roman camp but as a private house and does not even appear to have had a name until AD 927 when it was referred to as Villa Perpinianum. By the end of the century it had expanded considerably to become the headquarters of the Counts of Roussillon who, in turn, bequeathed it to the King of Aragon in 1172. This could have been awkward as the whole area had been looked on as a French possession since the days of Charlemagne but St Louis, with other things on his mind, made the arrangement official under the Treaty of Corbeil in 1258.

James I of Aragon immediately set about consolidating and improving his new possessions and created the Kingdom of Majorca for his younger son with Perpignan as its capital. This obviously meant building a palace, increasing the population and turning the whole place into the thriving city which obviously annoyed the rest of the family. They contained themselves for 68 years and then went out and captured it, only to lose it again to France in 1463. Perpignan objected to the change of ownership, rose in revolt and, although defeated, caused so much friction that Charles VIII gave it back in 1493. By this time the Kings of Aragon, through a combination of war and marriage, had united Spain so the Catalans found themselves ruled from Madrid and in the firing line whenever trouble broke out along the border. They put up with it for nearly 150 years and then proclaimed Louis XIII Count of Barcelona. The French King, accompanied by Richelieu, hurried down to take advantage of this stroke of good fortune but it was 1642 before the siege ended. Eight years later the Treaty of the Pyrenees divided up the area, giving Roussillon to France and leaving Barcelona and the country round it in Spanish hands. Because treaties do not necessarily mean the end of hostilities, the French were taking no chances and the fortifications round Perpignan were rebuilt and strengthened to the point where the city was thought to be impregnable. But war is one thing, progress is another. In about 1900 the town needed extra space so, instead of expanding outside the ramparts as everyone else had done, the authorities simply knocked them down and built some impressive avenues instead.

WHAT TO SEE

Perpignan, although French and proud of it, is very much a Spanish city in a lot of ways. Catalan is widely spoken and the music, the food and the festivals all originated south of the border to a greater or lesser degree. The Spanish influence is also noticeable in the main buildings which, for the most part, are grouped together between La Basse, a delightful canal that wanders through the old town to join the River Tel, and the enormous Citadelle into which they would all fit quite easily.

The **Palace of the Kings of Majorca,** right in the heart of the Citadelle, dates back to the late 13th century, although a lot of work remained to be done when the Kings of Aragon moved in to regain what they considered to be part of the family fortune. There is an impressive courtyard overlooked by the royal apartments, a throne room that seemed a bit chilly until three large fireplaces were discovered and a keep which includes two lovely old chapels, one on top of the other. Part of the building is still being restored but you can climb to the top of the keep to look down on the city and the country beyond. The palace is open from 9.30am until noon and from 2pm to 6pm but is closed on Tuesdays. You pay 5 F to go in but this also includes two permanent exhibitions tracing the art and history of Roussillon.

The **Cathedral of St-Jean,** in the Place Gambetta, was started a few years after the palace, was redesigned in 1433, consecrated about 70 years later and finally became a cathedral in 1601. It is extremely ornate inside with a great deal of gilt, rich fabrics, marble, carvings and sculptures. All this tends to heighten the impact made by the Dévôt Christ, a most disturbing dark wooden crucifix. The figure, instead of being pale and drooping with a certain air of peace, is of a man in dreadful agony which permeates every inch of the body. The head has fallen forward nearly as far as nature will allow and there is a superstition that when the chin finally rests on the chest the world will come to an end.

Small passages, even darker than the rest of the interior, lead to a chapel, which was part of the original church of St-Jean-le-Vieux, and to the chapter house and all that is left of the ancient cloister cemetery, said to be the oldest and largest of its kind in France. The bell, in its wrought-iron bird

211

cage on the top of the clock tower, dates from the early 15th century and can be seen to advantage from the Place St-Jean where it is sometimes possible to park near a very sturdy fountain.

The **Church of St-Jacques,** adjoining the Jardin de La Miranda, and the **Church of Ste-Marie-de-la-Réal,** the old royal parish church, are both quite interesting in their way and so are the four original mansions grouped around the Place de la Loge. The **Loge de Mer,** built in the 14th century, was where disputes were settled in the days when Perpignan was a thriving port and has a ship for a weathercock to emphasise the fact. It is fairly grand in the manner which was popular in Barcelona during the Middle Ages. The **Hôtel de Ville** next door is roughly 100 years older and, when you have admired Maillol's bronze statue called *The Mediterranean* outside, ask the concierge to show you the marriage hall where the old ceiling is painted very much in the Moorish style. The **Palais de la Députation** and **La Maison Julia** make up the quartet and gives you an idea of how things were in the 14th and 15th centuries.

Le Castillet/Casa Pairal, standing on the edge of the canal nearby, is all that is left of the city walls. It has been in turn a gateway and a prison and now provides a home for the **Musée d'Arts et Traditions Populaires du Roussillon.** The eight rooms are filled with examples of domestic and agricultural equipment and religious art. The ancient *Annals of Justice* provide a clue to the sort of people who were locked up there and just what they had done to deserve it. It is open from 9am until 11.30am and from 2pm to 5.30pm, is closed on Sundays and public holidays from mid-September to the middle of July and costs 2F.

You will come across several other small museums and interesting houses as you walk through the streets of the old town, perhaps the most memorable being the Rue des Marchands where quite a few of the shops have their original porches, painted ceilings and marble pillars. There are not a great many gardens apart from the Square Bir Hakeim near the modern Palais des Congrès but the new avenues and squares with their palms, plane trees and mimosa serve almost as well.

WHERE TO STAY

Contrary to expectations there are not many top-flight hotels in Perpignan and those that do exist are, like their more modest companions, scattered about the town.

The **Hôtel de la Loge,** in the Place de la Loge (tel. 68–34.54.84), is about the most central you will find. It is attractive and comfortable as well

212

as being quiet but there is no restaurant and no garage space for cars. Nor is it expensive with a double room costing 215 F.

The **Hôtel France**, 16 Quai Sadi-Carnot (tel. 68–34.92.81), looks out on to the canal, has a restaurant where you can eat for 90 F upwards, but not on Sundays or on Monday nights, and charges 250 F for a room. It is closed in December.

There are two or three camping sites, none of which is at all outstanding, but they would do quite adequately if you were stuck for the night.

EATING OUT

Whatever the state of your finances, you will find a restaurant to suit them perfectly.

The **Delcros**, 63 Avenue Leclerc (tel. 68–34.96.05), could be a little noisy because it is just off a busy intersection a short way from the river. However, it is easy to find and the food is good. The set menus, at anything from 160 to 220 F, are on the high side, so why not give them a miss and choose one of the delicious specialities instead? The restaurant closes on Sunday nights, all day Monday and from mid-June to mid-July.

The restaurant **Le Helder**, 1 Rue Courteline (tel. 68–34.98.99), is attached to a modest hotel of the same name, is close to the station and, for anyone who is economising, will do a set menu for 50 F with wine at comparable prices. The restaurant is closed for ten days in October and from the middle of December for a month.

FESTIVALS AND ENTERTAINMENTS

Perpignan celebrates at the drop of a hat, especially in the Place de la Loge where people may often be seen dancing after dinner. From June to September you can watch the *sardane* at least twice a week. It is the traditional dance of Catalan which is thought to have been introduced by the Greeks over 1000 years ago. It consists of one or more rings of people swaying from side to side in a series of complicated steps to music provided by anything from a single instrument to the traditional band. The tempo varies considerably and just as you think you are getting the hang of it the music stops and everyone disappears until the next time.

Each Good Friday there is a Procession of the Passion, not unlike the one that takes place in Seville every year. The Brotherhood of La Sanch laid down the rules in the 15th century and they are still obeyed today. Penitents gather at the church of St-Jacques wearing black or scarlet robes, each with a hood rather like a witch's hat but with the brim replaced by soft material that falls below the shoulders and has two holes for the eyes. They escort sacred images through the streets attended by young girls in national dress and watched by large crowds who may be devout or simply curious.

TOURIST INFORMATION
For details of anything else that may be happening while you are there, the best plan is to contact the information office on the Quai de Lattre-Tassigny beside the canal (tel. 68–34.29.94) and you will find that they can also help you with hotels.

Canet Plage and Canet

Canet Plage is the main seaside resort for Perpignan and as a result is geared to the more sophisticated demands of an urban population. It has also been in existence longer than several of the other *ports de plaisance* and so it is rather odd that no one has bothered about planting many trees or creating leisure parks. Once you have come to terms with these minor disadvantages, there is almost no end to the variety of attractions on offer. In the first place, endless sandy beaches stretch out invitingly on either side of the harbour where nearly 1000 moorings are available for boats of between 4½ and 23 metres (15 and 75ft). All the usual services are within easy reach and the Club Nautique can be relied upon for help if or when necessary.

The club itself (tel. 68–80.20.66) has a finger in several pies such as sailing, fishing, rowing, diving, swimming and even the Canet Model Club and will tell you where to hire a boat or a bicycle. There are also private clubs that welcome temporary members if you feel the urge to windsurf, play crazy golf or even parachute. Other centres for adults with separate ones for children appear along the beaches every season and if you have taken grandmother as well she will find all the appropriate activities available at the François Moudat Centre (tel. 68–80.34.07).

In the evenings you can divide your time between the casino and approximately half a dozen nightclubs and discos or have a quiet dinner at any one of about 30 cafes and restaurants. There are several hotels in the medium-price bracket, literally thousands of furnished apartments and 11 camping sites which can accommodate between 9000 and 10 000 tents and caravans among them.

Canet village, slightly inland, has a rugby-tennis club, a basketball centre and clay-pigeon shooting and is working hard to restore the local château. For any information you need here or at Canet Plage get in touch with the tourist office (tel. 68–80.20.65), which is in the Place de la Méditerranée at the Plage.

St-Cyprien Plage

A good road down yet another sandspit, with the sea lapping gently on one side and the Etang de Canet et de St-Nazaire spread out on the other, brings you to St-Cyprien Plage which has very nearly as many enticements as Canet Plage but varies the details somewhat. For example, there is a large sports complex with plenty of trees and a golf course where you can play either nine or 18 holes, depending on how the spirit moves you. The park, which borders on the lake, also has facilities for sailing, windsurfing, archery and mini-golf, but you will have to go to St-Cyprien village if you want a day out on horseback. The telephone number for the park is 68–21.01.71 and they will tell you whom to ring if you are interested in scuba-diving or hiring a bicycle.

The large marina is as efficient and well-equipped as all the others in this part of the world with space for about 1500 boats and at least three charter companies which will provide one if you have not brought your own. There are five hotels, not a great many good restaurants but plenty of cafes, and a large number of furnished flats and camping sites. St-Cyprien itself, on the road to Elne, has very little to tempt you off the beach apart from the bull-fights which are held between June and September. Dates and times, like all the other details you might want, are available from the tourist office (tel. 68–21.01.33).

Argelès

By the time you get as far south as Argelès with its attendant plage, you have reached the Côte Vermeille and the long sandy beaches are about to give way to a rocky coastline full of the most enchanting little bays. It is a large place that describes itself as the camping capital of the area, which is no wonder considering that it has 60 sites divided up into more than 20 000 different plots. In addition there are 30 hotels, 5000 furnished flats and eight holiday camps over and above the two which are set aside for children. Not content with all that, the authorities are planning a marina to bring the holiday population up to strength.

215

The sea front is littered with clubs during the summer where you can arrange to sail, windsurf or water-ski. Les Corailleurs are the people to ask about scuba-diving and there is no difficulty about hiring a boat, a bicycle or a horse. Nightclubs, cinemas, cabarets and the casino vie for attention with fêtes and exhibitions of folk dancing, Catalan-style. The Château de Valmy is open to visitors who want to taste the wine produced on the estate and possibly take a bottle or even a case away with them. To add to the general gaiety, a folklore festival is held at the château on the first Sunday in September. When you have had a surfeit of sea and sand, it is possible to join a walking tour up in to the mountains or visit the **hermitage of Notre-Dame-de-Vie** on the slopes of the Albères. It dates from the 17th and 18th centuries and is open throughout the year.

WHERE TO STAY
If you want to stay long enough to sample all the local delights, it might be an idea to take a room at the **Lido** on the sea front (tel. 68–81.10.32). It has a garden, a swimming pool and a restaurant where no dogs are allowed, serves meals in the open air and charges up to 300 francs a night. It is open from late May to early October and the cheapest set menu is 94 F.

At the other end of the scale is the **Solarium**, in the Avenue Vallespir (tel. 68–81.10.74), which has less to offer but, on the other hand, charges only 186 F for a room and 62 F for dinner.

As usual the fountain of information is the **tourist office** in the Place Arènes (tel. 68–81.15.85).

Collioure

Collioure differs from Argelès Plage in almost every respect. For example, it is an old town where fishing takes precedence over pleasure boating, medieval buildings occupy nearly as much space as the newer ones and the festivals are traditional rather than designed for tourists. As a result it does not really qualify as a *port de plaisance*, although there is a small marina with moorings for less than 100 boats.

The village came into being when the Greeks established a small port on the edge of the bay. It was taken over in turn by the Romans, the Saracens, the French and the Spanish, and for a brief period formed part of the kingdom of Majorca. During the short time they were in power the Kings of Majorca built a summer palace overlooking the water which is now used for

216

summer exhibitions and is open from 2.30pm to 7.30pm between late June and the end of September.

The late 17th-century church is built of black volcanic rock and has a prominent round tower with a pink dome that was originally a lighthouse. It faces the palace across a semi-circular stretch of water which, with others like it on either side, gives the bay a sort of clover-leaf appearance. Each one has its own sandy beach and between them they provide swimming, wind-surfing, sailing and scuba-diving. With so many fishing boats about it is hardly surprising that a trawler leaves at 6.30 every morning and will take up to ten people for a few hours' deep-sea fishing. Excursions are arranged by coach to places of interest in the area and you can play tennis, go bowling or join a walking tour.

Holy Week sees the first of the ancient festivals when penitents dressed in black tread the well-worn path through the village. It takes place at night and there is not a great deal of jollification. In contrast the Grand Patron Saint's festival on 15 and 16 August goes off with a bang, starting with a colourful parade and including entertainments like bull-running and a fire-works display over the water. Folk dancers are put through their paces at the hermitage of Notre-Dame de Consolation where you can also see a collec-tion of religious items and ex-votos. Bull-fights are held in the arena from June to September and are usually crowded to capacity.

Collioure is a delightful village to explore and almost any of the little streets that wind up the hillside between rows of houses with shuttered win-dows and iron balconies will provide something of interest, even if it is only a boutique or a small shop filled with local produce. Surprisingly there are a large number of places to park a car, two camping sites, a great many fur-nished flats and well over a dozen hotels. The most expensive is the pink **Casa Pairal,** near the castle; the most interesting you will find to be **Les Templiers** not far away with its famous collection of paintings; and the best value for money is likely to be **Le Bon Port,** slightly out of town on the coast road to the south. To get the most out of your visit to Collioure it is as well to call in early at the **tourist office** on the Avenue Camille Pelletan (tel. 68–82.15.47).

Port-Vendres

A winding road along the mountainside overlooking the sea links Collioure with Port Vendres, some 4 kilometres (2½ miles) away. This also had its beginnings in the olden days but has not a great deal left to show for it. However, it is a deep-water port which did military duty in the 17th century and ran a regular service to North Africa as long as there were enough passengers and cargo to make it viable. The one-time Port of Venus still dabbles in commerce and the large vessels, aptly called *Goddess*, are a splendid sight as they fiddle their way through to the inner harbour and tie up alongside. There is a marina with 200 moorings and all the facilities necessary for an enjoyable visit. You can take a boat trip along the coast, join a fishing party or hire your own craft if you prefer to be alone. Windsurfing and scuba-diving are among the attractions, as are tennis and bowling, but if you lean more towards walking there are route maps available at the tourist office on the Quai Forgas (tel. 68–82.07.54).

You will not find a great deal of sand, or even a lot of shingle, because the coast thereabouts is definitely rocky with plenty of trees, grass and mountains by way of compensation. Grapes are grown extensively in the area so you can improve your knowledge of local vintages by taking a guided tour round the co-operative wine cellars or ordering a bottle when you look in at the nightclub or discotheque. Folk music and country dancing are popular with the local inhabitants who also celebrate 14 July with a grand firework festival. There is one camping site that could well be full, a number of apartments and a few not-very-up-market hotels. The restaurants tend to be on the small side but many of them specialise in local dishes which can be anything from *fruits de mer* to *bouillabaisse* or beef to jugged hare with some very admirable cheese to follow.

Banyuls-sur-Mer

Just over the hill you run down in to Banyuls-sur-Mer which has several claims to fame, all of which are worth investigating. It takes its role as a tourist resort very seriously and insists, quite rightly, that you need not have a dull moment the whole time you are there. For the energetic there is swimming from a sandy beach, windsurfing, diving, sailing, and water-skiing. You can ride, play tennis or crazy golf, shoot clay pigeons or go parachuting. The aquarium, which is in a superior class where Mediterranean fish are concerned, is open every day from 9am to 6pm with two hours off for lunch and costs 8 F. It is attached to the Laboratoire Arago, founded in 1887 and named after a local astronomer, so it is interested in things that happen overhead as well as under water.

The marina has moorings for only about 300 boats but even so it takes up quite a large chunk of the bay. There are daily trips along the Spanish coast and fishing expeditions leave at 8.30am, returning at about noon. If you want to 'get culture', as an American of my acquaintance insisted on putting it, you will find a church dating back to the 12th century, the hermitage of Notre-Dame de la Salette, with a superior view of the coast and some interesting sculptures. They include a rather underfed party of dancers called *La Sardane*, a war memorial by Maillol depicting mourners at the side of a dying man and *La Pensée*, a nude woman deep in thought who watches over his tomb in the garden of Le Mas Maillol.

What you will not find are many hotels and restaurants and the three camping sites can muster only 190 individual places altogether. The **Hôtel les Elmes** (tel. 68–88.03.12), a short distance from the town, has its own little bay of the same name which was deserted in the spring but probably fills up later in the year. It has a restaurant specialising in local dishes where the oysters were by far the best we sampled anywhere along the coast. A room works out at 260 francs and the set menus range from 56 to 180 francs. Banyuls-sur-Mer is famous for its sweet white wine but it also produces something between a sherry and a port called Banyuls that is recommended before dinner and, when you have acquired the taste, is very pleasant. The hotel is open from March to September.

Cerbère

The last village before the Spanish frontier is Cerbère, which is running like mad to catch up with all the places that have gone before. So far there are only a couple of hotels, both with restaurants, and one small camping site, but you can find more than 70 'bedsits'. There is a forest which is open to the public and the attractions include tennis, basketball, bowling, diving and windsurfing with an invitation to join in celebrating St Sauveur's festi-festival during the first week in August. Apart from this there is not much to do other than find a place to park among the vineyards, gaze down at the Spanish coast and think beautiful thoughts.

HISTORICAL CHART

B.C.

1000   Ligurians occupied the Mediterranean coastal strip.

600   Greeks from Phocea established a trading post at Massalia, now Marseilles.

542   Carthaginians occupied Massalia for 60 years.

5th C ⎫ The Greeks opened up additional trading posts at several places as
to   ⎬ far apart as Nice, Antibes, Glanum, Arles and Agde. Celts invaded
4th C ⎭ the coastal areas.

218   Hannibal marched up from Spain to cross the Alps into Italy.

125   Marseilles asked Rome for help against the Celts.

123   The victorious Roman Consul Sextius established Aix.

51   Julius Caesar completed the conquest of Gaul.

49   Fréjus was built by Julius Caesar as a major port.

19   Agrippa built the Pont-du-Gard to supply water to Nimes.

A.D.

1st C ⎫ The Romans consolidated their positions everywhere, enlarging
to   ⎬ and fortifying centres like Cimiez (at Nice) Marseilles, Arles,
3rd C ⎭ Orange, Narbonne and Carcasso (near Carcassonne). The Aurelian Way from Rome to Spain was completed.

313   Constantine gave Christians freedom of worship under the Edict of Milan.

476   The fall of the Roman Empire was followed by the Dark Ages which saw repeated invasions by, amongst others, Vandals, Visigoths, Franks and Saracens.

800   Charlemagne was crowned Emperor of the West in Rome.

843   Charlemagne's empire was divided between three grandsons under the Treaty of Verdun.

855   Provence became a kingdom under his great-grandson Charles.

884   Maures was captured by Saracens who terrorised the region for a century.

962   The Holy Roman Empire was created and later included Provence

although the Counts retained a good deal of independence.

1095   The First Crusade was launched by Pope Urban II at Clermont.

12th C   Aix became the capital of the Counts of Provence.

1209   The Albigensian Crusade started with the Massacre of Béziers.

1258   St Louis renounced his claims to Perpignan and Roussillon under the Treaty of Corbeil.

1260   Carcassonne was built by St Louis near the Roman fort of Carcasso.

1270   St Louis died.
          The end of the Crusades.

1276   Perpignan became the capital of the short-lived Kingdom of Majorca.

1287   The University of Montpellier, the third oldest in France, was recognised.

1297   The fortress of Monaco was seized by François Grimaldi. The overlordship was bought from Genoa 11 years later.

1309   Avignon became the seat of the Popes and later of the Antipopes when Gregory XI returned to Rome.

1409   The University of Aix was founded.

1419   Nice was officially ceded to Savoy after being under its protection since 1388.

1434   René of Anjou became Count of Provence, ushering in an era of great prosperity.

1481   Charles of Maine, nephew of René, bequeathed Provence (except Nice) to France.

1486   The union of Provence with France was ratified at Aix.

1501   The Parliament of Provence was established at Aix with a degree of power over local legal and political affairs.

1562
to   The Wars of Religion between Catholics and Protestants. They ended with the Edict of Nantes allowing freedom of conscience to
1598   Protestants.

1622   Louis XIII captured Montpellier.

1629   Richelieu began a systematic destruction of Protestant strongholds throughout the South of France.

1659   Perpignan was annexed by France under the Treaty of the Pyrenees.

1681   The Canal du Midi was inaugurated.

1685   The Edict of Nantes was revoked, Protestantism was suppressed and Huguenots who failed to escape were persecuted.

1713	The Dutch House of Orange–Nassau ceded Orange to France under the Treaty of Utrecht.
1718	Nice became part of the new Kingdom of Sardinia.
1720	The Great Plague took its toll of the population, killing some 50 000 people in Marseilles alone.
1763	The English novelist, Tobias Smollet, started the fashionable habit of spending the winter on the riviera.
1787	The persecution of the Protestants was ended by the Edict of Toleration.
1789	The outbreak of the French Revolution.
1791	The Papal Protectorate of Avignon and the Comtat Venaissin became part of France.
1792	Volunteers from Marseilles marched to Paris singing the Battle Hymn of the Rhine which soon became known as "The Marseillaise".
1793	Louis XVI was executed in Paris. The siege of Toulon gave Napoleon a chance to prove his ability in action.
1799	Napoleon landed at St-Raphaël on his return from Egypt.
1804	Napoleon was crowned Emperor of France.
1814	Napoleon abdicated and sailed from St-Raphaël for Elba.
1815	Napoleon landed at Golfe-Juan and was defeated at Waterloo on 18th June.
1834	Lord Brougham set Cannes on the way to becoming a fashionable resort.
1844	Carcassonne was rebuilt by the architect Viollet-le-Duc.
1860	Nice, after years of vasselating, was finally united with France.
1865 to 1878	Monte-Carlo came into being, the Monte-Carlo Cassino was opened and Monaco was established as a leading winter resort.
1940	The Italians occupied Menton.
1942 to 1944	The Germans invaded the Vichy Free Zone and the French scuttled their fleet at Toulon. The South of France was liberated within a fortnight of the Allied landings in Provence.
After 1946	The Riviera started to be developed as a summer holiday resort. Industrial developments sprang up at several places along the coast. Motorways were built and ports de plaisance were created from the Camargue to Spain, some of which are still being completed.

FURTHER READING

Ault, Warren, O., *Europe in the Middle Ages*, D. C. Heath & Co., 1946.

Bergin, Joseph, *Cardinal Richelieu*, Yale University Press, 1985.

Brion, Marcel, *Provence*, Nicholas Kaye, 1956.

Bury, J. P. T., *France 1814–1940*, Methuen, 1949.

Cameron, Roderick, *The Golden Riviera*, Weidenfeld & Nicolson, 1975.

Chamberlain, Samuel, *Bouquet de France*, Gourmet Distributing Corporation, 1952.

Chamberlin, E. R., *Life in Medieval France*, William Clowes & Sons, 1967.

Charlton, D. G., (Ed.), *France. A Companion to French Studies*, Methuen, 1972.

Cobban, Alfred, *A History of Modern France* (Vols 1 & 2), Penguin Books, 1961.

Daudet, Alphonse, *Letters from my windmill*, Penguin Classics, 1978.

Fenwick, Hubert, *The Châteaux of France*, Robert Hale, 1975.

Fisher, M. F. K., *Two Towns in Provence*, Hogarth Press, 1985.

Hamilton, Ronald, *A Holiday History of France*, Hogarth Press, 1985.

Hanbury-Tenison, Robin, *White Horses over France*, Granada, 1985.

Hare, Augustus, *The Riviera*, George Allen, 1897.

Hennessy, James Pope, *Aspects of Provence*, Hogarth Press, 1961.

Maurois, André, *A History of France*, Jonathan Cape, 1949.

More, Carey & More, Julian, *Views from a French Farmhouse*, Pavilion, 1985.

Raison, Laura, *The South of France: An Anthology*, Cadogan Publications, 1985.

Stendhal, *Travels in the South of France*, Calder & Boyers, 1971.

Stevenson, R. L., *Travels with a Donkey*, Century Publishing, 1985.

Wardel, A. *Know France*, Osprey, 1974.

INDEX

227